William Miller
Rita M. Pellen
Editors

Libraries and Google®

Libraries and Google® has been co-published simultaneously as *Internet Reference Services Quarterly*, Volume 10, Numbers 3/4 2005.

Pre-publication
REVIEWS,
COMMENTARIES,
EVALUATIONS . . .

More pre-publication
REVIEWS, COMMENTARIES, EVALUATIONS . . .

" A s the first book-length treatment of this topic, THIS FASCIN-ATING COLLECTION OF DIVERSE PERSPECTIVES about the usefulness of google and its potential menace to libraries and scholarly communication is A CALL TO ACTION FOR LIBRARIANS. We ignore Google, or rail against it, at our peril. Many of the contributions focus on specific Google products that have already had an impact on libraries–Google Print and Google Scholar. These fine, practical pieces for librarians and publishers are the heart of this collection."

Kathleen Hoeth, MLS
University Librarian
and Director of Library Services
Florida Gulf Coast University

" N O LIBRARY ADMINISTRA-TOR, SYSTEMS TECHNICIAN, ELECTRONIC RESOURCES LIBRAR-IAN, OR REFERENCE LIBRARIAN CAN AFFORD TO IGNORE THIS IMPORTANT WORK. Among the many questions thoroughly covered in this volume are: Can Google play friendly with libraries? Can a Google-library partnership be as positive as the Google-Amazon partnership? To what extent can Google mine the Invisible Web? Can libraries successfully rely on Google to link to licensed and aggregated full text resources? Is Google a boon or a detractor to information literacy? And, is library partnership with Google a security or privacy risk?"

Christopher C. Brown, MLIS, MDiv
Reference Coordinator
Penrose Library
University of Denver

The Haworth Information Press®
An Imprint of The Haworth Press, Inc.

Libraries and Google®

Libraries and Google® has been co-published simultaneously as Internet Reference Services Quarterly, Volume 10, Numbers 3/4 2005.

Monographic Separates from *Internet Reference Services Quarterly*™

For additional information on these and other Haworth Press titles, including descriptions, tables of contents, reviews, and prices, use the QuickSearch catalog at http://www.HaworthPress.com.

Libraries and Google®

William Miller
Rita M. Pellen
Editors

Libraries and Google® *has been co-published simultaneously as* Internet Reference Services Quarterly, *Volume 10, Numbers 3/4 2005.*

The Haworth Information Press®
An Imprint of The Haworth Press, Inc.

New York • London • Victoria (AU)
www.HaworthPress.com

Published by

The Haworth Information Press®, 10 Alice Street, Binghamton, NY 13904-1580 USA

The Haworth Information Press® is an imprint of The Haworth Press, Inc., 10 Alice Street, Binghamton, NY 13904-1580 USA.

Libraries and Google® has been co-published simultaneously as Internet Reference Services Quarterly, Volume 10, Numbers 3/4 2005.

The development, preparation, and publication of this work has been undertaken with great care. However, the publisher, employees, editors, and agents of The Haworth Press and all imprints of The Haworth Press, Inc., including The Haworth Medical Press® and Pharmaceutical Products Press®, are not responsible for any errors contained herein or for consequences that may ensue from use of materials or information contained in this work. With regard to case studies, identities and circumstances of individuals discussed herein have been changed to protect confidentiality. Any resemblance to actual persons, living or dead, is entirely coincidental.

The Haworth Press is committed to the dissemination of ideas and information according to the highest standards of intellectual freedom and the free exchange of ideas. Statements made and opinions expressed in this publication do not necessarily reflect the views of the Publisher, Directors, management, or staff of The Haworth Press, Inc., or an endorsement by them.

Cover design by Kerry E. Mack.

Library of Congress Cataloging-in-Publication Data

Libraries and Google / William Miller, Rita M. Pellen, editors.
    p. cm.
    "Libraries and Google has been co-published simultaneously as Internet reference services quarterly, volume 10, numbers 3/4 2005."
    Includes bibliographical references and index.
    ISBN-13: 978-0-7890-3124-2 (alk. paper)
    ISBN-10: 0-7890-3124-8 (alk. paper)
    ISBN-13: 978-0-7890-3125-9 (pbk. : alk. paper)
    ISBN-10: 0-7890-3125-6 (pbk. : alk. paper)
1. Libraries and the Internet. 2. Google. 3. Web search engines. 4. Library materials–Digitization. 5. Digital libraries. 6. Libraries–Forecasting. 7. Communication in learning and scholarship–Technological innovations. I. Miller, William, 1947- . II. Pellen, Rita M. III. Internet reference services quarterly.

Z674.75.I58L535 2005
020'.2854678–dc22
                                 2005031476

Indexing, Abstracting & Website/Internet Coverage

This section provides you with a list of major indexing & abstracting services and other tools for bibliographic access. That is to say, each service began covering this periodical during the year noted in the right column. Most Websites which are listed below have indicated that they will either post, disseminate, compile, archive, cite or alert their own Website users with research-based content from this work. (This list is as current as the copyright date of this publication.)

(continued)

(continued)

*Special Bibliographic Notes related to special journal issues
(separates) and indexing/abstracting:*

- indexing/abstracting services in this list will also cover material in any "separate" that is co-published simultaneously with Haworth's special thematic journal issue or DocuSerial. Indexing/abstracting usually covers material at the article/chapter level.
- monographic co-editions are intended for either non-subscribers or libraries which intend to purchase a second copy for their circulating collections.
- monographic co-editions are reported to all jobbers/wholesalers/approval plans. The source journal is listed as the "series" to assist the prevention of duplicate purchasing in the same manner utilized for books-in-series.
- to facilitate user/access services all indexing/abstracting services are encouraged to utilize the co-indexing entry note indicated at the bottom of the first page of each article/chapter/contribution.
- this is intended to assist a library user of any reference tool (whether print, electronic, online, or CD-ROM) to locate the monographic version if the library has purchased this version but not a subscription to the source journal.
- individual articles/chapters in any Haworth publication are also available through the Haworth Document Delivery Service (HDDS).

Libraries and Google®

CONTENTS

ABOUT THE EDITORS

William Miller, PhD, MLS, is Director of Libraries at Florida Atlantic University in Boca Raton. He formerly served as Head of Reference at Michigan State University in East Lansing, and as Associate Dean of Libraries at Bowling Green State University in Ohio. Dr. Miller is past President of the Association of College and Research Libraries, has served as Chair of the *Choice* magazine editorial board, and is a contributing editor of *Library Issues*. Dr. Miller teaches courses in English Literature and Library Science. He was named Instruction Librarian of the Year in 2004 by the Association of College and Research Libraries Instruction Section.

Rita M. Pellen, MLS, is Associate Director of Libraries at Florida Atlantic University. Previously she was Assistant Director of Public Services and Head of the Reference Department at Florida Atlantic. Ms. Pellen has a BA from The Pennsylvania State University and MLS from the University of Pittsburgh. In 1993, she received the Gabor Exemplary Employee Award in recognition for outstanding service to FAU, and in 1997, the "Literati Club Award for Excellence" for the outstanding paper in *The Bottom Line*. She has served on committees in LAMA, ACRL, and ALCTS, as well as the Southeast Florida Library Information Network, SEFLIN, a multi-type library cooperative in South Florida. Honor society memberships include Beta Phi Mu and Phi Kappa Phi.

Introduction:
Libraries and Their Interrelationships
with Google

It is hard to remember that we are still in the early stages of our inter-relationships with Google, and that not so long ago Google did not even exist. The fact is that Google has become a powerful presence in our lives, and in the lives of almost all library users. It is the de facto search engine for factual inquiries, and its potential is only just beginning to be realized. Some librarians love it and embrace it, while others hate or fear it. The essays presented here, in what may be the first book-length collection of essays on the subject of libraries and Google, express all shades of opinion, both hopeful and fearful.

Love it or hate it, Google is here to stay. It is something of both a threat and an opportunity not only to libraries but also to publishers, in various ways, not the least of which is the current initiative to digitize considerable copyrighted material. There will be other threats to publishers as time goes on. Why use *Journal Citation Reports* to evaluate faculty applications for promotion and tenure, when you can just run their names through Google? Google will be a "disruptive technology," as Mark Sandler says in his important essay "Disruptive Beneficence," for many sectors of society, not only for libraries. However, Sandler calls for us to embrace the dislocation and the opportunities it creates.

[Haworth co-indexing entry note]: "Introduction: Libraries and Their Interrelationships with Google." Miller, William. Co-published simultaneously in *Internet Reference Services Quarterly* (The Haworth Information Press, an imprint of The Haworth Press, Inc.) Vol. 10, No. 3/4, 2005, pp. 1-4; and: *Libraries and Google®* (ed: William Miller, and Rita M. Pellen) The Haworth Information Press, an imprint of The Haworth Press, Inc., 2005, pp. 1-4. Single or multiple copies of this article are available for a fee from The Haworth Document Delivery Service [1-800-HAWORTH, 9:00 a.m. - 5:00 p.m. (EST). E-mail address: docdelivery@haworthpress.com].

Available online at http://www.haworthpress.com/web/IRSQ
© 2005 by The Haworth Press, Inc. All rights reserved.
doi:10.1300/J136v10n03_01

Ronald Milne, in his piece on "The Google Library Project at Oxford," similarly recognizes some limitations on that project but stresses the fact that it will help fulfill the wishes of Sir Thomas Bodley, founder of the Bodleian Library, who wanted the collections at Oxford to be open and available to all scholars.

For libraries, Google does have very profound implications, and is accelerating trends that would have developed eventually anyway, such as the digitization of library collections, and a shift to disintermediation which leaves many librarians feeling like fifth wheels, even while it empowers users and seemingly frees them from dependence on library buildings and collections. Quite simply, there are those, within libraries and outside of them, who think (or fear) that Google will make libraries obsolete. But there are others who believe that this company's products simply open up new opportunities for libraries which respond to them in positive and innovative ways. These two perspectives are illustrated by Rick Anderson's "The (Uncertain) Future of Libraries in a Google World: Sounding an Alarm," and Mark Herring's "A Gaggle of Googles: Limitations and Defects of Electronic Access as Panacea."

While popular interest centers on the general Google search engine, most of the discussion in this book centers on the Google Print and Google Scholar products, and their potential impact on libraries. One of the articles, Mary Taylor's "Using the Google Search Appliance for Federated Searching," discusses the technical aspects of purchasing and implementing Google's own searching product with proprietary vendor databases. Other Google products, some still under development such as Google Earth, Google SMS, Google Suggest, and "Site-Flavored Google Search Box," are too new even to be on librarians' radar screens as yet. No one would seriously doubt, however, that some of these will also have a great impact on libraries in the near future.

At the moment, librarians are focusing on Google Print and Google Scholar, which some are collectively calling "Schoogle." The pieces by Robert Lackie ("Google's Print and Scholar Initiatives: The Value and Impact on Libraries and Information Services"), Burton Callicott and Debbie Vaughn ("Google Scholar vs. Library Scholar: Testing the Performance of Schoogle"), and Francine Egger-Sider and Jane Devine ("Google, the Invisible Web, and Librarians: Slaying the Research Goliath") are typical of pieces which consider these two tools extensively, and illustrate the impact that they are having on the librarian psyche.

It is clear that, as Shelley E. Phipps and Krisellen Maloney say in their article "Choices in the Paradigm Shift," Google has redefined the playing field and marginalized libraries if our only role is that of gatekeeper. They maintain that we need to "move beyond our existing mental models and truly redefine our unique role based on the needs within the external environment." Maurice York, in "Calling the Scholars Home," similarly argues that "we must abandon the walls and go to them. The walls, in fact, have already disappeared around us even as we stolidly stood guard at the gate."

Not all the articles here are think pieces or overviews. Many pieces here are eminently practical, show us how to make the most of Google's products, and highlight the research strengths of librarians. Janice Adlington and Chris Benda, for instance, in "Checking Under the Hood: Evaluating Google Scholar for Reference Use," compare Google Scholar to traditional scholarly indexes and abstracts, and uncover both strengths and weaknesses that librarians need to be aware of as they integrate this tool into their panoply of resources. Rebecca Donlan and Rachel Cooke's analysis of problems encountered when beta testing the linking of licensed full-text databases with Google Scholar is a model of thoughtful scholarly inquiry.

In "Directing Students to New Information Types," Mike Thelwall concludes that "Google's link-based page ranking algorithm makes this search engine an ideal tool for finding specialist topic introductory material, particularly in computer science, and so librarians should be teaching this as part of a strategic literature review approach." Rachael Cathcart and Amanda Roberts discuss Google Scholar in terms of ACRL's Information Literacy Standards, in "Evaluating Google Scholar as a Tool for Information Literacy." Alan Dawson, in "Optimising Publications for Google Users," urges librarians to consider themselves as publishing when they digitize library resources, and suggests ways to make digitized library resources more accessible via Google.

Paul S. Piper, in "Google and Privacy," raises what he calls "the darker side" of Google: the fact that it "collects personal information about its users, and it aggregates third party information more effectively than many third world governments." The non-library world is now beginning to focus on this phenomenon also, as highlighted by the company's recent decision not to communicate with C-NET for a year because one of its reporters published considerable sensitive personal information about one of the company's founders–all of it found via Google itself.

Meanwhile, Google the corporate giant remains magisterially above the fray. The company is fascinating to librarians, as Ron Force points out in "Image: Google's Most Important Product." Michael J. Krasulski and Steven J. Bell, in "Keeping Up with Google," give us strategies for remaining up to date on both the company and its products. Clearly, the onus is on us. Google has essentially ignored the complaints and fears of publishers regarding possible copyright violations inherent in the Google Print initiative (although, as of this moment, it has suspended wholesale digitization efforts for a few months, and has invited publishers to opt out of having their copyrighted items digitized–if they specify exactly which ones they want omitted!)–and has sidestepped the concerns of librarians about the impact of Google Print.

We were not surprised when the company turned down our invitation to contribute to this publication. We have to face the fact that libraries are small potatoes in the Google universe. It will not accommodate itself to us; we will have to come to terms with it. As the essays here point out, there is potential for much good in our relationship with Google's products, but we must leave our comfort zones and rethink our relationships with our users, if we are to benefit from this phenomenon; if we do not do so, we risk being done in by it.

William Miller
Director of Libraries
Florida Atlantic University

Disruptive Beneficence:
The Google Print Program
and the Future of Libraries

Mark Sandler

SUMMARY. Libraries must learn to accommodate themselves to Google, and complement its mass digitization efforts with niche digitization of our own. We need to plan for what our activities and services will look like when our primary activity is no longer the storage and circulation of widely-available print materials, and once the printed book is no longer the only major vehicle for scholarly communication. *[Article copies available for a fee from The Haworth Document Delivery Service: 1-800-HAWORTH. E-mail address: <docdelivery@haworthpress.com> Website: <http://www.HaworthPress.com> © 2005 by The Haworth Press, Inc. All rights reserved.]*

KEYWORDS. Google Print, academic libraries, digitization, storage, futurism

---

Mark Sandler is Collection Development Officer, University Library, The University of Michigan, 920 North University, Ann Arbor, MI 48109 (E-mail: sandler@umich.edu).

Google® is a Registered Service Mark of Google, Inc., Mountain View, California. *Libraries and Google®* is an independent publication offered by The Haworth Press, Inc., Binghamton, New York, and is not affiliated with, nor has it been authorized, sponsored, endorsed, licensed, or otherwise approved by, Google, Inc.

[Haworth co-indexing entry note]: "Disruptive Beneficence: The Google Print Program and the Future of Libraries." Sandler, Mark. Co-published simultaneously in *Internet Reference Services Quarterly* (The Haworth Information Press, an imprint of The Haworth Press, Inc.) Vol. 10, No. 3/4, 2005, pp. 5-22; and: *Libraries and Google®* (ed: William Miller, and Rita M. Pellen) The Haworth Information Press, an imprint of The Haworth Press, Inc., 2005, pp. 5-22. Single or multiple copies of this article are available for a fee from The Haworth Document Delivery Service [1-800-HAWORTH, 9:00 a.m. - 5:00 p.m. (EST). E-mail address: docdelivery@haworthpress.com].

Available online at http://www.haworthpress.com/web/IRSQ
© 2005 by The Haworth Press, Inc. All rights reserved.
doi:10.1300/J136v10n03_02

5

We've all seen the story on TV soft news: a group of cafeteria workers, after years of paying into a lottery pool, hits a jackpot payoff worth hundreds of millions of dollars. Unaccustomed to the spotlight, the workers vow that their windfall good fortune will not change them. Perhaps they might buy a bigger house, pay off some bills, put away money for their kids' education, give some money to a favorite charity, and quit their jobs, but in the final analysis they will remain true to their underlying values and lifestyles. As viewers, we admire the integrity of the winners, but we also know what the winners seem not yet to realize: that life-changing events change lives. Good fortune is every bit as disruptive as an unanticipated disaster–a catastrophic flood or fire–and it requires extensive planning and soul searching to maintain some fundamental direction and stability in the face of an explosive change.

Since December 14, 2004, when Google announced[1] its intention to digitize the collections of several major research libraries, there has been a great deal of library, publisher, and reader interest in the *hows*, *whys*, and *whats* of that program. Google staff members, along with staff members from the partnering libraries, are making a good faith effort to explain the Google Print initiative to their respective communities, with the proviso that the program itself is a work in progress, not fully formed in anyone's mind. Conference programs have been filled to the rafters, and there are FAQs posted at the Google and partner Web sites.[2] Anybody wanting to know the stated intentions of the Google Print program can, in fact, know that at this time.

What these many press releases and panel presentations can't explain, however, is what this initiative, in the context of the already disruptive life-changes engendered by the advent of the World Wide Web, means for the future of libraries, the future of publishing, and the future of scholarship. Like our lottery winners, it is comforting to think that we'll all remain, at root, the same institutions; that after some minor adaptations to new circumstances we'll still be easily recognizable in fulfilling our core missions. This may prove true, of course, but it might also prove to be a naïve assessment of the scope of change we are facing.

Whether history shows that we have over- or under-estimated the effects of the disruptive technologies swirling about traditional institutions supporting scholarly communication, it is imperative that we engage the question and muster the courage to begin planning for the changes coming, even if our vision of the future is tentative and incomplete. In this article, very little time to is given to rehashing the specifics of the Google Print initiative. Rather, the focus is on the implications of a presumptively successful Google project, and the kinds of plans and actions that the library community, as a whole, might begin effecting in the face of this project.

WHAT GOOGLE IS DOING, AND WHY?

Google is working to digitize many millions of bound volumes held by major research libraries in North America and the United Kingdom. At the time of the initial press release, partner libraries for the Google Print initiative were Harvard, Michigan, New York Public, Oxford, and Stanford. Each of the partner libraries has agreed to contribute content to a different extent, Michigan and Stanford apparently offering the most comprehensive coverage of their holdings as of the time of the initial announcement. Google's intention is to work with each of these libraries to develop a mass digitization workflow of unprecedented scale. Google's conversion strategy and standards have been under development for a period of several years, and some of the partner institutions have had an opportunity to provide ongoing feedback on image quality, applying accepted library capture standards by comparing image samples to traditional preservation targets. Through this initiative, Google expects to make millions of print volumes searchable, and accessible worldwide without charge to end-users. This is clearly a breathtaking expansion of the democratization of human learning; probably the most significant since the advent of print technology attributed to Gutenberg in the 15th century.

As for why Google would commit to such an ambitious project, they say it is because it supports their company's mission "to organize the world's information and make it universally useful and accessible." In explaining the project, they describe their motivation as follows:

> [T]he project's aim is simple: help maintain the preeminence of books and libraries in our increasingly Internet-centric culture by making these information resources an integral part of the online experience. We hope to guide more users to their local libraries; to digital archives of some of the world's greatest research institutions; and to out-of-print books they might not be able to find anywhere else–all while carefully respecting authors' and publishers' copyrights.

Cynics might seek to look beyond such statements, and ask further why Google is *really* undertaking this effort? Is to make more money?

To enhance the value of their search engine? To preempt competitors from doing it first? Or, to make the world a better place? For those foolhardy souls who guess on multiple-choice exams, the best guess here might be, "all of the above." It is likely that Google sees the Library Print program as a worthwhile investment–a good business decision, but also a means of enriching the Web for the benefit of humankind. While the outcome of the Google Print initiative is itself uncertain in these very early stages of the work, even more uncertain is the surrounding technology and business environment in five to ten years when the project is targeted for completion. It seems unlikely that Google would waste its time laying firm business plans so far in advance of being able to foretell actual circumstances. Vaguely understanding the significance of this asset is probably enough to encourage one or more information companies to pursue such a direction, without firmly established plans for leveraging the asset.

WHAT ARE THE PARTNER LIBRARIES THINKING AND DOING?

One of the difficulties with the Google Library Print program is that it has been hard to learn what each of the partner libraries have agreed to, either with regard to the scope of the material being treated or the rights of a library to receive and use the Google files. Michigan, however, has made its Google contract public,[3] so at the time of this writing it is easiest to talk about that school, and see in time if others have a similar view of the process and their obligations. Michigan is already receiving back content from Google and doing systematic quality assurance review for the purpose of providing Google with further feedback on their capture metrics. Michigan's University Library has been acquiring additional file storage capacity, so that the returned digitized content can be stored electronically. At some point, likely within 2006, Michigan expects to make some of the out-of-copyright works available through its own online delivery mechanisms, i.e., DLXS, with much the same look and feel of other Michigan-hosted text resources like Making of America.

Accomplishing such an implementation for tens or hundreds of thousands of items (not to mention millions) is in no way trivial, even for institutions with considerable experience managing online resources. Metadata needs to be linked to the files by deriving headers from catalog records, and OCR text derivatives need to be correctly linked to page images. All of these pieces of the workflow may be understood, but there are a lot of files involved and each individual work needs to be correctly collocated for the overall "digital library" to be useful. Those who have worked in traditional print research libraries know all too well the frustration when the library catalog doesn't accurately reflect the status of an individual work in the stacks. Research librarians know that the successful management of a large library collection is accomplished one book at a time; managing the whole means accounting for the individual pieces. The same will be true for an online collection of millions of e-books–links need to work, searches need to lead readers to the correct page image, records need to accurately reflect the work in hand.

Without getting bogged down in the process of accomplishing the desired end (reminiscent of sausage making), the goal for Michigan is to provide online access in perpetuity to its collections. The publicly accessible cooperative agreement between Michigan and Google reads,

> [S]ubject to the restrictions set forth in this section, U of M shall have the right to use the U of M Digital Copy, in whole or in part at U of M's sole discretion, as part of services offered in cooperation with partner research libraries such as the institutions in the Digital Library Federation.

There is no intention, at least known to this writer, to do anything flashy with this content, or to compete with the Google implementation for the hearts and minds of worldwide users. Nonetheless, Michigan's Library has an obligation to make its collection conveniently accessible to its campus users; it is its core mission. Library staff will do this with all the energy and attention that they've devoted to servicing print collections for 150 years. The difference here, however, is that once this is being done for University of Michigan users, there is no reason–no marginal cost or competition for scarce copies–that would cause Michigan to impose access limitations upon outside readers. By developing a digital library for its core users, Michigan can serve others as well.

While we are all interested in what Google intends to do with the library resources they are digitizing, how they intend to manage these into the future, and how long the company's future might be, the library community should be comforted by the intentions of the partner libraries–some or all–to make their collections universally accessible. There should be little doubt that these institutions will represent the content in a manner consistent with the needs of academic users. And, there should be little doubt as well that these institutions will support the resource, as a reflection of their core collections, in perpetuity. Given these reassurances, it would seem that the library community as a whole needs to be thinking and talking about the implications of this initiative for how *libraries*, not Google, collectively manage this digital library collection into the future.

WHAT ARE THE REST OF THE WORLD'S LIBRARIES THINKING AND DOING?

Knowing what Google and its partners are up to is important, but it is equally important to know what other libraries–thousands of them–intend to do in response. Logic suggests three possible directions for the country's–or world's–libraries:

1. Ignore Google and carry on with locally driven activities as if the Google Print project doesn't exist.
2. Do nothing on the assumption that Google will take care of everything.
3. Develop strategies that aim to complement and extend what Google is doing.

1. Ignore the 800-pound gorilla–Ignoring Google by simply pretending it is of no relevance to Library users flies in the face of reality. Google is a primary information source for hundreds of millions of users each day. Perhaps some librarians would like to believe that they could better satisfy these hundreds of millions of users than can Google, in the same way that the producers of live theater undoubtedly believe they can deliver a richer entertainment experience than television. Well, maybe both are true–whatever "true" means here–but the reality is that the masses have already voted with their feet and their dollars. Libraries are not going to reclaim Google users as their own. They're gone; get over it. People like the Web and they like using Google to access the Web.

There is, however, a more compelling justification for moving forward as if the Google project doesn't exist. Libraries already committed to local conversion of print collections could quite reasonably decide to pursue their digital library strategy as if Google had not entered this market space. They don't, after all, know much about what the company or its partners are doing, don't have a good way to gauge their likelihood of success, and don't know if it will satisfy the needs of their institutional users. Librarians strive to understand and address the needs of their local users, on the assumption that these needs differ from place to place. Neither The University of Michigan nor Google is going to craft their content or delivery to address the needs of a professor of Danish linguistics at Bryn Mawr. Google is all about scale, not tailored services. They are the Wal-Mart of information providers–there is something for everyone, but you have to walk up and down a lot of aisles to find your item. Academic libraries, on the other hand, are more like boutiques–selective, coherent, and responsive to niche markets. These libraries cannot simply refer their users elsewhere and hope that the needs of those users will be adequately served. So, they could reasonably choose to pursue locally responsive projects, even in the face of massive conversion occurring elsewhere.

2. *Let others do it*–Doing nothing–as in "having the vision and courage to do absolutely nothing"–is a time-tested strategy in the face of profound and rapid changes. It should not seem unreasonable for a library to put local initiatives or acquisition decisions on hold until the Google initiative, and user interests in the face of that initiative, begin to take on some shape or predictable patterns. "Waiting for the dust to clear" is a safe and sensible management strategy, knowing that trying to go too far, too fast, makes no sense when the destination is uncertain and the direction of travel can't be determined.

Having said this, it is absolutely not the case that Google will "do everything," such that there will be no need for others to think about cooperation and take action. For one thing, the Google partner libraries don't hold everything–far from it. And even if these libraries did own the entirety of the world's known book output, their agreements with Google recognize large areas of exclusion. At Michigan, for instance, the independent business and law libraries are excluded. And, within the covered collections, various formats are excluded: such materials as newspapers, maps, microfilm, uncataloged collections, fragile items, unbound items, many categories of rare books, manuscripts, etc. In short, there are millions of exclusions that will live outside of Google's digital collection, so it is simply not the case that everything is already being done, so others can comfortably do nothing.

3. *Our complements (sic) to Google*–A third logical category of library response to Google is to try to understand the parameters of the Library Print project and act to complement it. The first two options characterized above suggest a number of directions for needed coordination and partnership. For one thing, non-partner libraries ought to be

busily identifying locally relevant resources that may not be held at the current Google source libraries. Local histories, municipal documents, university archives, etc., are valuable representations of a community, and are unlikely to be widely distributed among the nation's libraries–even the largest research libraries. Digitizing locally oriented collections would create a very rich resource when overlaid on top of a general academic library collection now being captured by Google.

Also, projects that focus on formats not being treated by Google–at least not in this first pass–would be a rich addition to the items currently being digitized. Rare books, for example, are protected at each of our libraries because they are . . . well . . . rare. By definition, they are unlikely to be held elsewhere. Also, rare books tend not to travel well, so often benefit from local treatment and onsite digitization. Converting the rare book collections of hundreds of research libraries would be a very important complement to the work of Google and its partners.

In other ways too, the library community as a whole could be working to complement the Google Print initiative. At best, Goggle Print will be a massive collection of undifferentiated books. Libraries and subject specialists need to be thinking of how this massive online collection can be optimized to better serve our users. Some obvious needs include:

- Curating communities of content that are responsive to the needs of specialized communities of users, and developing tools that would address the particular needs of these specialized communities of scholars.
- Identifying categories of material for selective upgrades, correcting OCR errors, enriching tagging, etc. These might include heavily used works, works of proven and enduring research and instructional value, and perhaps poetry or other genres that might be used in ways that may not be served well by Google digitization.
- Integration with other online collections–commercially acquired and locally produced. Users will not be well served by having to search a series of free-standing projects in their attempts to be comprehensive.
- Improving access through cataloging, indexing, applying taxonomies, creating analytics for series, and article level access for bound journal volumes, pamphlet collections, government reports, etc. Pinpointing retrieval is critical when the scale of available resources can so easily overwhelm a searcher.
- Archiving strategies should be collaboratively developed for both the digital files and their print source documents.

There is a great deal of traditional library work to be done to make the Google Print collection something of enduring value and utility to academic users and the general population of readers. Google's interests may not be congruent with the interests of academic or research libraries, and it would be unfair and unrealistic to expect that the five partner libraries could on their own do all that is required to ensure a comfortable fit for scholarly or specialized users. The partner libraries are already committing energy and resources to move print collections into the queue, and manage the digital files that are returned. For this to be a useful national resource, it will take nationally contributed library resources to shape and build it.

THE FUTURE OF LIBRARIES

To cooperate with Google or not to cooperate: that is a question (but probably not *the* question). If libraries cooperate with Google or "their kind," are they sowing the seeds of their own destruction? The easy answer here is that this is simply unknowable. Smart people will wax eloquent on all sides of this question, but in the final analysis "time will tell." We have these vector forces–some predictable and some not yet in our field of vision–speeding toward each other with explosive force. At the end of the day, after the big bang, what will survive and what shape will it have taken? Change in the society at large, and change in our world of scholarly communication, is so pervasive and so fast, it is folly to try to predict, no less control, a final outcome.

That being said, we do know that Google intends to digitize millions of books to a standard that meets its needs and the perceived needs of its users. It will organize these books in such ways that serve their user needs and, importantly, it will regulate the flow of access and delivery in accord with a business model that may or may not be known at this time, may or may not succeed, and will almost certainly change over time regardless.

The business model of the nation's largest research libraries is equally uncertain–the only certainty here being change. If you think your library will be more or less the same in ten years, then you are simply not thinking. Even the most stodgy and conservative libraries–those with large and historically rich legacy print collections–will be very different places in a decade's time. Online journal backfiles will allow for transformation of stacks space into group workspace. Reference resources such as dictionaries, encyclopedias, and directories will follow the path of abstracting and indexing services to e-only resources, clearing further space and untethering service functions from a collection in a particular space. Processing units will be small–no need to speculate about how small–but certainly not occupying large and central space that could more profitably be diverted to media centers, numeric and spatial data centers, interactive communication facilities, and spaces to support other bandwidth-intensive activities that are unlikely to be available in all corners of a campus or beyond. Print books will still be acquired, processed, and distributed in libraries, but they will not dominate the space as they do today.

DELIVERING THE GOODS

Libraries are cultural institutions, and, at root, cultural institutions (e.g., concert halls, museums, movie theaters, baseball parks) are retail outlets. Stores, gas stations, hotels, museums, hospitals, and libraries are distribution outlets for goods and services that the public wants or needs. As such, they are local outlets or distribution points for meeting community needs, which community members may pay for directly or which may be underwritten by a third party payer. So, rather than dealing with libraries as a special case, let's explore the fate of retail establishments in the age of the World Wide Web.

It turns out that the Web works very well for delivering certain kinds of goods and services to remote customers. Generally speaking, Web-conducive retail businesses include the following characteristics:

- Those that can deliver a product in a digital form, e.g., music, financial services, images (pornographic or otherwise), advice, print information, or research services.
- Those that can deliver a physical (corporeal) product cost effectively, and on time, from afar.
- Those that can permit a remote but adequate browsing and choice process online.

Retail businesses that have proven particularly vulnerable to Web shopping and distribution include music stores, banks, real estate, insurance agents, photo labs, pharmacies, travel agents, electronics stores, office supplies, movie theaters, casinos, prostitution, and greeting card stores.

For the most part, the above list includes types of services that can be delivered successfully from a central source, thereby undermining the need for a local outlet. Granted, the example of prostitution is extreme, but certainly many of those services provided locally and in person can be approximated on the Web, in a more private, safe, and convenient manner. So, it is not always a matter of whether an exact service can be replaced one-for-one via the Web, but if alternatives can be developed and delivered that satisfy an underlying need.

What kinds of goods and services are the least likely to be affected by the Web? Gas stations, for one, will still need to be widely distributed across the country. So too for hair stylists, dry cleaners, and tire stores. Food outlets–grocery stores, restaurants, and fast food joints–will continue to have a strong local retail presence because of the immediacy of demand (as in, "I'm starved!"), as will hotels and motels (as in, "I'm here, and I'm tired!"). Clothing stores will continue to do well, because for some shoppers the notions of a good or bad "fit" or "look" are so narrowly differentiated–so exacting–that it is hard to imagine that browsing, touching, and trying-on could be completely replaced by a cleverly designed Web site (although it is conceivable that custom-made clothing could return in a big way, consumers having their precise measurements on file for remote clothing manufacturers).

Highly personalized businesses such as spas, boutiques, cosmetic counters with full service consultations, and health clinics will likely continue to function as distributed retail outlets, as will tanning salons and tattoo parlors. Some things just can't be delivered remotely, be it pampering or pain.

LESSONS FROM THE RETAIL TRADE IN BOOKS

Libraries should take note that Amazon, the world's largest and most successful online retailer, has been none other than a supplier of books. Book browsing can be emulated online (Amazon's "search inside" feature), reviews and recommendations can surround a title, and shipping of the physical printed item is easy, with online delivery of electronic versions close at hand. Even more remarkable than Amazon's success in the new books retail market, is its success–along with eBay, ABE, Alibris, and others–in reselling used books. The Web is an efficient means for linking a private buyer to a private seller by transcending geographically bounded markets. This efficiency for recirculating used books has transformed the college textbook market even more dramatically than the clash of titan book retailers fighting for first sales. In short, books (new and used) have proven to be one of the most active areas of Web retailing, with yet more dramatic advances to come.

The real paradigm shift of retail book sales will come when an appliance is developed that has the appeal for reading that the iPod has had for listening to music. That will be the knockout blow for conventional notions of the book culture, and who can doubt that this is just one or two Christmas seasons away. People will buy a "gadget," (a "fashion accessory" as suggested by Gregory St. James of John Wiley and Sons) and they'll download texts on it that can be read or listened to. Newspapers, magazines, reference tools, retail catalogs, cookbooks, bibles and spiritual books, comics and graphic novels, travel guides, product manuals, work documents, novels, and much more will be delivered and stored this way, perhaps with some sort of convenient option for bulk end-user printing. Linear reading of print books will not disappear over night–nor, perhaps ever–but competitors will continue to emerge and compete for prominence among the several ways we receive information. This is not mere amateur soothsaying–these changes have already occurred, but the underlying technology requires further refinement and marketing before a significant cultural and economic shift will occur.

LIBRARIES GROW A LONG TAIL

Undeniably, retail service is changing, and book distribution is in many ways leading the way, which should give us some hints about the future of libraries in the age of Google. First and foremost, new retail models suggest that libraries have to get away from their accustomed role as book warehouses. Research libraries have always justified tremendous warehousing expenses as necessary to satisfy sporadic and idiosyncratic need. No for-profit, brick and mortar business could or would afford to maintain an inventory of several million items for which there may be (but often is not) one request over a period of ten or even fifty years. A working librarian may spend an entire career of thirty-five or forty years managing some number of books that are never touched. Space and management compete for scarce resources with other programs and services–some already existing and some envisioned as desirable. In the absence of demonstrable measures of utility or return, the warehousing of old books will be subject to increasing management scrutiny, that scrutiny coming either from library administrators or, more likely, from their funding sources. In an increasingly electronic age, it is reasonable and rational for a funding source to question the value of long-term management of little used resources (and we're ignoring the fact that these costs are borne redundantly by hundreds of libraries).

In contrast, projects like JSTOR's conversion of journal backruns, and the Google Print library partnership offer libraries the opportunity to reassess their role as repositories-in-perpetuity (R.I.P.) for little used print collections. In fact, this role is so well satisfied online, and so poorly satisfied in a tangible manifestation, that libraries will reassess the wisdom of dragging their historic collections through time like a giant ball and chain. It is true, of course, that most great research libraries don't truly want to be liberated from their historic print collections. They are a source of institutional pride, a source of distinction, and a measure of institutional value. If everyone in the world had exactly the same access to the same legacy collections, what would distinguish a top-ten university or library from a lower tier institution? If not aggregated print holdings, what will be used to measure excellence, and could this mean a reversal of fortunes and rankings in the library world?

In describing "the long tail" effect of successful online services, Chris Anderson directs our attention to the future of online retail services, and, by extension, invites a thoughtful reappraisal of research libraries.[4] His point is relatively simple: brick and mortar retail outlets, dealing with physical objects (be they books, CDs, or Twinkies), and limited storage and display space, need to make choices and ultimately commit space for items in highest demand. In a virtual world, however, there is little or no cost to storage or display space–both are infinite and affordable. Deterioration of inventory is negligible. Items can be maintained in stock, on display, and available for purchase forever. The effect of this is that items of little relative popular interest–an old library book, for instance–can be kept available to readers for almost no marginal cost. And, in the aggregate for a sales culture, these idiosyncratic unit needs can add up to a substantial overall business opportunity. When space is limited, we want to fill the shelves with a product that a million people want to buy (e.g., bestsellers). When, however, shelf-space is infinite, then sales of one item each to a million far-flung people has the same net result as betting on a few likely hits.

For the research library world, we have collectively done a wonderful thing by stewarding our print collections over a century or more to a time when it is possible to hand it off for repackaging and distribution through new channels. We are not, however, the gas stations of the future. We do not need to be in every community, hanging on to every book, on the off chance that today is the day a purposeful reader will walk through the door. Our low use collections need to be converted and made available electronically, and yes we need to establish one or several or dozens of cooperative print archives. Nobody needs to argue against the premise that the original print manifestation of a work could someday be important to some subset or readers. Libraries need to collaborate on a plan that ensures print availability for the increasingly rare circumstances that require access to the original published form of a work, but at the same time make it possible for 90% (or 99% or 50% or 80%) of others to get out of the print repository business.

The long-tail works for electronic resources, and we've seen this for years now in monitoring use of collections like the Making of America at The University of Michigan. Simply told, Michigan converted 10,000 low use monographs from its storage facility, and made them freely accessible over the Web. These low use 19th century materials were suddenly seeing between 500,000 and one million hits per month. In the past, these works were accessible to a base population of 40,000 students, faculty, and staff. That's about four readers for each book included in the project. When electronic versions of these works were made accessible to the entire world, suddenly 40,000 potential readers became 4 billion, and the odds of consumer interest jumped from 4:1 to 400,000:1. Add to that the extent to which Web access overcomes the impediments of physical delivery–request a book (sight unseen) from storage, wait twenty-four hours for delivery, come physically to the library to pick it up, etc. Electronically, we're talking about instant gratification of a one in a million need. This is a service dream come true for libraries and library users, especially those without immediate access to a great research library collection.

There are, of course, many other truths underlying digital storage and delivery. Desirable works are searchable and discoverable at the word level, not just by searching catalog records (author, title, subject fields) or abstracts or tables of contents. The more that is made searchable, the easier it is for the reader to connect to relevant resources. Second, multiple readers can use the same item at the same time, although that's probably not a leading concern for those lesser used items in the long tail. Nonetheless, it removes a longstanding need of libraries to limit access so that a primary service group would not be competing for scarce (one copy) resources with non-constituent users. Third, not only can a digital library support non-constituents without diminishing service to a primary constituency, it really doesn't matter where these non-constituents reside. While libraries have been generous in supporting interlibrary loan of books over the years, most have been unwilling to lend overseas. Distance matters in the print library world, but not so for a digital library.

When Ranganathan set forth his five laws for library science, he couldn't have written a better justification for moving forward on mass digitization of research library collections. In light of the above discussion, consider the contemporary relevance of these statements originally presented in 1931:

- Books are for use
- Every reader his/her book
- Every book, its reader
- Save the time of the reader
- A library is a growing organism

Who could better express how the current directions of library digitization are true to our most honored traditions: Ranganathan meets Wired!

IF NOT REPOSITORIES,
WHAT WILL RESEARCH LIBRARIES BE ABOUT?

Let's envision a time where all or most of a library's legacy collection is being pushed out electronically to readers near and far. The print basis for this collection is never called upon, and has been pushed off to a remote site for occasional access by researchers with unusual needs or methodologies. Current receipts are almost all electronic as well, maybe licensed by the library or maybe a new campus economy will be in place such that academic users pay for content directly. In such a world, what will the library as place, or, librarians as service providers offer the user?

To answer this question, we can look to many of today's traditional (for-profit) retail establishments. They are forced to manage two very different environments–an onsite store or stores and a Web accessible sales environment. As for the latter, and putting aside price competition, we need to understand why one Web retailer succeeds where others in the same market fail. The explanation is that more shoppers prefer the successful site to the others. Perhaps it is more attractive; perhaps better organized; perhaps shoppers are driven to it by endorsements or high service ratings; perhaps it has interesting textual descriptions of products; perhaps there are clever scripts to recognize and support return customers; or perhaps it can sense and present a local look and feel, regardless of from whence it emanates. As in the bricks and mortar world, there are hundreds of small reasons to prefer one service to another. Set free from the constraints of physical proximity, libraries in the future will compete nationally and internationally to attract users, and will therefore need to invest much more in their websites to attract and maintain readers.

In addition to building an excellent Web presence, what can we expect for the "library as space?" What will draw readers to the physical facility of an academic or public library, in a world where books are largely delivered to a desktop computer–or mobile BlackBerry, or whatever? We can expect in this environment, libraries will be aesthetically pleasing spaces. Comfortable spaces. Social spaces. Spaces with interesting exhibits and activities. And above all, they will be places of high service. Places where experts show a deep interest in an individual's needs, and provide knowledgeable assistance to meet these needs. The value they add will be the indulgence of personal relationship with the efficiency of expert retrieval. They will be high-end consulting centers. In short, they will be the cosmetic counters of the intellectual world. And, you'll be able to schedule house visits too!

And yes, there will still be books, and manuscripts, and maps and other "real" collections in our libraries. And there will be media centers with content and delivery systems that are not widely available to end-users. And maybe there will be high-speed print centers, and other support systems to facilitate scholarship. And, like now, much of the work of the library will be happening beyond the eye of the public. As they have been for centuries, library staff will most likely be organizing and contextualizing content in ways that make individual works more useful, and the work of individual users more productive. More and more of the works may be in an electronic format, and more and more of the users may be virtual visitors to the library, but the role of libraries and the role of librarians will still be valued by scholars and students, and perhaps more so by unaffiliated users who will be new and welcome constituents for our better utilized resources and services.

CONCLUDING THOUGHTS

Why should anyone have any confidence in the kinds of irresponsible predictions set forth in this article? Because, like so many futuristic predictions, a purportedly prescient vision of the future is little more than a scan of current and past practices–this stuff is already happening, and, in truth, the forces underlying these changes were unleashed before Google Print, and probably before Google, the brand or the concept, existed at all.

Google, to use the vogue phrase, is a "disruptive technology." Perhaps it is causing change, but more likely it is catalyzing changes already underway. To paraphrase Marx, "Technology is not in the saddle, and does not drive humankind." Nonetheless, technology does often serve as the jockey's whip, steering and speeding up sought-after social and economic change. For the relatively small world of scholarly communication, "disruption" does not call into question the ultimate goal–scholars must necessarily communicate with each other–but the means by which this will be accomplished is now shrouded with doubt. Will people still come to libraries or seek out library-licensed content? Will commercial abstracting and indexing services find ways to add search value to a degree that they will maintain their revenue base? Will scholarly publishers lose market share to those satisfied with fair-use protected snippets of information, and, if so, will this definition of fair-use survive the likely political and legal assault that lost revenues will engender? So, maybe Google is really less revolutionary than it is unsettling–it has introduced new possibilities, and in so doing has unleashed speculation about consequences that are, as yet, unpredictable. Given Google's creative energy, scale, and resources, it likely will have a profound impact on scholarly communication in the next decade. The nature of that impact is almost certainly unknowable to it, and absolutely unknowable for the rest of us.

More accessible for the library community, although in no way perfectly knowable, is how the Google print partner libraries will represent their collections in a digital world. These libraries should be, and are, talking with each other, and the library community as a whole should be engaging and embracing the project to make the most of it, for the most users. Nobody is saying that the Google initiative is a panacea that will render libraries irrelevant. If, however, the library community ignores the Google Print initiative, the success of Amazon, the ubiquity of the World Wide Web, advances in search engines, new and improved technologies for delivering content to users, and changing consumer preferences, how can we expect libraries to maintain relevance in a changed world? Yes, the print book was itself an amazing technology, and like all technologies will not be totally replaced by its successors. For the next hundred–maybe thousand–years, beachgoers or air travelers might still grab a paperback novel to help pass the time. This does not mean, however, that our society's predominant means for accessing present and past information won't be transformed in ways that will require substantial changes in "information stores" like libraries. Libraries, be they academic, public, or corporate, need to be planning the goods and services that will ensure their continued relevance to a community of information seekers, regardless of how we define "community," and it goes about the job of "seeking" and retrieving information.

Like Alexander and Hadrian before us, we're in the early days of thinking about how to organize, market, and deliver digital library services. This planning is a collective enterprise, and should include all those with an interest in the chain of scholarly communication–scholars, publishers, database providers, and librarians from all types of libraries. We can know in advance that much of what we decide will prove wrong, but this still has to be better than being too timid to look around, too self absorbed to seek help, and too entrenched in short term interests to embrace change.

NOTES

1. Google press release, Mountain View, CA, Dec. 14, 2004 <http://www.google.com/press/pressrel/print_library.html>.

2. <http://print.google.com/googleprint/library.html>; <http://library.stanford.edu/about_sulair/special_projects/google_sulair_project_faq>; <http://www.umich.edu/news/index.html?Releases/2004/Dec04/library/q&a#a>.

3. Cooperative Agreement between the Regents of The University of Michigan and Google, Inc. <http://www.lib.umich.edu/mdp/>.

4. Anderson, Chris, *Wired Magazine*, no.10, October 2004, pp. 171-177 <http://www.wired.com/wired/archive/12.10/tail.html>.

The Google Library Project at Oxford

Ronald Milne

SUMMARY. This article summarizes Oxford's participation in the Google Print project. *[Article copies available for a fee from The Haworth Document Delivery Service: 1-800-HAWORTH. E-mail address: <docdelivery@ haworthpress.com> Website: <http://www.HaworthPress.com> © 2005 by The Haworth Press, Inc. All rights reserved.]*

KEYWORDS. Google Print, digitization

When Sir Thomas Bodley founded the Bodleian Library in Oxford in 1602, his clear intention was that this new library should serve not just the University of Oxford, but also what he called the "Republic of Letters." By this he meant that the library should be open to all, and its collections made accessible to external readers whether they had an academic affiliation or not. Indeed, the Bodleian was referred to as "the publique library of the University of Oxford" at a time when most other libraries were essentially private and closed to all but those communities it was their primary function to serve. Oxford still respects, and is

Ronald Milne is Acting Director of University Library Services and Bodley's Librarian, Bodleian Library, Broad Street, Oxford OX1 3 BG (E-mail: ronald.milne@ ouls.ox.ac.uk).

Google® is a Registered Service Mark of Google, Inc., Mountain View, California. *Libraries and Google®* is an independent publication offered by The Haworth Press, Inc., Binghamton, New York, and is not affiliated with, nor has it been authorized, sponsored, endorsed, licensed, or otherwise approved by, Google, Inc.

[Haworth co-indexing entry note]: "The Google Library Project at Oxford." Milne, Ronald. Co-published simultaneously in *Internet Reference Services Quarterly* (The Haworth Information Press, an imprint of The Haworth Press, Inc.) Vol. 10, No. 3/4, 2005, pp. 23-28; and: *Libraries and Google®* (ed: William Miller, and Rita M. Pellen) The Haworth Information Press, an imprint of The Haworth Press, Inc., 2005, pp. 23-28. Single or multiple copies of this article are available for a fee from The Haworth Document Delivery Service [1-800-HAWORTH, 9:00 a.m. - 5:00 p.m. (EST). E-mail address: docdelivery@haworthpress.com].

proud of, its tradition of making its collections accessible to all who have need, to the extent that 60% of the Bodleian's registered users are not members of the University of Oxford.

For most of the 400 years of the Bodleian's existence, users have had to travel to Oxford to use its collections. Scholars and others who have been unable to travel or to stay long enough in Oxford to complete their projects have used analogue means of reproduction, such as microfilm, facsimiles, conventional photographs, and transparencies as surrogates, but the advent of the Internet and the ability to digitize and make available over the network complete bodies of text has opened up new models for delivery and sophisticated access to library collections.

With the generous help of the Mellon Foundation, five years ago, in 2000, recognizing the opportunities for enhanced access that digitization offered, Oxford established the Oxford Digital Library, with the intention of enhancing access to its collections over the Web. Consistent with the policy of making its collections as accessible as possible, Oxford has also been a major participant in projects such as Early English Books Online (EEBO) and Eighteenth Century Collections Online (ECCO).

Seen in the context of a 400-year history of making collections accessible to all, and of initiating and being involved in substantial digitization initiatives, Oxford's participation in the Google Library Project appears as a natural "next step."

Oxford's earliest significant library contact with Google was in late 2002 when, as a result of discussions between Reg Carr,[1] Director of University Library Services and Bodley's Librarian, and the University's North American Development Office, Google was identified as a potential partner in the "Hybrid Library" element of Oxford University Libraries Capital Campaign. Dr Carr was introduced to Raymond Nasr (Google's Vice-President, Executive Communications) at a *Silicon Valley Comes to Oxford* seminar held at the University's Said Business School. It was during lunch and an extended tour of the Bodleian that the possibility of Bodleian-Google cooperation was raised.

Clearly, the discussion had resonance. There appeared to be an obvious alignment between the two organizations and it made perfect sense to explore possible projects and collaborative efforts. Further contact with Google followed soon after the initial meeting, with David Drummond (Google's Vice President for Strategy and Business Development) visiting Oxford in January 2003 and Reg Carr being invited to visit Google a month later, in February 2003, to coincide with a scheduled Research Libraries Group meeting in Mountain View.

While visiting Google at Mountain View, Carr met with a number of senior members of Google staff and discussed ways of developing Google access to information sources "hidden" in the Deep Web and beyond the Web. Evidently, Google already had an emerging ambition to expose much more material to its Web crawlers and to digitize and index it, and the talk was of an "offline content project." This has proved to be a rough prototype of what eventually became known to the world as Google Print.

During the same visit, Carr presented a paper on seamless access to research resources which discussed possible Google/Oxford synergies, and he urged Google to have conversations with major research libraries, such as the Bodleian, about ways of providing Google Search access to research library materials, both electronic and non-electronic, as a means of enhancing the quality of search results. It was agreed that Google's long-term mission and Oxford's aim of digitizing and making its material available over the Web were well-matched, and it was proposed that discussions should continue.

During the next few months discussions about a library-related project continued by e-mail while, at the same time, Google was talking to publishers who were willing to allow the company to provide a shop window for digitized versions of current materials and/or publication backlists. Carr travelled to Mountain View again in November 2003, together with a member of staff from the University's North American Development Office, for more focused discussions on the exact nature of Oxford libraries/Google collaboration. Work with publishers and initial discussions with "a number of leading research libraries" was alluded to. Agreement was reached that "the Google team" would visit Oxford as early as possible in January to view the set-up at the Bodleian, to progress the matter and, more specifically, to firm up on the detail. The Oxford visit to Mountain View concluded with a tour of Google's experimental in-house digitization operation.

In mid-January 2004 a four-man Google team visited Oxford for a full-day discussion with senior library staff who might be involved in any future project. The team also toured the Bodleian. Agreement was reached that Google and Oxford would pursue an agreement whereby Google would set up a digitization operation in Oxford to create digital copies of public domain materials for mutual exploitation and benefit.

Between February and December 2004 there were frequent exchanges of drafts of the Agreement, discussion documents, and points for negotiation. Reg Carr continued to have oversight of the negotiation process while the author and the University's Director of Legal Services became more intensively involved in the fine detail of the discussions. The most senior officers of the University gave their support to the project and approval to proceed was given by the University Council. The Agreement was signed by the University's Registrar.

On 14 December, the announcement relating to the "Google Five" (the libraries of Oxford, Harvard, Stanford, and Michigan universities and the New York Public Library) was made and there was wide coverage in the international media. The project was covered by UK national television and newspapers, and the author spent the best part of a week responding to requests for interviews from the UK and around the world. It had not been possible to talk about our forthcoming deal with library colleagues in other institutions. Thus, for many, the news in the media was the first they had heard of the project.

January 2005 saw the appointment of Google's main Oxford project contact, and an existing member of Oxford staff, Frances Boyle, was appointed by Oxford as Oxford's Google Project Manager. In February the author and others from Oxford visited Google's headquarters in Mountain View where we began detailed discussions about practical issues. Google personnel are now visiting Oxford on a very regular basis, and the on-site Google project manager for the Oxford programme started work at the beginning of August. We expect to be scanning books by the end of the year.

What exactly is being digitized in Oxford? The project will undertake the digitization of nineteenth-century public domain material held principally in the Bodleian Library, but also in other libraries within the University of Oxford, such as the Radcliffe Science Library (which is the principal science library in Oxford and which holds scientific legal deposit material for the University), the Sackler Library (classics, archaeology and history of art) and the Taylor Institution Library (the University's modern languages research library). It is expected that between 1 and 1.5 million out-of-copyright books will be digitized under the Agreement. Although it is believed that the majority of books will be in the English language, as in the other Google libraries, books in other languages will also be scanned.

The Agreement is non-exclusive and digitization will take place on University premises. Google will retain the "Google Digital Copy" and Oxford will receive an "Oxford Digital Copy." The digitized book will be navigable, and there will be a link from the Oxford catalogue to the digital copy. Within certain constraints designed to protect the investment made by Google, a complete copy of any individual work digitized under the Oxford programme can be made available over the

Internet to anyone who has Web access. This is only possible because all works being digitized in Oxford are already in the public domain. The cost, infrastructure, and planning required to make the Oxford Digital copy available are such that, in the first instance, Google has agreed to host access to the Oxford copy.

As one might expect, a considerable amount of Oxford staff time has been spent in considering the fine detail of the project. An Oxford University Library Services "Google Steering Group" has oversight of, and provides direction for, working groups set up to deal with logistics and conservation, legal and personnel issues (relating, for example, to digital rights, to the lease of the University premises to Google, and the training of Google staff to follow agreed conservation standards), and systems and technologies. (How will Oxford make the Oxford Digital Copy accessible? What metadata standards will we use?) We tested our workflow over a three-day period during May. This was an exercise from which we learned a great deal! The trial involved the identification of holdings to be digitized, appraisal, transfer of the material by van to the scanning centre, barcoding of books and associated bibliographic work (the Bodleian does not lend, and none of the stock is currently barcoded), and return of material to the Bodleian. The real challenge proved to be the bibliographic work associated with barcoding, but also of interest, and an issue for us to resolve, is that a survey of nineteenth-century stock held in the Bodleian revealed that approximately 20% of holdings are wholly or partially uncut. This is perhaps not surprising, given that much of the stock has been acquired by legal deposit. The percentage is much lower in other Oxford libraries.

The process of digitization will be on an industrial scale, and it will quite simply not be possible to "cherry-pick" individual items for digitization. The Google scanning process is non-invasive, but Oxford maintains the absolute right to say that particular items may not be digitized for conservation reasons. Subject to any concerns we may have relating to fragile material, we expect to digitize everything within our nineteenth-century printed collections with which the Google scanning technology can currently cope. The scope of nineteenth-century printed material held within the Bodleian and other libraries is immense and covers an extraordinarily wide range of interests. We intend to digitize printed material in every subject area and will cover all works, including those which would have had no particular academic interest when they were first acquired by the library (but may do so now). Thus trade and post office directories, railway timetables, travel guides, and recreational magazines will be digitized alongside academic books and journals.

We expect the outcome to be of considerable value to scholars and to the intellectually curious, wherever in the world they may live. The Google Library Project undoubtedly represents a step-change in the facilitation of access to information resources and Oxford is proud to be associated with the initiative, not least because it contributes very significantly to fulfilling Sir Thomas Bodley's desire that collections in the library that he founded should be available to all. Surely he would be pleased that the Bodleian ethos has found expression in the Digital Age.

NOTE

1. I am indebted to Reg Carr for allowing me to use his personal notes as a source for this article. I further acknowledge as a source his contribution to the Opening Plenary Panel session of the CNI Spring 2005 Task Force Meeting, Washington DC, 4 April 2005.

The (Uncertain) Future of Libraries in a Google World: Sounding an Alarm

Rick Anderson

SUMMARY. Libraries are in competition with other entities that provide information access to students, scholars and the general public. This constitutes a radical change in the information environment. The library profession's failure to take seriously the change that has taken place in the information environment, and to respond with fundamental changes of its own, may well spell disaster for the library as we know it. *[Article copies available for a fee from The Haworth Document Delivery Service: 1-800-HAWORTH. E-mail address: <docdelivery@haworthpress.com> Website: <http://www.HaworthPress.com> © 2005 by The Haworth Press, Inc. All rights reserved.]*

KEYWORDS. Google, Internet, patron behavior, online resources, search engines, traditional libraries

---

Rick Anderson is Director of Resource Acquisition, University of Nevada, Reno Libraries, 1664 North Virginia Street/MS 322, Reno, NV 89434 (E-mail: rickand@unr.edu).

Google® is a Registered Service Mark of Google, Inc., Mountain View, California. *Libraries and Google®* is an independent publication offered by The Haworth Press, Inc., Binghamton, New York, and is not affiliated with, nor has it been authorized, sponsored, endorsed, licensed, or otherwise approved by, Google, Inc.

[Haworth co-indexing entry note]: "The (Uncertain) Future of Libraries in a Google World: Sounding an Alarm." Anderson, Rick. Co-published simultaneously in *Internet Reference Services Quarterly* (The Haworth Information Press, an imprint of The Haworth Press, Inc.) Vol. 10, No. 3/4, 2005, pp. 29-36; and: *Libraries and Google®* (ed: William Miller, and Rita M. Pellen) The Haworth Information Press, an imprint of The Haworth Press, Inc., 2005, pp. 29-36. Single or multiple copies of this article are available for a fee from The Haworth Document Delivery Service [1-800-HAWORTH, 9:00 a.m. - 5:00 p.m. (EST). E-mail address: docdelivery@haworthpress.com].

Available online at http://www.haworthpress.com/web/IRSQ
© 2005 by The Haworth Press, Inc. All rights reserved.
doi:10.1300/J136v10n03_04

In order to understand the impact that Google is having on libraries, it is important to take a step back and remember what life was like only 15 years ago. Things have changed so dramatically and quickly in that time, and we have absorbed those changes to such a degree in our everyday lives, that it is becoming increasingly difficult to remember what life was like in the B.G. (Before Google) period.

In the late 1980s, it was not easy to locate or gain access to relevant, high-quality information. If one needed to know about the annual migration patterns of dolphins in the Pacific Ocean, or about the synthesis of two chemical compounds, or about the gross national product of Luxembourg, a trip to a library was probably one's only option. Once in the library, it would not always be clear where one should start. One might try an encyclopedia first, or *Chemical Abstracts*, or one might search the library catalog for a book about dolphins or a compilation of European economic data. The likelihood of finding exactly what one needed in the first resource one located was relatively low.

Eventually one might ask a librarian for help, and that might do the trick. But depending on the size of the collection and the specificity of one's research need, there was always a good chance that one would have to be referred to another, larger library. With luck, that library would not be very far away. With even more luck, that larger library would have the needed information–though again, depending on the nature of one's query, there was a good chance that the second library would fail to meet one's need as well. For those without access to a major research collection, gaining access to needed information might require several trips to different libraries and hours (if not days) of research.

In 2005, we live in a dramatically different information world. Huge amounts of high-quality information are now available at no charge to anyone who has Internet access, and Internet access is almost as universally available as television. Reliably accurate answers to most general reference questions can be found almost instantly online using remarkably simple search strategies. Public information services that only a few years ago required dedicated buildings, expensive collections of books, and a full-time professional staff are now provided on a free, self-serve basis, 24 hours a day, in the homes of those who need them.

The fundamental nature and radical effects of this change in the world's information economy can hardly be overstated. If a similar revolution had taken place in the housing economy or the bond market, it seems likely that significant social and economic upheaval would have resulted. But while the information revolution has certainly not gone unnoticed or commented upon, and it has had many significant impacts on the way people function in society, for the most part the world has simply taken its effects in stride. We have, for example, incorporated e-mail (a communication method unprecedented in its power, speed, efficiency, and flexibility) and online news services (unprecedented in their ability to communicate a wide variety of perspectives on world events in real time to billions of people simultaneously) into our professional and personal lives with a mixture of pleasure and frustration, but with little explicit fanfare. This is simply the way the world is now. Today's children and adolescents have no direct memory of the information environment of the late 1980s, and are aware of its historical existence in much the same way that Baby Boomers and members of Generation X are aware that there was once a world without television. For today's students and future researchers, the world is simply a place where they can get most of the information they need immediately and without assistance–and certainly without driving across town to the library, there to spend hours of fruitless searching in crudely indexed, incomprehensibly organized, out-of-date printed books.

This information revolution is, in itself, a matter of deep import to librarians and library services. But the almost unconscious ease with which the general public has adapted itself to these fundamental changes is even more important, and our profession's response to that adaptation will determine (if it has not already) whether we are able to retain an important place in the lives of those we have been hired to serve. There is a great danger that we will not be able to do so–that, in fact, our unwillingness to adapt our practices to the new realities of a fundamentally changed world has already crippled our ability to serve the information needs of our users in a meaningful and useful way.

One symptom of this problem can be seen in our profession's response to the emergence of Google. That response has typically been one of public derogation coupled with private adoption. Our public statements are often deeply wrongheaded. Comparing Google search results to fast food, for example, (Bell, 2004) may give us a *frisson* of condescending satisfaction, but it is not an apposite comparison. The Internet is much less like a McDonald's than a supermarket–McDonald's offers a small, limited menu of unappetizing fast food, whereas a supermarket offers shelves and shelves (more than one could ever consume) of fresh produce, candy bars, poisonous chemicals, baking supplies, canned vegetables, seasonings, etc. The problem, of course, is that the Internet is not organized the way a grocery store is, with the produce in one corner and the candy, cleaning products, and canned vegetables all arranged in separate aisles.

In fact, the Internet is not organized in any way at all. Hence, librarians would say, the need for libraries to organize it and present it in a more rational form to end users. Some commercial enterprises have agreed. Yahoo! was an early (and fairly successful) attempt at organizing the Internet in a way similar to the way a grocery store organizes food, with entries categorized and placed in virtual sections. This is also the way a library organizes books. Yahoo!'s approach was moderately successful until Google came along. Google took a very different tack. Using Google to search the Internet is like walking into a grocery store that has no organizational structure whatsoever, saying the words "milk lowfat quart" and then having someone appear (in less than one second) with a cart full of food items whose descriptions include those words. Some of those items will actually be quart containers of lowfat milk. Others will not be. The amount of time and trouble it takes the end user to formulate an effective search strategy and then to cull what is wanted from the search results will determine whether she returns to that store again.

By any reasonable standard, Google has succeeded wildly at finding its users the information they want in return for a minimum investment of time and energy. The librarian response to this fact has been to point out that Google falls short of perfection. First, it often returns huge lists of search results, which may be overwhelming to users, and in which the best (most accurate, relevant and timely) information may be deeply buried. Second, it searches only the open Web–those online documents that are freely available to the public. This means that a user who thinks he may have appendicitis will get only a partial answer to his urgent medical queries by using Google, since many high-quality medical resources are unavailable to the nonpaying public. And third, most people are not trained researchers and may not know how best to formulate good search strategies. Many users do not even know that it is possible to search for phrases in Google, or how to isolate search terms in page titles. They may think they have found what they wanted, whereas much better (more accurate, more complete, more relevant) information would have been available to them in the library or through the library's Web site.

All of these points are true, as far as they go. But they are irrelevant, for several reasons. First, they ignore how much closer Google and the Internet get to a perfect information solution than libraries do. While it is true that the Internet offers more information than users can absorb, this is also true of libraries–except for those libraries that offer less than users need, of which there are a great many. A rational user, given the choice between a surfeit of information from which the relevant piece must be plucked on one hand and a lack of relevant information on the other, will very possibly (and quite rationally) choose the former. Conversely, while it is true that Google offers only limited access to high-quality information, it is also true that it provides high enough quality to meet most users' needs quite adequately, compared to the available alternatives. (The appendicitis sufferer may not get all the information he needs on the open Web, but how much better would he do in his local public–or even academic–library? And at how much additional cost in energy and time–time being perhaps the more important variable in his case?) Second, while it is true that the average person's expertise as a searcher is limited, this limitation applies equally to that person when he is in a library. Yes, librarians are often (though not always) available to help, but tutoring is a far less effective and efficient solution to the problem than fixing the search interface, which is exactly what Google has done.

Let us not mince words. For libraries in the 21st century, the situation is dire. The library as we know it was designed to meet the needs of a society whose chief information problem was one of scarcity: information was stored primarily in one format (print) and had to be found, purchased, organized, and housed carefully in central buildings in order for people to have access to it. Libraries did a good job of meeting this need, but the radical changes of the past two decades have left traditional library practices behind. Information is no longer stored primarily in print formats; most published information is created and stored electronically–printing comes later, if at all–and a tremendous amount of it is made freely available to the general public through the Internet. The defining characteristic of today's information world is not one of scarcity, but of glut.

There are those who grumble that libraries are not adapting to this reality, but they are wrong. Libraries *are* adapting to the new information world, but they are doing so slowly, reluctantly, and ineffectively. As a profession, we are holding onto practices and attitudes that stopped making sense almost two decades ago, and are losing our patrons as a result. This is not an indication of weak character or laziness on the part of our patrons. It is an indication of rationality on the patrons' part, and of stubborn foolishness on ours.

In the current environment of information surfeit, content is no longer king. Content is cheap and ubiquitous. Today the scarcest, and thus most valuable, commodity in the information marketplace is *attention*. The amount of publicly-available information has skyrocketed, while the length of a day has remained, stubbornly, at 24 hours. This means that those who wish to provide information services to researchers in an effective and attractive manner must find ways to do so that minimize the amount of time researchers have to invest in the process. Libraries have not only failed to do this, they have presented that failure as something of a moral crusade. To make information gathering too quick and easy, we say, would be to "dumb down" the research process, or to "spoon-feed" our patrons. This attitude is both wrongheaded and self-destructive. As a profession, we are doing a very good job of marshalling carefully an abundant commodity (information, which we catalog, organize and preserve with unflagging vigor) while squandering an increasingly rare one (our patrons' time and attention).

What, specifically, does Google do well that libraries have traditionally done poorly? There are three general areas:

1. *Service on demand.* Google, and the Internet in general, give users information when they need it, and without requiring them to travel to get it. Libraries traditionally have offered information only *when* librarians were willing to give it (during business and some evening hours) and only *where* they were willing to give it (within the confines of the library building). In response to the online juggernaut, one response of librarians has been to point out the reliability of the print collection–or, as more than one librarian has said to this author, "at least you know the print collection is not going to go down." However, precisely the opposite is true–a print collection goes down every night when the library locks its doors, and it remains down until the doors open again the next morning. A library that closes at midnight every night and opens at 8:00 the next morning is "down" for fully four months out of every year. Not even the least reliable online database comes anywhere near that level of patron disservice.

2. *Service at the article level.* Google provides a highly granular level of service. Because it searches the full text of online documents, it provides access to individual articles and pages. Libraries generally provide access at the title level–they catalog journals and books, not articles and chapters. This poses a serious problem for the patron who is seeking actual information, rather than physical containers of information. Knowing that the library has holdings in *Brain Research* is suggestive of whether the library has a

particular article that is relevant to his or her topic, but does not actually give the patron what she or he needs. What the patron needs, in most cases, is not to know that the library subscribes to *Brain Research*, but access to a specific article from *Brain Research*. Historically, libraries have provided only crude tools (such as printed indexes) to help patrons zero in on specific, relevant journal articles.

3. *Full-text searchability.* Traditionally, libraries have required their patrons to learn and adapt their searching behavior to the requirements of prescribed search languages and strategies, and have offered searchability only at the title/author/subject level. Library catalogs do not interrogate the actual content of the collection. Instead, they search descriptions of the content, and the descriptions they search are not written in plain English, but in "librarianese." Google allows the user to pick his own terms and phrases and use them to interrogate the full text of documents on the open Web.

When these issues are pointed out to librarians as explanations for the massive migration of users to the Internet, the response has been along these lines: "Libraries are better than the Internet because they offer more focused and high-quality content selected by knowledgeable professionals, and because they offer expert help. Our users need this help; most are not trained researchers, and they will miss valuable documents if they are not guided to well-selected sources and assisted in their searching."

The problems with this response are several. First of all, it is quickly becoming less and less true that libraries offer more high-quality content than the open Web does. It is true that there will always be essential information that costs money–often more than individual users are able to pay. But there is no longer any reason why a traditional library needs to act as the broker for that kind of information. Statewide database purchases, for example, are becoming more common–such deals may be brokered by libraries, but they do not need to be.

Second, while it is true that most information seekers are not expert researchers, it is also true that the librarian's ability to turn them into expert researchers has always been extremely limited and that most users have gone without that help. Even more relevant is the speed with which Google is turning itself into a portal for high-quality scholarly information. Google Scholar and the nascent Google Print program are poised to make high-quality scholarship available through the very same search strategies that people now use, successfully, to find driving directions and nude pictures of celebrities.

Many libraries are responding appropriately, if belatedly, by making more and more of their services and resources available online. But the traditional attitude remains deeply rooted in the librarian psyche: by making information more easily available we are "dumbing down" our services; patrons need to learn research skills, not have information handed to them on a silver platter; online is not necessarily better than print; print is reliable and permanent, whereas online is unreliable and ephemeral. Some of these attitudes are normative, even religious, and not terribly susceptible to reasoned debate; others are debatable observations of empirical reality. All of them are utterly irrelevant to the question of whether, and how, libraries will survive in a Google world.

REFERENCES

Bell, Stephen. "The Infodiet: How Libraries Can Offer an Appetizing Alternative to Google." *Chronicle of Higher Education* 50, no. 24 (2004), p. B15.

A Gaggle of Googles:
Limitations and Defects
of Electronic Access as Panacea

Mark Y. Herring

SUMMARY. In recent years, Google has expanded at a furious rate and so have its competitors. While these sources are important to libraries and play an important role within the library, they are neither a substitute nor a panacea to information access as is often thought. Serious weaknesses exist in Google and the rest, and librarians should resist the hype of enthusiasts who believe libraries are no longer important, or are becoming obsolete. *[Article copies available for a fee from The Haworth Document Delivery Service: 1-800-HAWORTH. E-mail address: <docdelivery@haworthpress.com> Website: <http://www.HaworthPress.com> © 2005 by The Haworth Press, Inc. All rights reserved.]*

KEYWORDS. Libraries, Google, electronic access, information access, library obsolescence, paperless society

Mark Y. Herring is Dean of Library Services, Winthrop University, Dacus Library, 824 Oakland Avenue, Rock Hill, SC 29732 (E-mail: herringm@winthrop.edu).

Google® is a Registered Service Mark of Google, Inc., Mountain View, California. *Libraries and Google®* is an independent publication offered by The Haworth Press, Inc., Binghamton, New York, and is not affiliated with, nor has it been authorized, sponsored, endorsed, licensed, or otherwise approved by, Google, Inc.

[Haworth co-indexing entry note]: "A Gaggle of Googles: Limitations and Defects of Electronic Access as Panacea." Herring, Mark Y. Co-published simultaneously in *Internet Reference Services Quarterly* (The Haworth Information Press, an imprint of The Haworth Press, Inc.) Vol. 10, No. 3/4, 2005, pp. 37-44; and: *Libraries and Google®* (ed: William Miller, and Rita M. Pellen) The Haworth Information Press, an imprint of The Haworth Press, Inc., 2005, pp. 37-44. Single or multiple copies of this article are available for a fee from The Haworth Document Delivery Service [1-800-HAWORTH, 9:00 a.m. - 5:00 p.m. (EST). E-mail address: docdelivery@haworthpress.com].

In the *Cabbala* (or as it is sometimes called *Kabala*), a collection of Jewish myths of anonymous authorship, one of the more familiar stories finds God discussing his proposed creation of man with Fire (one must suppose the crucible of creativity) in his lap. Hilariously, Fire advises against it.

I see this myth as having some generalizability to Google. The Web is a good idea, even a great one; and Google, too, has its multitudinous advantages. No one can gainsay that. Furthermore, though the title of this essay plays on the name, there is a gaggle of Googles out there now: Google, Google Images, Google Scholar, Google News, Google Groups, and of course Froogle, Google's answer to E-bay. Who can say how many will come later? But even before Google, we had versions of the same, some of which remain, in Netscape, Hotbot, ILOR, Lasso, Wisenut, and Yahoo, Google's chief competitor. Even before many of these, we had versions of Google's current aspirations in Xanadu, the Gutenberg Project, the now defunct netLibrary (resurrected under OCLC), and the on-again, off-again, on-again-sort-of Questia, an *omnium gatherum* of books online. Each of these enterprises has its merits as each has its defects. While none to my knowledge have claimed to make libraries obsolete, it should be clear by now that this is a possible unintended effect, and something more bean-counters that we would like to admit wish would happen, at least to *some* degree.[1]

Now comes word from the paper of record that the University of Texas is giving up on books.[2] One might say, as the late Ronald Reagan did, "There they go again," meaning of course those who want the world to be paperless. For the better part of my career (which now spans almost three decades) I have been hearing about the coming paperless library and yet we are no closer than we were three decades ago. But of course it will come and surely this time is the right time. With Google and her gaggle in tow, how can all of this be anything but a great ripening of so much electronic fruit whose harvest has come?

It has ripened all right, and then some. Try overripened. Not only has the Web sunk to new depths, what with its 100 million porn sites added yearly, its hate sites, its grand and somehow shameless disinformation (not to mention its misinformation, too), but also the efforts to create a new Web sans these defects is having about as much success as former Vice President Gore's new television network. For all its luster, the Web often acts like a barber shop in a town of bald-headed men. It's needed, but often not like this, and not yet. Add to this the aforementioned news that yet another digitizing enterprise is underway by the magnate, Google. Well, here they go again. Google is rushing to tread where others feared not to and stumbled (Questia, Xanadu, Gutenberg, netLibrary, etc.). A month into this new enterprise and we still do not know whether Google's project will include 15 million complete books, 15 million parts of some as yet uncounted books or 15 million book bites (a la sound bites). When you add it all up, the Web, that once great idea sounds more and more like the making of one of those old-fashioned Hollywood disaster films. And bear in mind it is this same disaster film that threatens to replace libraries.

Disaster film? Isn't this overkill? Consider the facts we already know about the Web in general. First, we know not everything is on the Web, nor is everything that's there all indexed in one place, not on Google or any other search engine.[3] To date only about 25 percent of all known academic serial publishing is on the Web and the vast majority of that is not free.[4] Some part of academic publishing, because it is so esoteric, will never make it to the Web. Most of what gets added to aggregate databases is driven, for lack of a better word, by popularity. Journals that are desired by only a handful of scholars will never make it to first-choice databases. Moreover, these esoteric journals are also the likely ones that are cancelled in paper since so few actually need them, making them effectively available to no one. In some cases this is no real loss since too much unnecessary publishing goes on in academia. But many fine titles fall by the wayside far too quickly. Perhaps the worst case scenario endgame of this was played out at Johns Hopkins when an Internet-only search proved a possible drug protocol safe to administer.[5] After one healthy young woman died, a second, conventional paper search was done. Surely enough, there in the buried paper literature were papers contraindicating the very drug protocol used.

The Web, even with Google, is like some gigantic haystack and the user is faced with finding that one needle. Google, for example, somewhat proudly tells us that 3.5 million hits have been returned in 1.245 seconds. What we practitioners in the world of information access know is that the screen really holds four or five, and that *the first four or five* are all that any student will look at, regardless of quality. In rare cases this may work out just fine. In most others, the results are of dubious quality. For example, a simple search on the "White House" can turn up the government site as easily as it can its parody. While *some* adults will see the difference immediately, it can no longer be assumed that even the high school aged can tell the difference. Take, for example, http://www.dhmo.org/, a Web site devoted to broadcasting the dangers of dihydrogen monoxide. So well-done was this parody that some of its bogus research ended up fooling members of Congress and other international organizations.[6] Having 5 million hits at your fingertips gives you a Wal-Mart sized library at the click of a button for every research project. But that isn't all that helpful when you think about it. Sure, the information may be there but isn't finding the *right information* the whole point of what we information access practitioners do?

Similarly, there is no quality control. Even Google recognizes this and so Google Scholar has evolved.[7] While this *may* well develop into something useful, for now its beta self is chock full of easily located medical and scientific information and little·else. What there is, is also available in other, more easily accessible entities. Add this to all the misinformation and disinformation, and you have a howling waste, as one wag once called the Web.

Even when we purchase aggregate databases what we don't know may well hurt us. Footnotes get dropped. Some images will not print. Graphs are at times missing, unprintable, hard to read, or display as the famous "broken image" icon. All of this we are to applaud and accept without question. Of course, if any library purchased an academic journal with pages missing or footnotes cut off, we'd file a claim immediately. Apparently with the Web, users are treated roughly and made to like it. We'll pass on that for now and continue with the litany of ills we are forced to accept as advantages and be thankful about to boot.

About every 10 months we hear about the demise of the book or print with the advent of a new digitization project. As mentioned above, Google is embarking on one to great fanfare. Yet as more news comes out about it, the more we come to know that this union of Web and library we have married isn't a man (or woman) at all but a dog, and a mangy one at that. If such ventures do not end in Chapter 11 (such as those that have been mentioned above) then they end up limping along (like Questia or the Gutenberg Project). Further, Google has recently revealed that those 15 million will not all be new books but predominately ones printed before 1923, or those in public domain. If all of this were not enough, we further find the projected corpus will be most if not all English-language materials. So irritating did this prove to be that even the French, *mon Dieu*, finally got angry about something and threatened to do their own project. So far no word about cost, though we already know that if one were to fully digitize (i.e., indexing every word) even a modest library of 500,000 volumes, it would be most formidable.[8] Even accepting Google's faith that it can do the project for next to nothing, no one has factored in any of the costs for all the paper patrons will use to print out anything more than three pages long.

Always in the discussion of would-be Google projects are e-books, though one hears less and less about them. Could it be that's because e-book readers do not work, or do not work very well? The only ones I've seen that are easy to read cost about $2,000 each, not exactly the basement bottom, fire sale prices we were promised. My favorite e-book reader story is the one that was advertised as simulating a page turning each time you clicked "next page." This is the sort of thing that makes you go, hmm.

We're still waiting for those paperless libraries, too. Several such libraries were once talked about and yet we still do not have one even after the first one which was promised in the mid-nineties. Those small libraries that boast of being fully automated turn out either to have a small cadre of books on hand, making the paperless claim only, well, on paper, or to give patrons access to other conventional libraries in the area. Meanwhile, the Internet remains a mile or two wide and an inch or less deep. Even the famed Google Scholar isn't delivering as planned. Yes, of course it's only Beta right now, another word for "shell game"; but it cannot deliver without making money and in order to do that, it will have to remain pretty much like the Web. As mentioned earlier, most of Google Scholar is made up of medical and technical papers, all already available on the Web. Whatever else will be added will be marginal as most aggregate databases will not give their content up without a fee. When that fee is added in, Google Scholar will either have to charge or have to advertise to recoup cost. Call me old fashioned, but I'm not too keen on getting a pop-up about erectile dysfunction in the middle of *The Taming of the Shrew*.

To worsen all this news is the utter (and at times dismaying) capitulation made by so many within our profession. At a digitizing conference in early 2000, I registered some of these complaints and the *librarians* on the dais were quick to come to the rescue of the electronic representatives. Oh, that's all going to be fixed, don't worry, I was told. Here we are a half decade later and it's still the same. In 2002, I offered the American Library Association my poster, "10 Reasons Why the Internet Is No Substitute for a Library." I could understand someone telling me it just wasn't very good, or that the idea was a silly one. What astonished me was the word from the committee: most members thought it too negative about the Web and didn't want to be thought of that way.[9]

Go back to Blumenthal's article[2] about the University of Texas. The chief proponent there is another librarian singing the praises of a library without books. Oh, yes, go ahead and say it. Say I am *laudator temporis acti*, I am praising old things only because they are old. But please, tell me: when are we going to address the concerns raised here if we are going to have these bookless buildings we once called libraries (taken, I might add, from *liber*, for book)? What I fear most is that we will not have this discussion but rather like what happened with the middle and high schools in Europe, there will be no discussion at all and libraries will vanish. Only bare ruin'd choirs where late bound books used to sing will remain. Perhaps libraries will become digitaries and we'll all gladly become digitarians.

What are we to make of all this? By now it's too late for me to plead I'm no Luddite. Webgasmic readers have breathlessly dismissed me at the first paragraph, or argued that my points are overdone, overheated, over the top, or all three. But for those of you who are still reading, let me clarify what I'm trying to say. The Web has a place in libraries. What I lament here is that it's not the panacea many are making it out to be. For serial literature of 10 years' duration, there is hardly any better avenue. For serial literature that must remain, there is JSTOR. Fun facts and endless trivia should be placed on the Web and the more the better. I would also not remove any public domain materials if for no other reason than they are already there. If I could, I would outlaw pornography, the Web's number one content. Apart from the serious matter of demeaning women and making intercourse a commodity, it's rapidly making libraries the new peep-show outlets. "The eye," said Horace, "is more easily influenced than the ear." Anyone who thinks we are, as a society, unblemished by this bilge water is simply blind to the obvious. But beyond these few things the Web in general and Google in specific have little more to offer us but overreach without the grasp.

All of which is to put too fine a point on it: the Web in general, and Google in specific, along with all the rest have serious problems that remain unaddressed, or worse, simply ignored. Meanwhile, libraries are taking a beating or has that, too, gone unnoticed? The Web isn't going anywhere and there are likely to be changes in technology that will make some of my points obsolete in about 40 or more years. While God may have had good advice from the Fire in his lap, we librarians have only smoke and mirrors so far from those in the library brain trust. It would appear that all have bowed the knee to Google. But there is still a chance to regulate all this if only we will. Let Google be what it's supposed to be, a tool, and let's prevent libraries from becoming, as Thoreau put it, the tools of our tools.

The Web *is* a good idea but it isn't going to replace books unless we outlaw reading, a possibility I no longer lightly dismiss, given the state of public education. Libraries will have to remain more or less conventional in coming years, offering the best the Web has to offer (doubtless via proprietary, aggregate databases) but also holding on to the best that print culture has wrought for the last 500 years. The Web has its place but not as the panacea for book-filled libraries. Those of us charged to conserve them must continue to sound the alarm against any view to the contrary, not because we value our jobs (of course we do) but because we know a library without the lifeblood of books is useless, ephemeral, and likely to do as much harm as good (see the Johns Hopkins story above).

Every librarian who has anything to do with budgets or feels the pressure to come up with some way to cut costs knows this to be unswervingly true. If you doubt it, ask any librarian working as a media specialist in a high school or elementary school library. Most European counterparts have already reduced their high school and elementary library equivalents to electronic sources alone. The trend has crossed the Atlantic and now threatens to undo us here. Further, any librarian who makes the case that it can *all* be done on the Web should have his library card burned on the front steps. Yes, various combinations of aggregate databases and a discontinuation of duplicated materials can help hold down the cost of information in combination with a discipline-specific approach to collection building (as opposed to a title-specific one). But to ask that we become electronic libraries only now or even 50 years from now is to express how little one knows about the current state of affairs or its progress.

We need perspective here about the Web, one already provided by history when other similar trends rushed to "make the library obsolete." Thirty years ago, educrats prophesized that educational television would replace schools, colleges, and universities. It didn't, obviously. (Rather television just made us more dimwitted and less able to realize that our educational framework was [and is] crumbling.) Twenty years ago, library experts claimed that microforms would shrink libraries to the size of shoeboxes. Again, they didn't, obviously. (Our declining budgets are doing that just fine.) Do we really need two or three decades to figure out that the Web isn't going to replace libraries, or do we need to lose a few hundred of them before we figure that out? I surely hope not, but I am not overly optimistic.

As I have written elsewhere, libraries are icons of cultural intellect, totems of the totality of knowledge. To claim, as many now do, that the Internet (or Google or both) is making libraries obsolete is as silly as saying that shoes have revolutionized walking and so have made feet unnecessary.

REFERENCES

1. It's harder to look at these gigantic book digitization projects with any but a jaundiced eye, however. About this, more later.

2. Ralph Blumenthal. "College Libraries Set Aside Books in a Digital Age." *New York Times* (May2005), viewed at <http://www.nytimes.com/2005/05/14/education/14library.html?incamp=article_popular>.

3. These 10 are reprised from my "10 Reasons the Internet Is No Substitute for a Library." *American Libraries* (April 2001): 76-78 <http://www.ala.org/ala/alonline/selectedarticles/10reasonswhy.htm>. A poster (22 × 36) of same is available by contacting the author at herringm@winthrop.edu. A facsimile of the poster may be viewed at <http://www.winthrop.edu/dacus>.

4. This is an industry estimate. It's virtually impossible to find exact data on this. ACRL estimates that there are about 100,000 unique serial titles in North America. Only about 25,000 of these are available at any one time on several aggregate databases. This will change over time of course but is unlikely ever to rise past 35 percent for reasons that are given in the text which follows.

5. To prove I'm no Luddite, let me cite here Eva Perkins' "Johns Hopkins' Tragedy: Could Librarians Have Prevented a Death?" <http://www.infotoday.com/newsbreaks/nb010806-1.htm>, on a *Web site*, no less.

6. See <http://www.dhmo.org/> for more on this clever spoof.

7. And what, praytell, happened to Internet II, that Internet without all the ads and its profligate wastes?

8. See <www.dlib.indiana.edu/workshops/alioct03/costs.ppt> and <http://www.rlg.org/preserv/diginews/diginews3-5.html#feature> where the costs are about $1,600 per book or nearly a billion for a library of 500,000 volumes. Google estimates that its cost will be a mere $10 per book, an astonishingly small amount, given earlier estimates. What, exactly, is being digitized and how will it be accessed?

9. Incidentally, I published it myself and have sold more than 1,500 by word of mouth alone. Apparently there was a market after all. See note 3 for more details.

Using the Google Search Appliance for Federated Searching: A Case Study

Mary Taylor

SUMMARY. This article discusses the University of Nevada, Reno's experiment of federated searching with version 4.1 of the Google Search Appliance. The project's testbed included locally held CONTENTdm and geospatial data collections and a sample of records from EBSCO's Academic Search Premiere database. The latter set of records revealed the GSA's limitations in being able to index and retrieve content that is dynamically generated and that requires third party authentication. *[Article copies available for a fee from The Haworth Document Delivery Service: 1-800-HAWORTH. E-mail address: <docdelivery@haworthpress.com> Website: <http://www.HaworthPress.com> © 2005 by The Haworth Press, Inc. All rights reserved.]*

KEYWORDS. Academic Search Premier, dynamically generated content, EBSCO Academic Search Premier, Google Search Appliance, XML

Mary Taylor is Metadata Services Coordinator, University of Nevada, Reno Libraries, 1664 North Virginia Street/MS 322, Reno, NV 89434 (E-mail: taylormk@unr.edu).
Google® is a Registered Service Mark of Google, Inc., Mountain View, California. *Libraries and Google®* is an independent publication offered by The Haworth Press, Inc., Binghamton, New York, and is not affiliated with, nor has it been authorized, sponsored, endorsed, licensed, or otherwise approved by, Google, Inc.

[Haworth co-indexing entry note]: "Using the Google Search Appliance for Federated Searching: A Case Study." Taylor, Mary. Co-published simultaneously in *Internet Reference Services Quarterly* (The Haworth Information Press, an imprint of The Haworth Press, Inc.) Vol. 10, No. 3/4, 2005, pp. 45-55; and: *Libraries and Google®* (ed: William Miller, and Rita M. Pellen) The Haworth Information Press, an imprint of The Haworth Press, Inc., 2005, pp. 45-55. Single or multiple copies of this article are available for a fee from The Haworth Document Delivery Service [1-800-HAWORTH, 9:00 a.m. - 5:00 p.m. (EST). E-mail address: docdelivery@haworthpress.com].

Available online at http://www.haworthpress.com/web/IRSQ
© 2005 by The Haworth Press, Inc. All rights reserved.
doi:10.1300/J136v10n03_06

INTRODUCTION

As the Metadata Services Coordinator for the University of Nevada, Reno Libraries, one of my areas of interest includes federated searching. During the past year, I served on a committee to review and evaluate federated search products. After numerous meetings with vendors and several product trials, the committee's conclusion was that the functionality offered by these products did not merit the price quotes. During my first days in this position, I asked what would be the five most important tasks for my position. The Dean of University Libraries, Dr. Steven D. Zink, mentioned that finding out the cost and technical requirements for implementing the Google Search Appliance (GSA) should be at the top of this list. The GSA is an off-the-shelf combination of a 2U standard rack-mountable server hardware (commonly known as "The Google Box"[1]) and an administrative software module that can be configured to perform searches on a defined network (such as an intranet or Web site) of over 220 different types of file formats.

Dr. Zink, who is also the university's Vice President of Information Technology, had made inquires with Google several years earlier about the cost of implementing the GSA as a federated search product. At that time, the cost of GSA was too great to justify an in-depth investigation. As part the federated search committee, I decided to make a new inquiry for the sake of due diligence. I also wanted to learn more about how libraries could use the GSA for searching their digital collections and also the price for the non-profit and education sector. The Dean supported this idea, especially because Google offers potential customers a 60-day trial period to install and test the GSA. Our attitude was that even if the cost of the GSA was still too expensive, Google's policy of offering a free trial made it worthwhile to at least bring in the GSA for a test. At that time, the model was version 4.1 and our greatest interest was in evaluating its ability to do federated searching of digital collections and resources.

CROSSWALKING THE GOOGLE SEARCH APPLIANCE WITH ACADEMIC SEARCH PREMIER

During the summer and fall of 2004, we held several conference calls with sales and systems engineering staff from Google's Enterprise Search group. The main question that we posed was how the Search Appliance would work with the types of content that libraries manage. We gave them an overview of our digital collections, including the online library catalog (Innovative Millennium), GIS and map data, CONTENTdm collections, electronic journals, and third party vendor databases. As an initial test, our colleagues at Google had a demonstration server that emulates the GSA index and retrieves content from the GIS and CONTENTdm collections. Ideally we wanted to be able to use the GSA as a single point of access for vendor databases and electronic journals.

As a result of the conference calls, we gained a basic understanding of how the GSA works. It follows the document model, which is a representation of an item's physical and logical structure. The GSA crawls and caches content based on URL or filename. The cache index stores this information as the item's unique identifier in order to link it back to subsequent search results: "The Google Search Appliance crawls your content and creates a master index of documents that's ready for instant retrieval using Google's search technology whenever a customer or employee types in a search query."[2]

During the first conference call, we gave our counterparts an overview of vendor databases like Academic Search Premier and how articles in these databases are dynamically generated and contain session-generated URLs. As an example, the Persistent URL (PURL) for an article about granting "most favored nation" status to China contains information about the port that authenticates UNR access to EBSCOhost (innopac.library.unr.edu:80) and also the identifiers for the article's storage database (db=f5h) and item number (an=9609131521):

http://0-
search.epnet.com.**innopac.library.unr.edu:80**/login.aspx?direct=true&**db=f5h&an=960
9131521**

A session-generated URL for the same article is longer and, in addition to information about its storage database (db=f5h), it also includes the session identifier (sessionmgr5) and search query (2DChina++% 22most++favored++nation):

http://0-
web18.epnet.com.**innopac.library.unr.edu**/citation.asp?tb=1&_ug=sid+D7C7A13A%2
D8CB9%2D443D%2D8E41%2DC47B312BF7BA%40**sessionmgr5+dbs+f5h**+cp+1+50
E5&_us=frn+1+hd+True+hs+True+cst+0%3B1+or+Date+ss+SO+sm+KS+sl+0+dstb+K
S+mh+1+ri+KAAACB1B00094089+DF6E&_uso=tg%5B0+%2D+db%5B0+%2D**f5h**+h
d+False+clv%5B1+%2DY+clv%5B0+%2DY+op%5B0+%2D+cli%5B1+%2DRV+cli%
5B0+%2DFT+st%5B0+%2**DChina++%22most++favored++nation%22**+mdb%5B0+
%2Dimh+0817&cf=1&fn=1&rn=1

Because we wanted to determine if the GSA could function as a point of entrance to vendor databases and electronic journal collections, we needed to find a database to crosswalk with it. EBSCO's Academic Search Premier database would be ideal because of its wide subject coverage and appeal to undergraduate and novice library users. Having the GSA as its point of access would make it an easy and attractive research tool for these users and hopefully increase its overall usage. After speaking with the staff at Google's Enterprise Search group, we then contacted EBSCO's Chief Information Officer, Michael Gorrell, for two conference calls. The first call was to give him an overview of the Google Search Appliance and to see if EBSCO would be willing to allow use of Academic Search Premier for a test of the GSA. The second conference call included the Systems Engineer for Google's Enterprise Search Group, John Gregory, to discuss with Gorrell how their products would work together. EBSCO agreed to participate in a small test, in which the demo servers would index and cache content from Academic Search Premier.

The bulk of digital collections in libraries are vendor databases containing session-generated URLs, which makes it hard to answer the question of how the GSA would cache this content. If an article's URL changes from session to session, whatever information that the GSA stores in the cache would direct subsequent search results to an Error 404 page because the referring URL no longer exists. It was not clear how the GSA could link the session-generated URLs stored in the cache back to the originating articles. While explaining this potential barrier to Google, we asked if they had customers who use the GSA to search dynamically generated content. Some of their customers do use the GSA to search Customer Relationship Management systems, which have dynamically generated content. However we did not learn the specific details about how these customers had resolved this issue. A short time after completing the test, we found a review of the latest release of the GSA that mentioned its inability to integrate with content or document management systems.[3]

Gregory suggested three possible solutions to how the GSA could index and cache session generated URLs. The library's authentication process is a proxy rewrite, so we could investigate how to rewrite a session-specific URL back to its persistent URL (PURL) before caching. Another solution would be to see if the proxy rewrite could strip out the session-generated sections of a URL, such as the search query, and then pass the remaining information to the GSA as the URL. This solution was problematic partially because the session specific information included in the URL is located in different sections and not at the beginning or end of the URL string. More important was that the Systems Office had already invested time and effort into implementing a proxy rewrite for the library's vendor database and electronic journal collections. Neither of these options was realistic for our institution. Gregory also suggested that EBSCOhost generate a list of all of Academic Search Premier's persistent URLs (about 18 million) for the demo servers to crawl. Again, this suggestion was not realistic given the strain it would place both on EBSCOhost's network and staff.

Gorrell proposed a fourth alternative that eventually proved to be the most efficient process for the test–EBSCO's OEMDirect XML Service is a database interface that employs a Simple Object Access Protocol (SOAP) interface.[4] SOAP is an XML-based format for exchanging information in a decentralized environment. The advantages of using this format instead of the traditional Z39.50 standard are that it makes it possible to search content that is in other formats besides MARC, such as journal databases. Customers can access the SOAP interface through EBSCOhost or can locally host a database of XML formatted records.

One concern that EBSCO had about the test was the potential strain that the demo servers could place on Academic Search Premier. Gorrell provided a sample set of XML records to host on our network for Google's demo servers to crawl and index. The Systems Office loaded these records onto a server and then generated a URL. It quickly became clear that the GSA could not return meaningful search results for these records because it could not differentiate between markup tags and article content. It treated both equally as text. In order for the demo server to be able to crawl and index only the text from the article, there needed to be a way to transform the records into HTML. I asked the libraries' Webmaster, Araby Greene, for her opinion about the best way to transform these records. She experimented with two different approaches to make the files "interpretable" to the demo servers.

The first approach was to create an index page and corresponding XSLT style sheet to generate an HTML file from the persistent URL embedded in the XML file. Gregory reviewed these files and replied that even with the style sheet to transform the persistent URLs unlike a Web browser, the demo server cannot interpret tags from within a file. Given this feedback, Greene returned to the question of how to transform the XML files to HTML in a manner that would work with the GSA. The solution was to write and run a script that generated an HTML file for each of the XML files. This transformation was successful, except for an error message for two files, which required manual correction. Subsequent attempts to use this script for transforming XML files have been successful with none of the files requiring manual correction. She also determined that if the GSA could crawl the files starting from the home page, it would be more efficient to change the folder holding the sample records into a subweb on the library's network. This approach was successful and keyword searches about the two topics Gorrell selected for the records (the 1989 Tiananmen Square Protests and granting "Most Favored Nation" status to China) generated meaningful search results.

CHALLENGES OF IMPLEMENTING GSA VERSION 4.1

Despite the successful outcome for the test, the final decision was to delay bringing in the GSA for an onsite trial. Working with the sample records from Academic Search Premier raised both technical and financial issues. While we knew that the GSA would be able to cache and index CONTENTdm and GIS collections, doing a full test on Academic Search Premier content would have required switching to the SOAP-based interface and taking an additional charge to our existing contract with EBSCO. It made no sense to make a significant financial investment in a database interface that we would potentially have no other use for besides the test. We had also not gained any insight into its ability to pass through the authentication process for a third party site or if it was capable of indexing and caching dynamically generated content or database records. The only option that we knew could make Academic Search Premier work with the GSA would be to locally host the XML formatted records. Using that approach would entail additional costs to our contract with EBSCO and also the investment of time and effort to create scripts and style sheets for transforming the XML files into HTML. Greene estimated that she spent at least ten hours figuring out this process.

Most of the case studies[5] on the Enterprise Search section of Google's Web site list clients who are using the GSA for publicly accessible Web sites or intranets. Considering how Google had primarily developed and marketed the GSA for these types of digital environments, one explanation was that the GSA might only be able to search either completely inside or outside of a firewall. In fact, the GSA section of Google's Web site includes two categories for its case studies, "Intranet Deployments"[6] and "Public Web site Deployments."[7] Another factor to consider is that the content in these environments generally consists of discrete documents and stable URLs, making it easier for the GSA to create a stable unique key to store in its cache. An evaluation of the GSA version 4.1 backs up this conclusion: "[The GSA is] best used in tactical external or internal intranet installations where content need not be indexed directly from dynamic repositories."[8]

Oxford University published a brief article in *Ariadne* about its trial of the GSA that supports this theory. They also had issues with being able to index both public and restricted sections of its network.[9] Their conclusion was that the most straightforward–though expensive–solution would be to implement two models, a GSA for publicly available content and another for restricted content:

> . . . one for outside the firewall and one for inside. The most likely involved routing all searches through a proxy server maintained separately, which would check all accesses to see if they would work from outside the firewall, and annotating the database accordingly. It is worth noting that if all Oxford Web sites had put their restricted material on a separate Web server (e.g., oucs-oxford.ox. ac.uk) or used a naming convention (e.g., oucs.ox.ac.uk/oxonly/), it would be easy to configure the box to provide the external search as needed.[10]

Our original reason for looking into a test of the GSA was Google's policy of offering a free trial period. Paying an additional charge for the SOAP interface to EBSCOhost meant that the test would no longer be free. The other option of hosting a local version of Academic Search Premier on our network would also include an additional charge to our contract with EBSCO and also require additional support from the Systems Office. The most serious financial issue for implementing the GSA is that it not only uses the document model for content indexing and caching, but also in setting the price. At present there are four different versions of the GSA. The recently released "mini" GSA starts at $3,000, can search up to 100,000 documents and is marketed to small and medium-sized businesses.[11] The model that would most likely fit within a library's budget and collections requirements, the GB-1001, starts at around $30,000 and can search up to 500,000 documents.[12] Considering the huge amounts of data stored in an average vendor database, such as the 18 million unique articles in Academic Search Premier, using the document model as the basic pricing unit would increase the GSA's cost far above $28,000. Even the highest end model of the GSA (the GB-8008 which costs around $450,000)[13] would not be able to cache and index the full scope of Academic Search Premiere.

FOLLOW UP WITH NELLCO
AND SEARCH APPLIANCE RELEASE 4.2

During the conference calls with Google, they mentioned that the next scheduled version for the GSA (Release 4.3) would include added functionality that could resolve its issues with dynamically generated content and authentication. Several months after the decision to delay an onsite trial of the GSA, a colleague located a summary of presentations at the International Coalition of Library Consortia's April 2005 meeting in Boston. The New England Law Library Consortium's (NELLCO) presentation about federated searching and the GSA, "NELLCO's Blue Sky Thinking–a possible alternative to federated searching"[14] discussed familiar issues. Like us, they had completed an unsatisfactory review of the federated search products and consequently started looking at the GSA as an alternative. At the time of the presentation, they were planning a test of the GSA's ability to search local collections and vendor databases.

Out of curiosity, I contacted NELLCO's executive director, Tracy L. Thompson, who delivered the presentation, to ask about the presentation. This contact led to several other telephone and e-mail conversations about the GSA both with Thompson and Roberta Woods of the Franklin Pierce Law Library. I shared with them our notes from the conference calls and test and they in turn discussed the research that they had been doing for an upcoming meeting with Google and an interested vendor about testing the GSA at the Franklin Pierce Law Library. During these conversations, Thompson made the very astute observation that while Google Scholar might provide an adequate short term solution for applying Google's PageRank technology for searching scholarly content, it also means that collection development occurs based on whatever publishing companies and institutions decide to participate, rather than local needs and policies. At present, Google Print (the division that oversees the Google Scholar and the "Google for Libraries" initiatives) has declined to name all of the participating publishers. Furthermore, organizations such as NELLCO's member institutions have discovered that niche publications, especially for professions such as theirs, are not yet making it into Google Scholar.

XML FEEDS AND AUTHORIZATION API IN RELEASE 4.2

Speaking with Thompson and Woods helped to further refine our technical knowledge about the GSA. Woods located two key pieces of information that we had unsuccessfully requested during our conference calls. Information about how to cache and authenticate third-party content is not found on the Search Appliance section of Google's Web site, but instead in the Code section. According to the documentation, Release 4.2 of the Search Appliance has a "Third-Party Content Feed API" that makes it possible to handle dynamically generated content by converting search results into XML. We were able to find a case study on the Search Appliance section of Google's Web site, about Sur La Table's e-commerce Web site, which discusses the process of converting the search results for dynamically generated content from a third-party database into an XML feed:

> Because the Google Search Appliance gives administrators access to Google results as an XML data feed, Grant was able to integrate the results easily into a Cold Fusion environment. Pointing the Google Search Appliance at an offline product database, Grant then mapped the search results to live URLs using a few simple scripts.[15]

> Both the announcement for release 4.2 and the accompanying documentation for its new "Database Crawler[16] feature, mention that the GSA can now crawl and index content held in "standard enterprise relational."[17] However from a review of the documentation, it appears that this function works for locally held databases (i.e., on one's own network) that do not require authentication for users outside of a firewall. Finally, the document model for pricing appears to also be in place for database content, in that "each database record is counted as a 'document' toward the license limit."[18]

Woods also located the documentation about the Authorization Application Protocol Interface (API), for release 4.2, the "Secure Content API," although after the answer given to us during the chat session, it still is not clear how authentication scales to the level of working with electronic journals and databases, where access is for a large and distributed user base and requires more than a single user id and password. The latest developer's guide to the Application Feeds Protocol, released on June 2nd 2005, does describe a process similar to the one we used for our test:

> To create a feed, you will convert your data to XML. You will then upload the XML to the appliance using a web form or a script. A

script that creates the XML data and pushes it to the appliance is known as a custom connector. The XML data that you push to the appliance is the feed.[19]

CONCLUSIONS

Despite the "plug and play" statements in their promotional materials, doing a full implementation of the Google Search Appliance in the library environment not only requires purchasing costs and annual licensing fees, but also additional manpower and unforeseen costs like having a SOAP database interface. At present, our institution has decided to defer doing an onsite trial and seriously considering it as a federated search tool until it becomes clearer how it can best authenticate and index/retrieve dynamically generated content from third-party databases. The short-term solution has been to enable the library's link resolver to join Google Scholar. This decision does not mean that we have abandoned the idea of using the Search Appliance, but instead that we want to gain a better understanding of the technologies underneath it and to also advocate for development that can address these needs. Our impression is that working with this type of content, especially when it consists of dynamically generated, discrete documents, is new to Google, especially given its use of the document model for pricing. It will likely take more work by Google and customer input in order to make the Search Appliance be a "plug and play" solution for third-party, dynamically generated content. We continue to stay in touch with our contacts at Google and EBSCO and are following the work that NELLCO is doing with their experiment to test the Search Appliance on Franklin Pierce's collections.

REFERENCES

1. Bryan Mjaanes. "Review: Implementing the Google Search Appliance in an Intranet environment." Available at http://www.macosx.com/articles/review-implementing-the-google-search-appliance-in-an-intranet-enviro.html (accessed March 12, 2005).

2."Google Enterprise Solutions: The Google Search Appliance." Available at http://www.google.com/enterprise/gsa/ (accessed January 10, 2005).

3. Mjaanes, Ibid.

4. Endeavor Information Systems Incorporated. "Endeavor, EBSCO partner for XML gateway development providing dependable search and retrieval functionality." (Des Plaines, IL.: Endeavor Information Systems Incorporated.), press release. Avail-

able at http://www.endinfosys.com/cgi-bin/news/viewer.cgi?ID=55 (accessed July 29, 2005).

5. Google Enterprise Solutions. "Customers." Available at http://www.google.com/enterprise/customers.html (accessed January 10, 2005).

6. Google Enterprise Solutions. "Intranet Deployments." Available at http://www.google.com/appliance/intranet.html (accessed January 10, 2005).

7. Google Enterprise Solutions. "Site Search." Available at http://www.google.com/appliance/sitesearch.html (accessed January 10, 2005).

8. Ann Bednarz. "Google upgrades search appliance." Available at http://www.networkworld.com/news/2004/0607google.html (accessed June 25, 2005).

9. Sebastian Rahtz. "Looking for a Google Box?" Available from http://www.ariadne.ac.uk/issue42/rahtz/ (accessed January 10, 2005).

10. Ibid.

11. Google Enterprise Solutions. "The Google Mini." Available from http://www.google.com/enterprise/mini/ (accessed January 10, 2005).

12. Google Enterprise Solutions. "Google Search Appliance: Product Models." Available from http://www.google.com/appliance/products.html (accessed January 10, 2005).

13. Google Enterprise Solutions. "Google Search Appliance: Product Models."

14. Tracy Thompson (2005, April). "NELLCO's Blue Sky Thinking a possible alternative to federated searching." Presentation at International Coalition of Library Consortia (ICOLC) Spring 2005 Meeting, Boston, MA.

15. Google Enterprise Solutions. "Google Search Appliance–Database Crawler Feature Snippet" Available from http://code.google.com (accessed May 25, 2005).

16. Google Enterprise Solutions. "Product Features–What's New Snapshot." Available from http://www.google.com/enterprise/gsa/features.html (accessed June 5, 2005).

17. Google Enterprise Solutions. "Google Search Appliance–Database Crawler Feature Snippet" Available from http://code.google.com (accessed May 25, 2005).

18. Google Enterprise Solutions. "For licensing purposes, how are 'documents' counted with respect to database records?" Available from http://www.google.com/support/gsa/bin/answer.py?answer=16586&topic=-1 (accessed May 25, 2005).

19. Google Code. "Google Search Appliance Feeds Protocol Developer's Guide." Available from http://code.google.com (accessed June 25, 2005).

Google's Print and Scholar Initiatives: The Value of and Impact on Libraries and Information Services

Robert J. Lackie

SUMMARY. Google regularly makes headlines with new Web-based tools, but two recent projects promise to have profound implications for the future of librarianship. With Google's recent big push to add content from books and journals into its database via its expanded Google Print and new Google Scholar initiatives, today's academic libraries and publishers, among others, are taking notice. Many are sitting back and watching how others deal with these initiatives, while some are raising their voices in question, praise, or protest. *[Article copies available for a fee from The Haworth Document Delivery Service: 1-800-HAWORTH. E-mail address: <docdelivery@haworthpress.com> Website: <http://www.HaworthPress.com> © 2005 by The Haworth Press, Inc. All rights reserved.]*

KEYWORDS. Google, Google Print, Google Scholar, general-purpose search engines, libraries

---

Robert J. Lackie is Associate Professor-Librarian, Franklin F. Moore Library, Rider University, Lawrenceville, NJ 08648 (E-mail: rlackie@rider.edu).

Google® is a Registered Service Mark of Google, Inc., Mountain View, California. *Libraries and Google®* is an independent publication offered by The Haworth Press, Inc., Binghamton, New York, and is not affiliated with, nor has it been authorized, sponsored, endorsed, licensed, or otherwise approved by, Google, Inc.

[Haworth co-indexing entry note]: "Google's Print and Scholar Initiatives: The Value of and Impact on Libraries and Information Services." Lackie, Robert J. Co-published simultaneously in *Internet Reference Services Quarterly* (The Haworth Information Press, an imprint of The Haworth Press, Inc.) Vol. 10, No. 3/4, 2005, pp. 57-70; and: *Libraries and Google®* (ed: William Miller, and Rita M. Pellen) The Haworth Information Press, an imprint of The Haworth Press, Inc., 2005, pp. 57-70. Single or multiple copies of this article are available for a fee from The Haworth Document Delivery Service [1-800-HAWORTH, 9:00 a.m. - 5:00 p.m. (EST). E-mail address: docdelivery@haworthpress.com].

Available online at http://www.haworthpress.com/web/IRSQ
© 2005 by The Haworth Press, Inc. All rights reserved.
doi:10.1300/J136v10n03_07

57

INTRODUCTION

When asked in early April this year to write an article about Google for this special volume, this author enthusiastically responded. Librarians and users of the Web in general may not agree on the best starting places for conducting scholarly research, but when asked about their favorite search engine, Google consistently ranks high in the responses, and has for several years now. It truly is amazing how this brain-child of founders Sergey Brin and Larry Page continues to inhabit the lead paragraphs and front pages of so many newspapers, magazines, and blogs. Many have watched the fledgling Mountain View, California company exponentially grow over the last few years, making a lot of people rich and many others (maybe us?) wishing they had bought stock in Google last year, even when many were wondering about the company's future worth. Well, Brin and Page, both in their early 30s now, are each worth about $9 billion apiece, according to *The Guardian*–and their stock continues to climb (Teather 2005).

Not bad. However, what this author finds more interesting–even astonishing–is that Google so regularly makes headlines not for the amount of money it makes (although mentioned often), but for the new Web-based tools it continues to offer, many of them "graduates" from the Google Labs "technology playground" (Google Labs 2005). Two of these tools, both still in beta, that promise to have "profound implications for the future of librarianship" (Banks 2005), because they directly relate to and involve libraries, published information, and access to that information, are the focus of this article–Print and Scholar.

With Google's recent big push to add content from books and journals into its database via its expanded Google Print and new Google Scholar initiatives, today's academic libraries and publishers, among others, are taking notice. Many are sitting back and watching how colleagues deal with these projects, while others are raising their voices in question, praise, or protest. Some are viewing Google Print's plans as highly controversial and possibly illegal, challenging the search engine company's authority or goals. Others are praising Google's efforts, especially regarding Scholar, to get information out to and for the good of the public, not to mention jumping in to partner with it. Conflicts often arise among these factions. This article will briefly look at the background of each of these two projects and explore and discuss how libraries and other information services view the value and impact of these two Google initiatives.

BACKGROUND ON GOOGLE PRINT AND GOOGLE SCHOLAR

Google Print

When Google first introduced its experimental program to index books in late 2003, it received some media attention and controversy, but many in libraries were not as interested as some publishers or authors, who were the target audience for the Google Print initiative because it presented a way for them to promote their books on Google for free. It was, however, immediately compared by Chris Sherman (2003) in a December online newsletter with Amazon's "Search Inside the Book" program that was just getting started: Amazon was making the full text of books available for readers online, while Google Print was only indexing small excerpts. Google Print was also compared with other producers of online books, even though Print is really a marketing program (another billboard on which Google can place its sponsored advertisements) rather than an online library. It was and is still often compared with Michael Hart's *Project Gutenberg*, "the oldest producer of free electronic books on the Internet," comprising 16,000+ pre-1923 "literary works that are in the public domain in the United States" (2005). Other providers include John Mark Ockerbloom (2005) at the University of Pennsylvania's *Online Book Page* (20,000+ works), and the *Million Book Project* (10,000+ books thus far) coalition of Carnegie Mellon University (2005), with assistance from the Internet Archive (http://www.archive.org/) and other libraries around the world–to name just a few other free projects. Of course, OCLC's NetLibrary and ebrary, Inc. are examples of fee-based services that provide online books as well, but Google Print was projecting to offer millions of online texts over the next several years–a very significant projected increase in the number of texts available via current or proposed digitization projects.

As mentioned earlier, Google Print received some attention when introduced, but the project exploded with media attention when the company announced its significant expansion of the program in December 2004 to include the digitization of library books with its new partnership of four leading academic research libraries (Harvard, Oxford, Michigan, and Stanford) and the New York Public Library. According to *Reading Today*, the five libraries combined hold "more than 56.9 million books" (Googling 2005, 22:7), but most of them have only granted Google conditional scanning rights to their holdings. For example, the University of Michigan will allow Google to scan all 7.8 million of its books. "Oxford is allowing Google to scan all of its material that was published prior to 1900, while Harvard, Stanford, and the New York Public Library have only authorized the scanning of "parts of their holdings as part of a trial program" (7). For instance, Harvard mentions on its site that it has authorized the scanning of only 40,000 volumes of its 15 million volumes for this pilot digitization project (Harvard 2004). Nevertheless, Harvard and other libraries have now embarked on the Google digitization adventure.

The mission of Google Print (2005), available now at its own beta site, is "to organize the world's information and make it universally accessible and useful" by placing book content online in Google. At the time of this writing, Google Print does not have an advanced search page, but a search on its basic search screen will result in the ability to browse through either the whole book, or if under copyright still, the bibliographic data and a snippet or excerpt; search for words highlighted within the text; find online reviews of the book; locate related information from other Web sites; buy the book from a list of online booksellers; learn about the publisher of the text; and if the book is a library book, find it in a local library. You, however, cannot print or copy the text or images from the pages, as this has been disabled. Google has added a lot of general information and FAQ's about the Print product that can be found easily under the "About Google Print" link on the main page (print.google.com).

Even though the project is currently underway, "Google's digitization effort will be expensive and time consuming," according to a very recent *Technology Review* article, as the average time for a single book-scanning machine to scan one book is thirty minutes, at an estimated cost of $10 per book (Roush 2005, 58). *Technology Review* provides a very interesting "Books to Bits" chart that lists twenty of the United States' largest libraries, along with Oxford University, estimating the number of volumes and scanning costs. A quick addition of the estimated figures provided in the chart indicate that it would take a single book-scanning machine about 12,632 years to scan the approximate 206 million volumes of books from those 21 libraries, at a estimated cost of 20.6 billion dollars! Of course, as the author of the article points out, "the more machines in use, the sooner they'll finish" (58), and this author wishes to emphasize that Google has only partnered with five of those libraries thus far to digitize only about 15 million of their volumes.

Recent and near-future innovations in book-scanning technologies could significantly decrease the time table to accomplish their task, but a February *Information Today* article stated that "estimates circulate that the [current digitization] project may take Google 10 years, or even longer, and could run into the hundreds of millions of dollars. Naturally, Google has no comment on such pesky details" (Quint 2005, 7). Whatever the final cost to Google (a *BBC News* story [France mobilizes 2005] cited $200 million), it is probably pretty safe to assume that the current 5-library partnership deal will keep their scanners and accountants quite busy for the next few years.

Google Scholar

Not one to rest on its laurels, or have only one major project in the pot, the Mountain View-based company announced the Scholar initiative in November 2004, making front page headlines again for Google as a "new search service aimed at scientists and academic researchers" and "intended as a first stop for researchers looking for scholarly literature" (Markoff 2004, C6), just a month before the announcement of the significant library expansion of the Print project mentioned earlier. The mission of Google Scholar (2005), also available on its own beta site, is to "search specifically for scholarly literature, including peer-reviewed papers, theses, books, preprints, abstracts and technical reports from all broad areas of research" in many different formats. The site recommends using Scholar "to find articles from a wide variety of academic publishers, professional societies, preprint repositories and universities, as well as scholarly articles available across the Web."

As happened with Google Print, immediate comparisons were made between Google Scholar and other existing search engines or products. For instance, as Pike mentioned in his *Information Today* article (2005, 16), "no good deed goes unpunished. Less than a month [after Scholar was introduced], Google was on the receiving end of a trademark infringement lawsuit by the American Chemical Society (ACS)," because the ACS already had a search tool available on the market with "scholar" in the title: SciFinder Scholar. An interesting quick read on the facts and merits of the case, and opinions of the court, can be found in the "ACS sues Google" article (Mehta 2004, 13). An engaging comparison of Elsevier's free Scirus scholarly science search engine and Google Scholar has occurred in a recent issue of *Searcher* magazine (Felter 2005). In addition, *Online* magazine (Wleklinski and Ojala 2005) just finished conducting a fairly in-depth study of Google Scholar, as did renowned reviewer Dr. Peter Jacso (2005). We will discuss these reviews and opinions of Scholar later in this article.

For now, though, what can you do with Google Scholar? Well, of course, you can, as the site states, "expand the universe of important scholarly papers available to your users by including Google Scholar on your site for free" (scholar.google.com/scholar/scholarsearch.html) to find "peer-reviewed papers, theses, and other scholarly materials." The advanced search interface, introduced in late December 2004, provides useful options to increase the "accuracy and effectiveness" of searches by including publication restrict and date restrict options–only available via the advanced screen. The "Advanced Search Tips" and "Google Scholar Help" links are also descriptive and useful, as are the recently updated "Support for Libraries" and "Support for Publishers" links.

Google's advanced search interface for Scholar does seem to make it easier to conduct searches for scholarly material. After conducting a search for information on Scholar, below each paper or book citation or link, you may find "Cited by" and "Web Search" links. These links provide citation analysis, as well as a general search via Google to find material about that topic on the Web, respectively. Contrary to popular belief, not all results provide full text, and many searchers using Scholar do not know if a source is available within their own library, except when a source was a book record available via the Open WorldCat Program, which allows the user to click on the "Library Search" link below the book citation to reveal local and worldwide libraries that own the book. By the way, "for its records to be available via Open WorldCat, a library must be a member of the OCLC cooperative and have contributed library ownership information and metadata" (OCLC 2005).

For articles that are not available full-text within Google Scholar but that are available full-text within the library in which the user is conducting the search, link resolver products can provide seamless access to those materials. From February to early May 2005, about 30 libraries in the United States had been "testing institutional access in a pilot project . . . using the link resolver product each has purchased," such as SFX (Ex Libris), Article Linker (Serials Solutions), and 1Cate (Openly Informatics) software (Oder 2005, 17). Earlier this year, this author read an article in *Feliciter* magazine which discussed how librarians could help searchers identify content in their libraries when searching Google Scholar. The author keenly suggested adding "the address for Google Scholar to a list of services that is detected by the institution's proxy server," so that seamless access to the full-text held within the library could occur when searching Scholar (Rhyno 2005, 51:10). This is happening now, and he further points out that "Northern Light attempted to provide integrated access to licensed content and general Internet resources" (10) long before Google Scholar. The very recent collaboration of Google and Project MUSE (2005) allowing MUSE subscribers to use Scholar to search MUSE holdings for scholarly materials, as well as the May expansion of Google Scholar allowing "any library or institution that has the proper link resolving software" to now connect to Scholar and "provide direct links to articles found via a GS search" (Price 2005) proves that Google is beginning to listen to the academic community and is taking some of their recommendations to heart. According to a May online *Chronicle of Higher Education* article, "more than 100 colleges and universities have made arrangements with Google that will give people using the Google Scholar search engine on their campuses more direct access to library materials there" by including direct linking to online copies of materials as well as "data on printed works in a library's collection" (Young 2005). You can bet that a lot more institutions will be joining their ranks soon.

THE VALUE AND IMPACT ON LIBRARIES AND INFORMATION SERVICES

Google Print–Value and Impact

If there is one thing that the Google Print projects (for publishers and libraries) have shown, it is that it is possible to conduct large scale digitization. Of course, when Google is footing all of the bills, it makes the project much easier to swallow, even though it will mean more work for those libraries involved. Still, just like many other librarians, this author was also "swept up in the positive publicity surrounding the project, because it is inspiring to contemplate the democratization of knowledge that has been previously sequestered inside some of the world's leading research libraries," as Marcus Banks at the New York University Medical Center expressed so elegantly (2005). After all, many organizations, such as the National Library of Medicine and Project Gutenberg, have been digitizing and providing full-text books online for free for some time, to the joy of many who find them. Authors and publishers of the books that can be searchable online expect increased revenues generated from sales due to the books' greater visibility, and anyone searching Google Print will be able to seamlessly search a wide variety of libraries' collections and publishers' holdings, connecting themselves to books from around the globe to read, check out, or buy. Sounds good. So, why all the controversy lately?

There have been several concerns raised and many responses from librarians and publishers since the expansion of Google Print into libraries was announced. Jean-Noel Jeanneney, head of the French National Library, "called for a European 'counter-attack' against the Google [Print for Libraries] project" earlier this year, warning Europe that Google's digitization plans "could result in the crushing domination of the U.S. in shaping the worldview of future generations" (France to develop 2005). Basically, it seems that he does not like that Google has only partnered with five "Anglo-American" libraries for this book digitization project. Just too American, it seems, for France and the European Union (EU). According to *NewsMax.com* in early May, "the Europeans fear that the continent's contribution to the pillars of recorded knowledge will be crushed by a profit-oriented California company and may end up presenting a U.S.-centric version of the world's literary legacy . . . Now six heads of state and 23 national libraries in Europe have pledged their support for the continent's own book-scanning project, dubbed the European Digital Library" (France mobilizes 2005). The EU, however, is not the only organization upset with the newly expanded Google Print.

According to *American Libraries Online*, the Association of American University Presses (AAUP) raised an alarm concerning the Google Print for Libraries plan to digitize library book collections and make them available online. AAUP Executive Director Peter Givler sent a letter on May 20, 2005 to Google Executive Alexander Macgillivray giving him a list of questions regarding copyright and fair-use. He "asked for 16 points of clarification about the Google Print for Libraries project, indicating that 'it appears to involve systematic infringement of copyright on a massive scale'" (University publishers 2005). The AAUP and other publishing groups believe that scanning copyrighted books could violate copyright. As of the writing of this article, no response to those questions of concern has been published. For the entire text of the May 20 letter, see the May 26 issue of *Business Week Online* (University Press 2005).

Even if the in-depth, widespread scanning is determined to be legal and continues to go forth, many still question the project. Roy Tennant, User Services Architect of the California Digital Library, believes that "Google hype to the contrary, blind wholesale digitization [of pre-1923 books] is no more a good thing than buying books based on color, . . . as [we may] soon find ourselves in a world where incorrect, dated information trumps current, accurate information through circumstance" (2005, 27). Others have voiced opinions about whether this digitization will physically harm the texts, or what Google or the libraries will do with the texts once scanned. Some concerned citizens wonder if Google will help financially with long-term physical storage of the scanned materials, or if those library holdings will "become another instance of the JSTOR effect, where big libraries get rid of low-use items simply because they can now subscribe to databases that offer pretty good searchable likenesses of them?" (Baker 2005, 10). As Tennant mentions early in his article, "the news articles [on Google Print for Libraries] were long on hype and short on specifics" (2005, 27), and months later, not much of that has changed.

This author is certainly interested in knowing what type of documents will be digitized and how the digitized images will be stored, not to mention how Google will deal with copyright and fair use issues. But many of us are waiting for Google's response to the AAUP's questions. And watching and waiting for what happens next. But until then, Google is still moving forward with its Print projects, as the very recent launch of Print beta site highly suggests. Many of us just hope that Bloomsbury chief executive Nigel Newton's warning does not come to pass. He believes that "we are being given an opportunity to undermine our industry. It may not seem inherently scary at the moment. But my concern is what this will lead to in 10 years. We are opening a Pandora's box, and we have no idea where it will lead. We just don't know, once they have this material, what they will do with it" (Jones 2005). Banks basically agrees with this assessment, worrying that in their "admirable desire to improve access to their collections, some of our best libraries may have struck a Faustian bargain" (2005). Let's hope that possible forecast does not come to pass and that many of the librarians and archivists that are still "ecstatic" about the [Print] project are correct when they say "it will likely be remembered as the moment in history when society finally got serious about making knowledge ubiquitous" (Rouch 2005, 108:56). It will be quite a while before we really see the impact of the Print library project, but one thing is for certain now—it has been and will likely continue to be a major source of controversy for some time.

Google Scholar–Value and Impact

The Google Scholar initiative, on the other hand, is not embroiled in controversy. There are certainly differing opinions on the worthiness of the new scholarly search engine. In the February 2005 issue of *Searcher*, during the comparison of Elsevier's Scirus and Google's Scholar, the author voiced some complaints about Scirus [i.e., its advanced search features "confound our users and prompt comments such as, 'Why can't it be more like Google?'" (Felter 2005, 44)], and Scholar [i.e., it "lacks the clear identification of full text availability, . . . tak[ing] quite a bit of clicking (or an experienced user) to know which of the multiple sources could lead to a full-text source" (45)], but she generally thought that both were products worthy of information professionals' immediate attention. Generally, the advice to librarians within this article is to "embrace Google Scholar as well as Scirus and prepare for their widespread use . . . [as well as to view] Google Scholar as an opportunity to introduce our researchers to what they can access and to teach them search habits that best integrate Google Scholar and/or Scirus with institutional resources" (Felter 2005, 48). This author tends to agree with her advice, because for one thing, students are telling us that they are using it, even if other free scholarly services such as Scirus tend to be much better tools for performing sophisticated scientific searches.

The Google Scholar site, especially after very recently expanding its free institutional access feature, makes everything seem so familiar and easy–that is, if your library has the database software tools to connect Scholar to library-owned database collections. Even so, when conducting a search for an article on Scholar, as Carol Tenopir, Professor at the School of Information Sciences, University of Tennessee, again points out, "easy access to multiple sources unwittingly highlights a multiple version problem. Preprints, revised versions, and final versions of articles all get retrieved" (2005, 32). This author's searches on Scholar have also presented different versions of basically the same article, and they have revealed the service certainly not to be anywhere nearly as comprehensive and current as many scholarly, proprietary library databases.

As briefly mentioned earlier in this article, two excellent, revealing reviews of Scholar that librarians everywhere should read to bring them up to speed on Google Scholar have appeared very recently in *Online* magazine and on *Peter's Digital Reference Shelf–June 2005*. Marydee Ojala, editor of *Online*, stated recently that although most "academic librarians reacted to the initial introduction of Google Scholar with a mixture of glee and horror," many are beginning to teach Scholar, including its "limitations (not everything is in there, search results can't be sorted by date, no automatic mapping between synonyms)," while demonstrating what the online and print library collections can do to enhance their searches, especially "before pulling out [their] credit card to pay for things you find in Google Scholar" (Wleklinski and Ojala, 24). In their article, these authors effectively combine humor with a serious discussion of the results of tests they performed on the Google Scholar database, explaining the mistakes Scholar makes, its coverage, and sharing opinions of what academic libraries are now doing with Scholar–it's a good read.

Peter Jacso's review is quite lengthy and in-depth (he has spent "hundreds of hours using Google Scholar"), and many would say it is very critical (although this author found it humorous), but he concludes that Scholar is "great for the have-nots or individuals not affiliated with an academic library" (2005) who need free access to scholarly materials but do not have access to academic libraries' scholarly proprietary databases [i.e., PsycInfo, Scopus, Web of Science, ScienceDirect]. What was definitely disappointing to Jacso was that the newest Scholar update in April did not improve much or address many previous critiques highlighted earlier in this article (Wleklinski and Ojala, Tenopir, Price, Felter).

Additionally, Jacso complains that there are still no browsing options available for authors or journal names. Scholar does not allow exact phrase searching for journal names and it lets you search for only one variant journal name at a time. Regarding searching by publication year, or a range of years, to limit the number of hits, Jacso's review showed this search limit to be very misleading. His analysis on sorting by author or date: "Forget about it, as author names . . . are in the format of first initial then last name (such as ME Koenig). Perfect [he is being facetious here] for sorting a bibliography by first initial. And don't even think about sorting by date as Google Scholar does not know how to determine the correct publication date" (2005). Ouch! He was not happy with the results of his "citedness score test" of Scholar either, comparing it to Scopus and Web of Science. Obviously, Jacso has studied Scholar much more than many other librarians, and even though he believes that many searchers will not care about his in-depth study, he does also believe that "librarians, other information professionals and scholars should be aware of the limitations of Google Scholar and not join the Google-for-president crowd by dispensing careless endorsements and hollow sound-bites for the press, faculty, students and staff"–sounds like very good advice.

Google Scholar is, however, still in beta, meaning that Google is still fine-tuning the service, and it is not meant to replace our databases for in-depth scholarly research. But as it continues to improve and grow, Google still has not provided users with definitions of what it considers "scholarly" material, a listing of that material or the comprehensiveness of its sources (as do the scholarly, free, full-text PubMed Central [http://www.pubmedcentral.gov/] and HireWire Press [http://highwire. stanford.edu/]). Nor does Google Scholar indicate how often or when the database is updated–answers to these questions and more are sorely needed. Unfortunately, Anurag Acharya, a Google engineer who started the Google Scholar project, has been quoted as saying, "'We're not sharing detailed information at this point,' though he added that Google might eventually do so" (Young 2005).

CONCLUSION AND FUTURE CONSIDERATIONS

Not providing details that information professionals and scholars need regarding their Google Print and Scholar initiatives, especially by June 2005, is definitely annoying, but right now, Google seems to be calling all the shots on both of these projects. That could change very soon. Google has shown that it is beginning to listen to the academic community's complaints and make some changes (i.e., Scholar and using link resolvers). However, Acharya and others at Google should seriously consider studying the very recently published reviews on Scholar, highlighted earlier in this article (Jacso, Wleklinski and Ojala), and take some of their recommendations to heart. Regarding Google Print, it is probably too early to say–everyone is still waiting on their response to the AAUP's six pages of questions regarding the Print for Libraries project.

Whatever some may think of these two Google initiatives, the announcements and studies of Google Print and Google Scholar have obviously been serious wake-up calls to libraries and information services in general around the world. Many libraries and publishing groups may not be happy with the inventiveness of Google and the current or future plans of one or both of these Google creations, with good reason. On the other hand, Google has made itself a household name–even a verb–and librarians, publishers, and other information service providers could possibly draw inspiration from the Google team and see what they can do better because of them.

Headlines and stock prices do seem to indicate that Google is here to stay, along with the Print and Scholar initiatives. What does the future hold for these two projects? Who really knows, but many will still undoubtedly continue to sit back and watch the path that Google takes, especially regarding these two initiatives, while others will continue to raise their voices in question, praise, or protest. Amid speculation of Google Print and Google Scholar merging in the not-too-distant future, something this author thinks is likely to happen, Google officials at *Information Today*-sponsored conferences have said that they were not planning to do so, but that it remains an interesting possibility.

REFERENCES

Baker, Nicholson. 2005. Copy but don't "disband." *Library Journal*, February 15, 10.

Banks, Marcus A. 2005. The excitement of Google Scholar, the worry of Google Print. *Biomedical Digital Libraries*, March 22. BioMed Central. <http://www.bio-diglib.com/content/2/1/2> (accessed May 11 2005).

Carnegie Mellon University. 2005. Million Book Project. <http://www.library.cmu.edu/Libraries/MBP_FAQ.html> (accessed June 1, 2005).

Felter, Laura M. 2005. Google Scholar, Scirus, and the scholarly search revolution. *Searcher*, February, 43-48.

France mobilizes against Google. 2005. *NewsMax.com*, May 12. <http://www.newsmax.com/archives/ic/2005/5/12/151149.shtml> (accessed May 31, 2005).

France to develop Google rival. 2005. *BBC News*, March 17. <http://news.bbc.co.uk/go/pr/-/2/hi/europe/4358871.stm> (accessed May 31, 2005).

Google Labs. 2005. <http://print.google.com/> (accessed June 8, 2005).

Google Print. 2005. <http://print.google.com/> (accessed June 9, 2005).

Google Scholar. 2005. <http://scholar.google.com/> (accessed June 10, 2005).

Googling up books, academic material. 2005. *Reading Today*, February/March, 7.

Hart, Michael. 2005. Welcome to Project Gutenberg. Project Gutenberg. <http://www.gutenberg.org/> (accessed June 10, 2005).

Harvard University Libraries. 2004. FAQ: The University's Pilot Project with Google <http://hul.harvard.edu/publications/041213faq.html> (accessed May 31, 2005).

Jones, Philip. 2005. Bloomsbury exec warns against Google Print. *The Bookseller*, April 20. <http://www.thebookstandard.com/bookstandard/news/global/article_display.jsp?vnu_content_id=1000891650> (accessed May 31, 2005).

Markoff, John. 2004. Google plans new service for scientists and scholars. *The New York Times*, November 18, C6.

Mehta, Aalok. 2004. ACS sues Google. *Chemical & Engineering News*, December 20, 13.

Ockerbloom, John Mark. 2005. The online books page. <http://onlinebooks.library.upenn.edu/> (accessed June 1, 2005).

OCLC. 2005. Quick facts about the Open WorldCat program. <http://www.oclc.org/worldcat/open/facts/default.htm> (accessed June 9, 2005).

Oder, Norman. 2005. Google Scholar links with libs. *Library Journal*, April 15, 17-18.

Pike, George H. 2005. All Google, all the time. *Information Today*, February, 15-16.

Price, Gary. 2005. Google Scholar is now open to all libraries. <http://www.searchenginejournal.com/index.php?p=1694> (accessed May 30, 2005).

Project MUSE. 2005. Project MUSE linking partners. <http://muse.jhu.edu/about/muse/vendors.html> (accessed June 8, 2005).

Quint, Barbara. 2005. Up front: The day the world changed: Google takes command. *Information Today*, February, 7.

Rhyno, Arthur. 2005. Google goes scholarly? *Feliciter*, 51, 9-10.

Roush, Wade. 2005. The infinite library. *Technology Review* May, 54-59.

Sherman, Chris. 2003. Google introduces book searches. *SearchDay*, December 17. <http://searchenginewatch.com/searchday/article.php/3290351> (accessed April 20, 2005).

Tennant, Roy. 2005. Google out of print. *Library Journal*, February 15, 27.

Teather, David. 2005. Fusion–why the force is with Google. *The Guardian Unlimited Online*. <http://www.guardian.co.uk/online/news/0,12597,1490080,00.html> (accessed June 10, 2005).

Tenopir, Carol. 2005. Online databases: Google in the academic library. *Library Journal*, February 1, 32.

University Press Assn.'s objections. 2005. *Business Week Online*, May 23. <http://www.businessweek.com/bwdaily/dnflash/may2005/nf20050523_9039.htm> (accessed June 12, 2005).

University publishers question Google Print library project. 2005. *American Libraries Online*, May 27. <http://www.ala.org/al_onlineTemplate.cfm?Section=alonline&template=/ContentManagement/ContentDisplay.cfm&ContentID=95192>.

Wleklinski, Joann M. and Marydee Ojala. 2005. Studying Google Scholar: Wall to wall coverage? *Online*, May/June, 22-26.

Young, Jeffrey W. 2005. More than 100 colleges work with Google to speed campus users to library resources. *The Chronicle of Higher Education*, May 11. <http://chronicle.com/free/2005/05/2005051101t.htm> (accessed June 5, 2005).

Google Scholar vs. Library Scholar:
Testing the Performance of Schoogle

Burton Callicott
Debbie Vaughn

SUMMARY. How does the content of Google Scholar, a.k.a. "Schoogle," compare to that of subscription databases and the library catalog? Five sample research topics indigenous to undergraduate libraries were searched in Google Scholar, the College of Charleston online catalog, EBSCO's Academic Search Premier database, and a subject-specific subscription database. Points of consideration included document type, availability of full-text materials, local availability of materials (either in print or online), and relevance of materials to the research topics. Results showed that Google Scholar, while a substantive supplementary research tool, does not provide the same quality in terms of relevance for many research topics. *[Article copies available for a fee from The Haworth Document Delivery Service: 1-800-HAWORTH. E-mail address: <docdelivery@haworthpress.com> Website: <http://www.HaworthPress.com> © 2005 by The Haworth Press, Inc. All rights reserved.]*

Burton Callicott (E-mail: callicottb@cofc.edu) and Debbie Vaughn (E-mail: vaughnd@cofc.edu) are Reference Librarians, both at the College of Charleston, Addlestone Library, Charleston, SC 29424.

[Haworth co-indexing entry note]: "Google Scholar vs. Library Scholar: Testing the Performance of Schoogle." Callicott, Burton, and Debbie Vaughn. Co-published simultaneously in *Internet Reference Services Quarterly* (The Haworth Information Press, an imprint of The Haworth Press, Inc.) Vol. 10, No. 3/4, 2005, pp. 71-88; and: *Libraries and Google®* (ed: William Miller, and Rita M. Pellen) The Haworth Information Press, an imprint of The Haworth Press, Inc., 2005, pp. 71-88. Single or multiple copies of this article are available for a fee from The Haworth Document Delivery Service [1-800-HAWORTH, 9:00 a.m. - 5:00 p.m. (EST). E-mail address: docdelivery@haworthpress.com].

Available online at http://www.haworthpress.com/web/IRSQ
© 2005 by The Haworth Press, Inc. All rights reserved.
doi:10.1300/J136v10n03_08

KEYWORDS. Google Scholar, Google, subscription resources, Free Web, library databases, library research

INTRODUCTION

Google, the popular Internet search service, recently released a beta version of a new database called Google Scholar (http://www.scholar.google.com). Google Scholar, known in some circles as "Schoogle," is an Internet search engine that, according to Google's site, "enables you to search specifically for scholarly literature, including peer-reviewed papers, theses, books, preprints, abstracts and technical reports from all broad areas of research." The method by which Google indexers determine what material is "scholarly literature" has not been made public at this time. A simple search does bring up what look to be classic peer reviewed journal articles. This is, in essence, what Google Scholar is–a collection of Web files that look like scholarly journal articles with a smattering of scholarly support such as conference and technical reports, theses, and the like. Using special, secret algorithms, Google culls out items from their general database that fit their mold of a scholarly article. These pages are then dumped into a new, more specialized database–Google Scholar.

Following the launch of Google Scholar in late November 2004, there has been much hype and speculation about the effects the reigning search engine king will have on library usage and scholarly enquiry in general. Although Google Scholar is still in "beta" mode, the authors wanted to assay this new research tool to see how it compares to more traditional research avenues and finding aids. Five typical undergraduate research topics ranging from literary criticism to environmental pollution were chosen as a way to put Google Scholar through its paces. For each topic, Google Scholar, the College of Charleston library catalog, a general, and a subject specific online periodical index (library database) were searched with the aim of making a substantive analysis of just what constitutes Google Scholar and to find out what it means to "stand on the shoulders of giants," as the deceptively humble invitation that underwrites the Google Scholar search box encourages us to do. (This is a reference to an Isaac Newton quote: "If I have seen further, it is by standing on the shoulders of giants.")

A BRIEF BACKGROUND OF GOOGLE SCHOLAR

In order to enhance the content of Google Scholar, representatives from Google have made arrangements with willing journal publishers as well as journal aggregators (e.g., InfoTrac) to have citations, abstracts, and, in some cases, full-text articles added to Google's database. As Google notes in its help files, "a large fraction of scholarly literature is still offline, and until these papers are available online, citation-only results help researchers find as much relevant information as possible." This statement does not really tell the full story, as most Google Scholar searchers will soon discover. It would be more accurate to say that a "large fraction" of scholarly literature *is* available online, but it is not free to the public. Many publishers have digitized their content but they do not let just anyone access it, including Google. Many publishers are happy to facilitate "pay to peek" transactions and will lead researchers to secure sites that can quickly process credit card purchases so that users can download the full text of a given article or book chapter. There is no doubt that it will not take long for many publishers to see that there is quite an incentive to work with Google and add their content to Google Scholar, however limited by publication date coverage or availability of full text.

To further round out Google Scholar, Google is also encouraging individual authors to provide citations, abstracts, and, when warranted, entire articles they have written to the mix. In this regard, vanity is working in Google's favor. The first search most authors perform upon opening Google Scholar is their own name. The first "F.A.Q." under the link "Scholar Help" on the main Google Scholar page reads: "How do I find my own articles?" (F.A.Q. numbers 5 and 6 read "I'm an author, why would I want my articles in Google Scholar?" and "I'm an author and my articles do not appear in Google Scholar, how do I remedy that?"). Google offers many links here to facilitate communication between scholars and Google.

Having "free" access to journal citations from all of these various sources can be wonderful and incredibly frustrating by turns. Searching in the unspecialized, less mediated arena of Google Scholar will undoubtedly turn up articles and documents not found by the more traditional finding aids–MLA Bibliography, America: History and Life, Environmental Sciences and Pollution Management, etc. Because the real content, the full text, has monetary value, many of the "hits" in Google Scholar will lead only to a citation and abstract (and often a request for a credit card number). This can lead to furrowed brows and, in some desperate cases, an unnecessary loss of money. In theory, searchers affiliated with an institution will seamlessly be brought from the free world of Google Scholar to the subscriber world of the college or university. In other words, if a faculty member at the College of Charleston discovers an article in the *American Journal of Bioethics* using Google

Scholar, s/he should automatically be linked to the full text of that article. This juncture is still often problematic, but as libraries and content providers begin to work with Google, the connection is becoming smoother and more reliable.

In a move that signals that they have accepted and embraced a Googlefied world, OCLC freely dumped most of its WorldCat database into Google and Google Scholar. Researchers using Google Scholar for book references are bound to experience the unlikely discoveries and terrible frustrations inherent in journal article searches. Books that are not found in local library catalogs can, and undoubtedly will, appear in Google Scholar searches. Google programmers are at work on refining "find in a library" software that, in theory, will point searchers to the closest library that holds a particular title. Given the vast numbers of book records, often the closest library may be many miles away. This represents a potential boon for those with time and interlibrary loan resources and white knuckles for those with little time and no access to a book delivery service. Fortunately for libraries and librarians, due to the limitations of Google Scholar in terms of full text and search refinements, the new database should bring as many people to the library as it diverts.

THE LITERATURE

The Google search engine with its clean, uncluttered search screen and unique relevancy ranking system has been the darling of savvy Web searchers since 1999. The clever name and consistent results struck a chord with Internet researchers who had grown weary of the busy interfaces of Internet search tools such as Yahoo, Excite, Alta Vista, and the like. In an article entitled "I'm Feeling Lucky," which appeared in the February 2000 issue of *Internet Magazine*, Google co-founder Sergey Brin (2000) states that Google's home page is deliberately simple because "when people come to Google, all they want to do is search. . . . Being efficient about the search includes all aspects of the user interface, including how long it takes you to find the search box and type your terms."

With the advent of online databases and now Google, simplicity in searching is something that researchers, especially undergrads, have come to expect. Web page user testing at the College of Charleston confirmed this idea; 53% of participants were unable to successfully navigate the library's home page when asked to find a journal or magazine article on the *Great Gatsby*. One participant typified the sentiments of many in the user test when she exclaimed: "I just want a search box" while struggling to find an appropriate link (Vaughn and Callicott 2003, 8, 14). Though none have come close to the amount of white space found on Google search pages, libraries such as those at the University of Michigan and Texas A&M have attempted to mimic Google's Zen approach to Web searching. Using database driven/active server Web pages as well as site-wide search boxes, many libraries have attempted to pare down busy Amazon-styled home pages with the use of prominent search boxes on the front page (Cauffman 1999; Van Ullen and Germain 2002). Despite these efforts, the quest to emulate the simplicity of Google without compromising a hefty investment in subscription resources has yet to be fully realized (Klein 2003).

Google Scholar's arrival in 2004 has evinced serious soul searching and sparked numerous debates amongst librarians over the quality of resources and span of content. Google Scholar can be thought of as a beautiful acquaintance that seems to have it all: elegance (of interface), wealth (of content), and finesse (of yielding results). On the one hand, librarians naturally want to support its dive into academe; on the other hand, we harshly question its aims and goals–perhaps due to our own insecurity about our perceived shortcomings–and seek fault in an act of self preservation. As the gatekeepers of information, it is imperative that librarians test and retest Google Scholar's weight in the field of academic research to learn where it stands, even in its beta form, in the spectrum of scholarly information resources.

Despite its recent arrival, Google Scholar has already generated a number of articles including a handful that specifically investigate its content as compared to that of a library's catalog and its subscription resources. Carol Tenopir of the University of Tennessee, Knoxville, discusses sample searches in her article "Google in the Academic Library: Undergraduates May Find All They Want on Google Scholar" (2005). Tenopir searched the term "geysers" in Google Scholar, Google, Web of Science, Science Direct, and Academic Search Premier. She reports that though the Google Scholar content was "better" than that in full Google, the content available through subscription databases "showed a much wider range of journal titles than Google Scholar" (Tenopir 2005, 32).

Operating on the assumption that "most people search the simplest and cheapest sources first," Laura M. Felter excluded institutional and/or fee-based databases in her comparative examination of Google Scholar, "Google Scholar, Scirus, and the Scholarly Revolution" (2005). Instead, she compares Google Scholar to Scirus, Elsevier's free Internet search service. Though she does not investigate Google Scholar's offerings in light of subscription resources, Feltner makes the point that "we [librarians] need to help our researcher clients to integrate their tools of choice, whether Google Scholar and/or Elsevier's Scirus, with our offerings."

In his article entitled "Google Scholar: The Pros and the Cons," Péter Jacsó (2005) uncovered a potentially telling void in Google Scholar's content. Jacsó searched for information on tsunami alerts in Google Scholar and limited his results to articles published in the journal *Nature*. His search produced only one article, published in 2000. The same search executed using the Nature Publishing Group search engine brought up eight relevant hits, ranging in publication date from 1987-2003. Jacsó found similar results with *Science* magazine and the Astrophysics Data System that hosts the online version of the magazine. Like Feltner, Jacsó argues that Google Scholar is best considered a supplement to other research tools rather than a replacement.

The theme of Google Scholar as a supplement to scholarly research is echoed in Joann Wleklinski's article "Studying Google Scholar: Wall to Wall Coverage?" (2005). Wleklinski conducted research in both Google Scholar and regular Google on the author/scholar Ithiel de Sola Pool. Google Scholar led her to both scholarly materials as well as not-so-scholarly items, such as sites merely selling his book *Technologies of Freedom*. Regardless of the quality of the citations, few were available full-text without the benefit of a library subscription or a credit card. Though Wleklinski did not compare her findings with those from subscription resources, she states that, when it comes to Google Scholar, "all roads frequently lead back to the library" (26). She goes on:

> The Google Scholar Pool search let me know some of the books he'd written, plus who was citing him and his work. Those citations led me to other books that might be helpful to the subject I was researching. Google Scholar led me to information that I could then mine elsewhere in a much more responsible manner. (24)

The author's own research produced similar results. Like clues that lead to the buried treasure, Google Scholar often gestured towards relevant literature that could be found only by abandoning Google and switching over to the library/the library Web page. For example, full-text access to information cited in Google Scholar was often literally buried beneath institutional access to Ingenta content (which is sometimes buried within InfoTrac). Nonetheless, Google Scholar could, indeed, be a "helpful beginning."

THE RESEARCH

Working at what is primarily an undergraduate institution with a well regarded, broad-based curriculum, reference librarians at the College of Charleston main library receive requests for assistance with research help on a variety of major subjects ranging from the humanities to the "hard sciences." In an effort to test the depth and breadth of Google Scholar as it may relate to the College of Charleston, five sample research topics were chosen in an effort to reflect typical undergraduate research projects:

- Zora Neale Hurston's *Their Eyes Were Watching God*
- Martha Stewart and female entrepreneurs
- Mosquito control spray and its effects on the environment and public health
- Andy Warhol and the pop art movement
- the Triangle Shirtwaist Company fire

Each topic was searched in Google Scholar, the College of Charleston online catalog, EBSCO's Academic Search Premier, and an appropriate subject-specific subscription database (MLA International Bibliography, Business Source Premier, Environmental Sciences and Pollution Management, Art Full Text, and America: History and Life, respectively).

Search terms and phrases were deliberately constructed to resemble those a typical undergraduate researcher might use. These terms and phrases were varied slightly as warranted for each search tool to reflect variations in search capabilities such as subject authority, the use of Boolean operators between search boxes, filtering, etc. (see Figure 1). For each search, material type and relevance were noted for the first 100 results (see Figures 2-6). Results were classified by material type as books, full-text articles, not full text articles (article citations or abstracts), "citations" (specific to Google Scholar), Web sites, and other (dissertations, theses, newsletters, working papers, white papers, reports, lesson plans, and other documents neither monographic nor peri-

FIGURE 1. Search Terms Varied Among Each Search Tool

Zora Neale Hurston's *Their Eyes Were Watching God*	
Database	**Search Terms**
Google Scholar	Zora Neale Hurston Their Eyes Were Watching God
CofC Catalog	Hurston, Zora Neale. Their eyes were watching God. *(as subject)*; Hurston Their Eyes Were Watching God *(as keyword)*
Academic Search Premier	Zora Neale Hurston AND Their Eyes Were Watching God *(as keyword)*
MLA Bibliography	Their Eyes Were Watching God (1937) *(as primary subject work)*

Martha Stewart and female entrepreneurs	
Database	**Search Terms**
Google Scholar	Martha Stewart women entrepreneurs
CofC Catalog	Stewart, Martha.*(as subject)*; Martha Stewart *(as keyword)*
Academic Search Premier	Martha Stewart AND entrepreneur *(as keyword)*
Business Source Premier	Martha Stewart AND entrepreneur *(as keyword)*

Mosquito control spray and its effects on the environment and public health	
Database	**Search Terms**
Google Scholar	mosquito control pesticide spray environment pubilc health
CofC Catalog	Mosquitoes Control *(as subject)*
Academic Search Premier	Mosquitoes Control *(as subject)* AND (public health OR environment) *(as keyword)*
Environmental Sciences and Pollution Management	culicidae AND (control OR pesticide* OR spray*) AND (environmental effects OR public health) *(as keyword)*

Andy Warhol and the pop art movement	
Database	**Search Terms**
Google Scholar	Andy. Warhol pop art
CofC Catalog	Warhol, Andy, 1928–Criticism and interpretation. *(as subject)*; Andy Warhol pop art *(as keyword)*
Academic Search Premier	Andy Warhol AND pop art *(as keyword)*
Art Full Text	Andy Warhol AND pop art *(as keyword)*

Triangle Shirtwaist Company fire	
Database	**Search Terms**
Google Scholar	Triangle Shirtwaist Company fire
CofC Catalog	Triangle Shirtwaist Company *(as subject)*; Triangle Shirtwaist Company *(as keyword)*
Academic Search Premier	TRIANGLE Shirtwaist Co. *(as company entity)*; Triangle Shirtwaist Company fire *(as keyword)*; Triangle Shirtwaist Company *(as keyword)*
America: History and Life	Triangle Shirtwaist Company *(as subject)*; Triangle Shirtwaist Company *(as keyword)*

FIGURE 2. Results by Search Tool and Material Type for Zora Neale Hurston's *Their Eyes Were Watching God*

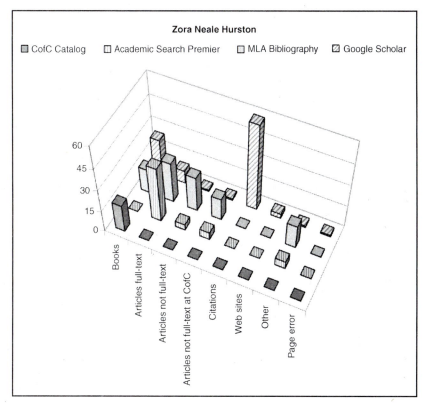

odic in nature). For article citations and abstracts that were not readily available full text online, College of Charleston holdings (print or electronic) were searched to determine local availability.

Though admittedly somewhat subjective, efforts to determine relevance were guided by a strict interpretation of the thesis for each topic. Results that were only tangentially related were counted as "not relevant." For example, in the case of Martha Stewart and female entrepreneurs, a document discussing Stewart's business tactics, success, and popularity in the domestic industry was considered relevant; a document referencing "entrepreneur Martha Stewart" and her time in prison was considered not relevant.

FIGURE 3. Results by Search Tool and Material Type for Martha Stewart and Female Entrepreneurs

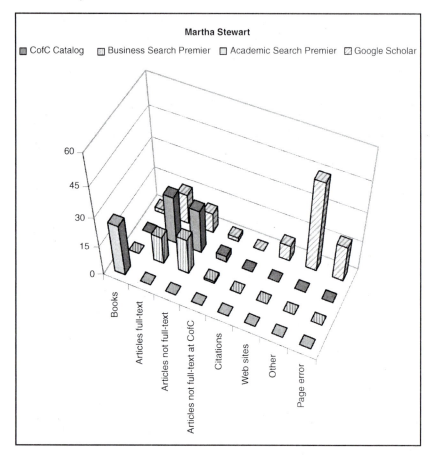

THE RESULTS

Despite claims in much of the literature as well as early encounters with the database, in general Google Scholar measured up favorably when compared to more traditional, fee based online finding aids in terms of quality and quantity of results. As can be seen in the tally for searches on Zora Neale Hurston and mosquito control, more than half of the search hits were relevant to the research topics and included many

FIGURE 4. Results by Search Tool and Material Type for Mosquito Control Spray and Its Effects on the Environment and Public Health

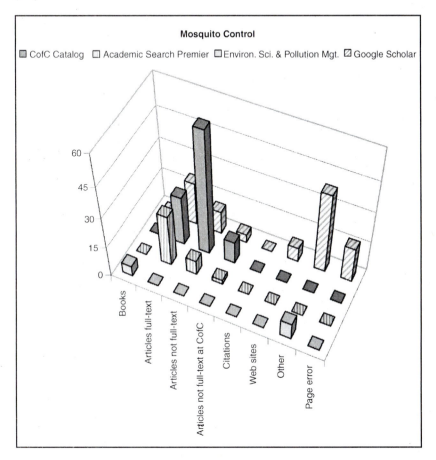

reputable, scholarly sources. This was not the case, however, with all of the test subject searches. Google Scholar generated a rather paltry six percent relevancy rate in terms of citations for Martha Stewart and female entrepreneurs (though the other, "traditional" search tools generated few relevant results as well). Results in terms of relevancy were not much better for searches on Andy Warhol and the Triangle Shirtwaist Company fire (see Figures 5 and 6).

FIGURE 5. Results by Search Tool and Material Type for Andy Warhol and the Pop Art Movement

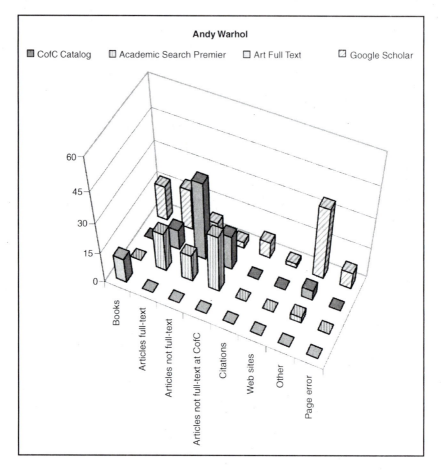

Despite claims that scientific literature has been quicker to embrace the Web and electronic systems of distribution, Google Scholar's results in the humanities were surprisingly solid, relevant, and full of full-text links. In the short time that the authors investigated Google Scholar, some improvements in the database were observed. The quality of the search results appeared to improve somewhat as the size of the database grew to some extent. The fact that results are presented in an

FIGURE 6. Results by Search Tool and Material Type for the Triangle Shirtwaist Company Fire

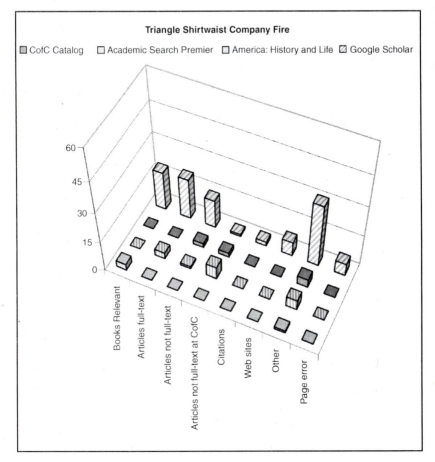

unsorted fashion with book citations, dissertations, journal articles, lesson plans, etc., all jumbled together, can mean that researchers spend lots of time sifting and weeding through various entries. What Google Scholar labels "[CITATION]" in its result list can be frustrating, as these citations are often incomplete. A Google Scholar citation that appears in the first 20 hits for Zora Neale Hurston includes the following:

[CITATION] Watching God
ZNTEW Hurston - Beautiful African American Janie Crawford
grows up in the . . .
Cited by 1 - Web Search

Clicking on "Web Search" executes a new Google Scholar search with apparently random key words from the citation. Not a single time was such a search useful or successful in terms of generating the full citation or even other relevant citations. However, the "Cited by" link is potentially very useful as it is a true citation index that brings up every record in Google Scholar's database that cites that particular article.

FINAL MUSINGS

As Google Scholar and subscription library content become more integrated, Google Scholar stands to be a more reliable and respectable

FIGURE 7. Results by Search Tool and Relevance (Graphically)

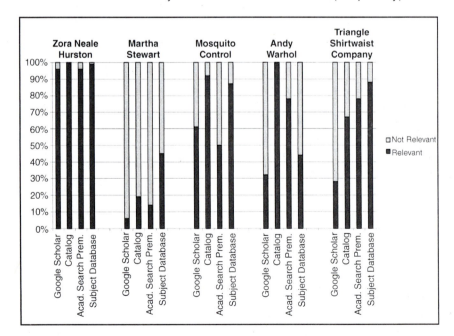

FIGURE 8. Results by Search Tool and Relevance (Numerically)

Zora Neale Hurston	Relevant	Not Relevant
Google Scholar	96%	4%
Catalog	100%	0%
Acad. Search Prem.	96%	4%
Subject Database	99%	1%

Martha Stewart	Relevant	Not Relevant
Google Scholar	6%	94%
Catalog	19%	81%
Acad. Search Prem.	14%	86%
Subject Database	45%	55%

Mosquito Control	Relevant	Not Relevant
Google Scholar	61%	39%
Catalog	92%	8%
Acad. Search Prem.	50%	50%
Subject Database	87%	13%

Andy Warhol	Relevant	Not Relevant
Google Scholar	32%	68%
Catalog	100%	0%
Acad. Search Prem.	78%	22%
Subject Database	44%	56%

Triangle Shirtwaist Company	Relevant	Not Relevant
Google Scholar	28%	72%
Catalog	67%	33%
Acad. Search Prem.	78%	22%
Subject Database	88%	12%

* Page errors in Google Scholar results were counted in the "Not Relevant" category.

source of scholarly information. In the wake of OCLC's move to release formerly protected, revenue generating catalog content to the wilds of the free Internet, many libraries are considering similar schemes to Googlefy their resources. As the results from this study indicate, Google Scholar shows great potential as a means to introduce novice researchers to library resources and scholarly literature. Until or unless Google Scholar begins to provide more sophisticated search capabilities and revise its relevance ranking system to accommodate scholarly research, it will continue to function best as a sort of training database that users will abandon as their research needs become increasingly sophisticated.

In the realm of scholarly research, Google Scholar's biggest strength, its simple, single search box, is also its biggest weakness and cause for some concern. Just as with Google, searchers are pretty much guaranteed to get some results, regardless of what they type in the Google Scholar search box. As many librarians and instructors who assign library research projects have discovered, many students are satisfied with results from simple searches that satisfy only the simplest search parameters and may miss or bury some of the most relevant and pertinent material available. Without the ability to construct more complicated searches and to limit for particular types of material–peer reviewed journal articles, books, magazines, etc.,–Google Scholar will always cater to the lowest common denominator and discourage thorough research. Though they can appear unwieldy and bulky, search screens for more sophisticated databases such as MLA Bibliography and America: History and Life often encourage more sophisticated search techniques and offer an array of limiters and expanders to ensure a more complete review of the literature.

Regular Google's unique relevancy ranking system, which factors in the number of times that other sites link to a particular Web site to gauge its significance, is ill-suited to the world of scholarly research. To account for the fact that the most popular articles may not be the best articles, Google Scholar employs its own relevancy ranking system:

> Google Scholar doesn't rely on how many websites link to a particular paper or book. Instead, it examines who wrote it, who published it and how many other scholarly works cited it. Based on those sorts of criteria, dissertations, peer-reviewed papers and other scholarly literature can float to the top of search results. (Gaither 2004)

Arguably revolutionary in its own right, Google Scholar's relevancy ranking system is far from perfect. Much work still needs to be done to really make this ranking system meaningful and reliable. Over and above the technical considerations, Google Scholar's approach implies some potentially troubling considerations. First of all, representatives at Google Scholar have been very secretive and protective of the algorithms and specific criteria that they use to rank results. Ideally, searchers would have some control over this including an ability to set their own preferences even in a limited capacity. At the very least, Google Scholar searchers should have some basic understanding of the system, so that they may tweak searches and interpret results appropriately. Though a system taking into account author credentials, publisher standards, published reactions, etc., may be an improvement over traditional online indices ranking results primarily by date of publication, it does take an aspect of critical thinking out of the equation. Inexperienced researchers who cut their scholarly teeth with this kind of finding aid may never learn to make their own judgments in terms of quality and reliability of source material.

As more and more research is "published" online, distinctions between monographs and various types of periodicals may become irrelevant. The fact that Google Scholar lumps together dissertations, white papers, drafts, books, citations, scholarly articles, and the like in a willy-nilly, one-stop-shop fashion could also cause problems for novice researchers who do not fully understand the differences between various material types and their significance in terms of content. Steven Abram (2005) provides a colorful and apt description of Google Scholar when he likens it to a newborn baby:

> Today we can recognize Google Scholar as a newborn. Even as a toddler we'll not fear it because it won't be perfect or even really good for scholarly research yet. However, when it hits the terrifying threes, beware if you haven't adapted your service to respond to it. You want to be around to see its teens. Google Scholar– just the kick in the pants we need!

Certainly Google Scholar has its shortcomings, but it is growing and evolving intelligently. Because its popularity continues to rise, it would be a mistake to ignore Google Scholar just as it would be to steer new library patrons away from it. As this article was going to press, Google's stock was trading at $280.94 a share (up from its initial public offering of just under $100.00 a share), and its price was expected to increase. Many new dictionaries include an entry for "Google, v. to search for information," and many colleges and universities are registering IP ranges with Google so that their resources will mesh with Google search results. Those involved in the dissemination of scholarly literature are hedging their bets that Google and Google Scholar are going to dominate the playing field for some time. To fully embrace their mission of assisting patrons with using the best research tools at their disposal, contemporary librarians need to be aware of Google Scholar and monitor its growth, innovations, and limitations. Until Google, or some other entity, completely eclipses all other library databases, however, librarians need to stress to library patrons that Google Scholar is just one tool among many.

REFERENCES

Abram, Steven. 2005. "Google Scholar: thin edge of the wedge?" *Information Outlook*, January, 44-46. InfoTrac OneFile Plus (accessed May 31, 2005).

Brin, Sergey. 2000. I'm feeling lucky. *Internet Magazine*, February, 34. InfoTrac OneFile Plus (accessed May 31, 2005).

Coffman, Steve. 1999. Building earth's LARGEST library: driving into the future. *Searcher*, March, 34, InfoTrac OneFile Plus (accessed May 31, 2005).

Felter, Laura M. 2005. Google Scholar, Scirus, and the scholarly revolution. *Searcher*, February, 43-48. InfoTrac OneFile Plus (accessed May 27, 2005).

Gaither, Chris. 2004. "Google designs an engine for eggheads: with its Scholar research software, the Web giant hopes to tap into a new source of traffic–and revenue." *Los Angeles Times*, December 27, C1. Lexis-Nexis Academic Universe (accessed May 27, 2005).

Jacsó, Péter. 2005. Google Scholar: the pros and cons. *Online Information Review* 29(2): 208-214.

Klein, Leo Robert. 2003. The expert user is dead. *Library Journal*, October 15. <http://www.libraryjournal.com/article/CA323336.html>.

Tenopir, Carol. 2005. Google in the Academic library: undergraduates may find all they want on Google Scholar. *Library Journal*, February 1, 32.

Van Ullen, Mary K. and Carol Anne Germain. 2002. Business as usual: Amazon.com and the academic library. *The Journal of Academic Librarianship* 28: 319-324.

Vaughn, Debbie and Burton Callicott. 2003. Broccoli librarianship and Google-bred patrons, or what's wrong with usability testing. *College & Undergraduate Libraries* 10(2): 1-18.

Wleklinski, Joann M. 2005. Studying Google Scholar: wall to wall coverage? *Online*, May-June, 22-26.

Google, the Invisible Web, and Librarians: Slaying the Research Goliath

Francine Egger-Sider
Jane Devine

SUMMARY. Effective Web research must include both Visible and Invisible Web resources and reference librarians have an important role to play in mediating the research process. The Google search engine is the public's tool of choice and dominates Web searching even though it accesses a limited portion of the Web. The Invisible Web is less well-known to the public and harder to access but contains a greater wealth of resources. Reference librarians should help guide people to the best solutions for their information needs: at times Google, at other times the diverse tools that access the Invisible Web. *[Article copies available for a fee from The Haworth Document Delivery Service: 1-800-HAWORTH. E-mail address: <docdelivery@haworthpress.com> Website: <http://www.HaworthPress.com> © 2005 by The Haworth Press, Inc. All rights reserved.]*

Francine Egger-Sider is Coordinator of Technical Services (E-mail: fegger@lagcc.cuny.edu); and Jane Devine is Chief Librarian (E-mail: jane@lagcc.cuny.edu), both at the Library Media Resources Center, LaGuardia Community College, Long Island City, NY 11101.

Google® is a Registered Service Mark of Google, Inc., Mountain View, California. *Libraries and Google®* is an independent publication offered by The Haworth Press, Inc., Binghamton, New York, and is not affiliated with, nor has it been authorized, sponsored, endorsed, licensed, or otherwise approved by, Google, Inc.

[Haworth co-indexing entry note]: "Google, the Invisible Web, and Librarians: Slaying the Research Goliath." Egger-Sider, Francine, and Jane Devine. Co-published simultaneously in *Internet Reference Services Quarterly* (The Haworth Information Press, an imprint of The Haworth Press, Inc.) Vol. 10, No. 3/4, 2005, pp. 89-101; and: *Libraries and Google®* (ed: William Miller, and Rita M. Pellen) The Haworth Information Press, an imprint of The Haworth Press, Inc., 2005, pp. 89-101. Single or multiple copies of this article are available for a fee from The Haworth Document Delivery Service [1-800-HAWORTH, 9:00 a.m. - 5:00 p.m. (EST). E-mail address: docdelivery@haworthpress.com].

Available online at http://www.haworthpress.com/web/IRSQ
doi:10.1300/J136v10n03_09

KEYWORDS. Google, Visible Web, Invisible Web, reference librarians, search engines

INTRODUCTION

When we began to discuss the differences between researching in the Visible Web using Google and researching in the various databases that make up most of the Invisible Web using the numerous tools available, we were amused that both of us envisioned David vs. Goliath imagery. In the course of the discussion, however, it became clear that our images were different. One of us perceived Google as a giant because of its popularity and dominance in Web searching. She argued that the smaller, lesser-known tools that access the Invisible Web are in fact often more valuable than Google because they access a vaster, richer resource. The other saw the Invisible Web as a giant, albeit a cumbersome giant, lacking a single search tool, dwarfing the Web that is accessible to Google. In spite of the size and value of Invisible Web resources, the Google search engine remains the public's tool of choice for Web searching because it is quick and easy to use. This paper will argue that both visions are valid, that research on the Web must cover both the Visible and Invisible Web, and that librarians have an important role to play in mediating the research process with the most effective tools for the specific research question.

Clearly the determining factor in the relative preeminence of searching the Visible vs. the Invisible Web rests on the researcher's awareness of the Invisible Web and its role in reference and research. Many people, including some librarians, do not know what the Invisible Web is or why it should be important to them. Many people have false beliefs about search engines like Google and how much of the Web they are actually designed to search. But it would be hard to find anyone doing Internet research who is unfamiliar with Google.

The Visible and Invisible Web are closely related. Search engines such as Google use programs that are designed to search and index the Web. These programs, often known as spiders or crawlers, are created with parameters that determine how deeply they will search and index a Web site, how often they will revisit sites to pick up new content, what type of formats they will include, and similar characteristics. The Invisible Web is made up of all the World Wide Web content that is not found by all-purpose search engines like Google. In fact, each search engine could be said to create its own version of the Invisible Web. Each search engine divides the World Wide Web into what it indexes and the "everything else" that it does not cover. In that respect, each search engine has its own Invisible Web counterpart.

Given its convenience and speed, why should what Google finds be considered insufficient? Why need anyone worry about what Google does not find? Why are librarians concerned about Google's Invisible Web counterpart? Why has Google not simply added more Invisible Web content to its own indexing? It is true that Google does continually add content and reshape the Invisible Web: innovations such as Google Scholar or Google Video take material away from its Invisible Web counterpart. And Google is easy, fast, colorful, and pervasive. Indeed, the Invisible Web is not better known because, in fact, Google does such a good job.

But the Invisible Web "leftovers" that do not make the grade for inclusion in Google's indexing actually contain remarkably valuable material. The Invisible Web dwarfs the Web that Google and other search engines can crawl. Much of Invisible Web content resides in databases that are excellent sources of information but are not accessible to search engines like Google for a variety of technical, political, and economic reasons. The Invisible Web is not well documented. No single tool comparable to Google accesses and indexes the Invisible Web. Searching the Invisible Web may mean relying on multiple tools and hard, time-consuming work. It may also mean relying on a reference librarian to guide the way.

However, the riches available on the Invisible Web mean that the Web according to Google does not always win the research war. In many situations, people are using Invisible Web content without realizing that they are doing so. Anyone required to do comprehensive searching will need to go beyond a general search engine. Businesses may subscribe to Invisible Web search services to make sure that they keep abreast of industry developments. There are fee-based services that market Invisible Web searching to the business world. The Invisible Web is a major component in the field of competitive intelligence; a "supersearcher" must be an Invisible Web expert.

This article will explore the role of both the Visible Web according to Google and its Invisible Web counterpart in reference and research and how librarians can guide people to the best solution for their information needs.

USER PATTERNS

It is not uncommon for an undergraduate student to come to the reference desk with a question such as: "Can you please help me find this poem on Google?" Nor is it uncommon for a student, after a few minutes of waiting for the reference librarian to search the library's online catalog or a subscription database, to leave in exasperation, muttering, "I'll just go on Google," or "Can't you just find it on Google?" There seems to be no limit to students' reliance on Google, to the point where in students' minds today, information retrieval is simply anonymous with Google. Getting immediate results seems to be the primary concern.

More and more studies show that today's students start their research with a search engine on the Internet rather than on a library's home page or with a reference librarian. A 2001 study by the Online Computer Library Center in Ohio (OCLC) of 1,050 college students found that students gravitate first toward a search engine when undertaking research: "The first-choice Web resources for most of their assignments are search engines (such as Google or AltaVista)."[1] Similarly, the 2002 Pew Internet & American Life Project, entitled The Internet Goes to College, found that

> an overwhelming number of college students reported that the Internet, rather than the library, is the primary site of their information searches. Nearly three-quarters (73%) of college students said they use the Internet more than the library, while only 9% said they use the library more than the Internet for information searching.[2]

In the more recent 2005 Pew survey of 2,200 adults 18 years of age and over, Search Engine Users, the researchers concluded that "[in] impressive numbers, users trust their search engines"[3] and that younger users are more confident users.[4]

Both of the Pew studies reinforce the notion that the younger the student is exposed to a computer and searching, the more at ease he or she will be with a search engine and the more he or she will rely on that search engine, bypassing all other methods of research, including the library. Christen Thompson, a graduate student in Library and Information Science at Simmons College in Boston, sums up the various studies in her article "Information Illiterate or Lazy: How College Students Use the Web for Research," and concludes that "They [students] consistently begin their search with commercial search engines instead of their library's home page."[5] She goes on to point out that, in view of the students' preference of doing their research on the Web and the unreliable nature of the Web, it becomes imperative for librarians not only to teach students how to search on the Web but also to teach them how to evaluate the information found.[6]

The authors have not found any comparable user pattern studies for the tools that mine the Invisible Web. However, this is not a surprise, given the nature of the Invisible Web–a myriad of separate entities such as databases, directories, and Web sites–and the complex array of tools that access them.

THE GIANT IMPACT OF GOOGLE

What makes Google so appealing to students? Why has Google garnered such a corner on the market? Google's most appealing characteristic is the simplicity of its interface. To execute a basic search, a student simply types a word or phrase in the single search box, clicks, and, presto!, a results list appears. Librarians, on the other hand, have often been faulted for front-loading the library home page. Todd Miller, writing "In Defense of Stupid Users," remarks that:

> One way this mind set [the assumption that its customers are stupid] is manifest in Google is in its emphasis on the back end instead of the front end of searching. In the library world, we spend a remarkable amount of time and energy larding up our search interfaces with umpteen filters, Boolean pull-downs, radio buttons, and so on.[7]

He goes on to ask why librarians are surprised that students turn to Google rather than the library's "'Cadillac of search engines'" for which we have to "proceed to 'educate' the user about constructing searches in native command languages."[8] The second main attraction of Google is the relevancy page ranking which the founders of the search engine have devised to display the results of a search. The algorithm displays first those sites that have the most links *to* them, thereby ensuring that the most popular sites appear at the top of the results list.

Coupled with the rise in popularity of search engines such as Google is a continued decrease in traditional library services such as reference. Studies from the Association of Research Libraries (ARL) show a decline in reference statistics of 2% between 1991-1999 and 21% between 1991-2001.[9] Students do not feel that they need the expertise of a reference librarian to conduct the research for a term paper. The ease of use of Google gives students the illusion that they are obtaining data appropriate to their topic but, in fact, the students do not have the expertise to evaluate properly the websites retrieved through a Google search. As a result, many libraries are trying to emulate student experience with searching on the Web by offering various virtual reference services such as telephone reference, e-mail, instant messaging, chat, 24/7, discussion boards, FAQ Web pages, and the like. However early reports show little demand for these services.[10] No matter what libraries offer, students simply want to "Google."

Indeed, Google has reached such iconic status in our culture that today the word Google is used as a verb, "to google," with variants, "googling," "google-ize," and "google-izing." It has noun variants as well: "google-ization," "google-izers," "googlers." Another outgrowth of the status of Google as a cultural icon is that entire courses have been devoted to it. Simmons Graduate School of Library & Information Science in Boston offers a continuing education workshop entitled "Power Google: Top 20 Power Tips for Rapid Ready Reference."[11] The University of Washington Information School offered a one-credit graduate course in Winter 2004 simply called "Google," with the following syllabus description:

> Google–it's not just a search engine any more. Now the most popular way to search the web, Google has become a cultural phenomenon. In this course, we'll look at how it started and how it works, compare it to other search mechanisms (web-based and otherwise), look at its business model, technologies and competition, and examine its broader uses and significance.[12]

Sensing public interest, the *Seattle Times* described the University of Washington course in its Business & Technology section in February 2004.[13]

Some librarians are tailoring their services to Google in order to, at least, bring students into the library or, more to the point, have them use the library's home page as a starting point for their research. In a December 2002 article in *College & Research Libraries News*, "Facing the Competition: The Critical Issues of Reference Services," Virginia Massey-Burzio argues that if libraries can't compete with search engines, they should emulate them.[14] A panel discussion entitled "Googlizers vs. Resistors: Librarian's Role in a Googlized World," took place at the annual conference of the Pennsylvania Library Association in October 2004 in which panelists including librarians, publishers, and information specialists debated the place of search engines in the library world.[15] Some librarians are thinking of ways to harness the power of this search engine and perhaps use it to access the vast library collections available to students across campuses. In a June 21, 2004 *New York Times* article, Daniel Greenstein, the University Librarian of the California Digital Library notes that: "If you could use Google to just look across digital libraries, into any digital collection, now that would be cool."[16] One Baltimore school library has placed a large link to Google on every page of the library's Web site. The justification given by the librarian is that: "Our librarians are fully aware that Google is our students', our faculty's, and sometimes our own first choice to find information." Acknowledging criticism of the size of the link to Google on every page, the librarian replied: "[But] after observing hundreds of students (and faculty) in action, I changed my mind. Everyone starts with Google except librarians. So the prominence is not an accident, but a tip of the hat to the real world." [17]

THE GIANT VALUE OF THE INVISIBLE WEB

Google may be the search engine of choice these days and people may prefer its uncomplicated search screen but there are times when Google just does not get the job done. Research can be complicated and time-consuming work and the flexibility and accurate focus of a David is needed to defeat this research Goliath. Reference librarians have always played a role as mediator between information seekers and information resources. Increasingly, librarians may be responsible for leading people to resources that search engines cannot find–Invisible Web territory. There are two major characteristics of the Invisible Web, its size and the nature of its content, which librarians may be more prepared to deal with than the average Google user.

Bright Planet, a commercial provider of "Deep Web" searching for businesses, government agencies, and organizations, offers a list of the 60 largest known Invisible Web sites.[18] Their list includes both free and fee-based Web sites. Bright Planet projects that the content of these 60 sites alone is 40 times the size of the "Surface Web." As Google search results represent only the Surface Web, all of Bright Planet's Invisible Web content is non-searchable using Google's easy search screen. Much of the Invisible Web content resides in databases and while Google can lead a user to a database Web site, it cannot enter it and locate the specific information needed. Database answers to queries are dynamically generated and directed toward that particular question. The results are collected to answer a query and, when the user is done, disassembled. Each search can be said to have its own unique answer. Search engines cannot capture this type of fluid content.

Another look at Bright Planet's list of Deep Web content shows that 19 of the sites listed are subscription databases. Libraries provide these fee-based resources to their communities, so some of the names on Bright Planet's list will be familiar: EBSCOhost, JSTOR, LexisNexis. In addition to being inaccessible to Google because of their characteristics as databases, these resources are inaccessible to Google because of their proprietary status.

Another large grouping on the Bright Planet listing consists of federal government Web sites such as the Library of Congress, the Census Bureau, and GPO Access. These sites represent problems for Google in two ways. First, they are very content-rich sites. Google indexes only the first 101 KB of a Web site.[19] That means that the Library of Congress site, for example, is only partially indexed in Google; a great deal of its information is just too "deep" for Google to handle. The second problem with these types of Web sites for Google is that they may require researchers to use unique navigational tools to find specific information or that the user be somewhat familiar with how the information is grouped and how to identify the needed information. The simplicity of Google is stymied by the complexity of the information resources.

Other types of Invisible Web information may be found in formats not indexed by Google and other general search engines. Google lists all the formats that it does index but it leaves many formats untapped. For instance, Google has only recently introduced a video search which is in beta testing.[20] It still does not index audio files. All formats not indexed by Google become part of its Invisible Web counterpart. Google also cannot draw content from sites such as professional Web sites that require a user identification and login procedure.

The developers of the Bright Planet site conclude that their listing is incomplete because the Invisible Web is not yet well documented. There is no analog to Google that can search the entire Invisible Web. Many of the best Invisible Web search tools are directories, such as the *Librarian's Index to the Internet*, and many are hybrids that capture both Invisible Web and Surface Web resources. Directories, by their nature, are not used in the same way as search engines. While search engines use keywords for specific topic searching, directories arrange information by broad headings, requiring the user to drill down through a hierarchy of information to get at needed results. Searchers who cannot adjust to search modes other than Google's search box may need help with directory-type formats and may find themselves impatient with the process.

Even if librarians concede that Google represents the first stage of searching, there is ample scope for librarian research skills for more advanced searching. Who will need this kind of more advanced searching? Business people are primary candidates and, in fact, Bright Planet and other vendors market Invisible Web searching to corporate consumers. Students doing research for upper-level courses or for a thesis, professors writing for professional journals, and teachers looking for lesson plans all need the Invisible Web. Research and Development departments, and people in certain research fields, especially the sciences, medicine and technology will also need the Invisible Web (as well as print resources). When people or institutions need comprehensive information, they will have to turn to the Invisible Web.

What are the roles for librarians in this picture? In a world where users prefer "searching" over "navigating," librarians are needed to help people find information that lies below the surface. Librarians continue to develop interfaces that assist users with the many aggregator products and subscription databases. As Roger Strouse suggests in his article about content users, the "research specialist role will remain."[21]

Librarians rely on Google as much as any researcher and will continue to do so. However, librarians have a responsibility to know more than the average Google user. Rita Vine, in her article on Web searching, makes the point that "[w]hen librarians rely exclusively on Google for information seeking, they may inadvertently communicate to students that they know no more about Web searching than the student who is asking the question."[22] There are myriad questions that can be answered in a better way or with more reliable sources than those that Google will find. Reference librarians should always see themselves in the role of providing that value-added content–much of it from the Invisible Web. Otherwise, librarians "allow Google to become the arbiter of what is relevant."[23]

GOOGLE, THE INVISIBLE WEB, AND LIBRARIANS: SLAYING THE RESEARCH GOLIATH

It seems, then, that the Goliath in this story is the researcher's information needs and that both the Visible and the Invisible Web should be used to tackle them. How can librarians help researchers deal with massive information resources, using both Google and the Invisible Web tools as appropriate? Dennis Dillon of the University of Texas at Austin is quoted in *Library Journal* that libraries will need to provide added values to remain relevant: "We're looking at localization, customization, and providing services. Google owns the mass market, so we have to play around the niches."[24]

One value-added service is educational: to introduce researchers to the concept of the "Invisible Web" at the reference desk and in the library classroom. Students especially need to be taught "when information is needed and have the ability to locate, evaluate, and use effectively the needed information."[25] Students, as a rule, do not enter college with the necessary skills to properly evaluate online information. A class in Internet searching which delves into the various layers of Web site evaluation can help prevent a student from relying on a Web site found through a general-purpose search engine like Google but totally unacceptable for a research paper. Chris Thompson, quoted earlier, ends her literature survey of students' use of the Web aptly by noting that: "it is not only how to find information on the Web that must be taught to college students, but also how to evaluate the information once it has been found."[26] Students are not the only ones who need to be educated. Marketing the Invisible Web to all faculty becomes imperative as teaching faculty are ultimately responsible for the types of sources students use in their research. Librarians need to make faculty aware of the Invisible Web, through presentations, one-on-one discussions, and instruction classes to ensure that students use databases and get access to proprietary information rather than relying solely on general-purpose search engines.

Another value-added service is reference assistance that points students toward reliable and trustworthy sites and toward effective tools for finding such sites. If, for example, a student is looking for information on Shakespeare and starts his search in Google, he will be faced with an unmanageable plethora of results (18,000,000 on 5/9/05). A similar search in a database such as the *Librarian's Index to the Internet*, one of the predominant tools to mine the Invisible Web, will bring up 22 Web sites dealing with Shakespeare, giving the student a workable number of results to look at and evaluate for appropriateness to his particular topic. Another useful tool is *Infomine*, a database of scholarly resources put together at the University of California, Riverside. In *Infomine*, that same Shakespeare search brings up 318 results.

However, our hypothetical student who is researching Shakespeare must be reached by a reference librarian before he can be steered towards such reliable and trustworthy sources as the *Librarian's Index to the Internet* or *Infomine*. At what point in the student's research process will an encounter with a librarian take place? Will it be through a class in a course management system such as Blackboard, to which a reference librarian is assigned? Will it be through a more traditional library instruction class associated with the course in which the student is enrolled? Might the student faced with an onslaught of responses from a Google search wander towards the library's home page and find a 24/7 chat or e-mail or telephone reference service? In the student vision of the information landscape, there is such a disconnect between the Web according to Google and the Web resources offered through a library that the solution boils down to the ability of librarians to gain a foothold within the student's research process.

Librarians have been working for several years at offering students online access to specific course-related resources through course management software packages, Blackboard being the most heavily used. A simple link to the library's home page will sometimes suffice; in other cases, a librarian can offer online content by creating a list of specific course-related sources and posting them directly in Blackboard. Librarians are working alongside teaching faculty by inserting themselves into online discussions when appropriate. This is a new realm in which online reference services can be offered to an entire class.

On a grander scale, Steven Bell in his article on "Infodiet" appeals to librarians, faculty, and database producers to work as one to level the playing field between Google and databases which comprise the greatest segment of the Invisible Web: "Together we must begin by developing search systems and interfaces that provide an appropriate balance between the quality and sophistication of library catalogs and good aggregator databases, on the one hand, and the convenience and ease of Google-like search engines, on the other."[27] Various initiatives are underway along these lines, in particular ProQuest with its new interface which makes search terms more transparent to users, and "RedLightGreen," a book database drawn from the Research Libraries Group (RLG) union catalog, which offers a single search box and ranks the results by relevance.[28]

As students, faculty, and other researchers as well as librarians become more and more aware of multiple ways to harness the Web to meet research needs, it turns out that the research Goliath can best be attacked through a collaboration of Google searches and Invisible Web tools. Librarians need to become reference librarians in all their interactions and offer an alternative to such powerful magnets as Google when appropriate. Students will not stop using Google as a first step in their quest for research materials; librarians will have to re-double their efforts as information mediators to make online sources from the Invisible Web accessible and to publicize them at the reference desk and in the library classroom. It is up to information professionals to keep Google vs. the Invisible Web in balance in the reference arena, using Google when it can provide a quick answer but keeping it at bay when more appropriate Web sources can be tapped through Invisible Web content.

NOTES

1. *OCLC White Paper on the Information Habits of College Students: How Academic Librarians Can Influence Students' Web-Based Information Choices* (Dublin, Ohio: Online Computer Library Center, June 2002), 3.

2. Steve Jones, *The Internet Goes to College: How Students Are Living in the Future with Today's Technology* (Washington DC: Pew Internet & American Life Project, 2002), 12. Available: http://www.pewinternet.org. Accessed: January 24, 2005.

3. Deborah Fallow, *Search Engine Users: Internet Searchers Are Confident, Satisfied and Trusting–But They Are Also Unaware and Naive* (Washington DC: Pew Internet & American Life Project, 2005), 15. Available: <http://www.pewinternet.org>. Accessed: January 24, 2005.

4. Fallow, 24.

5. Christen Thompson, "Information Illiterate or Lazy: How College Students Use the Web for Research," *portal: Libraries and the Academy* 3, no. 2 (2003): 261. Available: <http://muse.jhu.edu /journals/portal_libraries_and_the_academy/v003/3. 2thompson.html>. Accessed: February 15, 2005.

6. Thompson.

7. Todd Miller, "In Defense of Stupid Users," *Library Journal* (March 2005): 51.

8. Miller.

9. James Casey Ashe, "Information Habits of Community College Students: A Literature Survey," *Community & Junior College Libraries* 11, no. 4 (2003): 17-25.

10. Carol Tenopir, "Rethinking Virtual Reference," *Library Journal* (November 2004): 34.

11. Simmons College, Graduate School of Library and Information Science, Office of Continuing Education, Online Workshops, "Power Google: Top 20 Tips for Rapid Ready Reference," October 6-November 7, 2003. Available: <http://www.simmons.edu/gslis/forms/CE_Fall_2003_Brochure.pdf>. Accessed: April 28, 2005.

12. University of Washington, Information School, "LIS 598 Google: Syllabus" (Winter 2004). Available: http://www.ischool.washington.edu/jwj/google/. Accessed: April 28, 2005.

13. Cynthia Flash, "Google for a Grade: UW Class to Study Popular Search Engine," *Seattle Times,* February 2, 2004, Business & Technology section. Available: <http://seattletimes.nwsource.com/html/businesstechnology/2001848831_google02. html>. Accessed: April 22, 2005.

14. Virginia Massey-Burzio, "Facing the Competition: The Critical Issues of Reference Services," *College & Research Libraries News* (December 2002): 774-775.

15. Kenny, Brian, "Googlizers vs. Resistors," *Library Journal* (December 2004): 44-46.

16. Katie Hafner, "Old Search Engine, the Library, Tries to Fit Into a Google World, "*New York Times*, June 21, 2001, A section. Available: <http://galenet.galegroup.com/>. Accessed: February 7, 2005.

17. Walter Minkel, "Going Gaga over Google," *School Library Journal* (September 2003): 37.

18. "Bright Planet, Largest Deep-Web Sites." Available: <http://www.brightplanet.com/infocenter/largest_deepweb_sites.asp/>. Accessed: April 25, 2005.

19. Greg R. Notess, "Review of Google," *Search Engine Showdown* (June 5, 2004). Available: <http://www.searchengineshowdown.com/features/google/review.html>. Accessed: January 12, 2005.

20. Google Video, Available: <http://video.google.com>.

21. Roger Strouse, "The Changing Face of Content Users," *Online* 28, no. 5 (2004): 27-31.

22. Rita Vine, "Going Beyond Google for Faster and Smarter Web Searching," *Teacher Librarian* 32, no. 1 (2004): 19-22.

23. Evan St. Lifer, "Guiding the Googlers," *School Library Journal* (January 2005): 11.

24. "Google to Digitize 15 Million Books," *Library Journal* (January 2005): 19.

25. Association of College & Research Libraries, Standards & Guidelines, "Information Literacy Competency Standards for Higher Education" (American Library Association, 2005). Available: <http://www.ala.org/ala/acrl/acrlstandards/informationliteracycompetency.htm#ildef>. Accessed: May 9, 2005.

26. Thompson, 3.

27. Steven Bell, "The Infodiet: How Libraries Can Offer an Appetizing Alternative to Google," *Chronicle of Higher Education* (February 20, 2004): B15.

28. Bell.

Choices in the Paradigm Shift:
Where Next for Libraries?

Shelley E. Phipps
Krisellen Maloney

SUMMARY. External factors are forcing libraries to seriously evaluate and redefine their purpose within higher education. Libraries have identified themselves as gateways to information. Google, and other Internet search tools, have changed the need and importance of the gatekeeper role in libraries. The authors argue that libraries have a role that is broader than that of gatekeeper. It is necessary to move beyond our existing mental models and truly redefine our unique role based on the needs within the external environment. To develop this broader role, libraries must develop collaborative relationships and leverage existing tools and services. *[Article copies available for a fee from The Haworth Document Delivery Service: 1-800-HAWORTH. E-mail address: <docdelivery@haworthpress.com> Website: <http://www.HaworthPress.com> © 2005 by The Haworth Press, Inc. All rights reserved.]*

Shelley E. Phipps is Assistant Dean for Team and Organization Development (E-mail: phippss@u.library.arizona.edu); and Krisellen Maloney is Team Leader, Digital Library and Information Systems Team (E-mail: maloneyk@u.library.arizona.edu), both at the University of Arizona Library, Tucson, AZ 85721.

Google® is a Registered Service Mark of Google, Inc., Mountain View, California. *Libraries and Google®* is an independent publication offered by The Haworth Press, Inc., Binghamton, New York, and is not affiliated with, nor has it been authorized, sponsored, endorsed, licensed, or otherwise approved by, Google, Inc.

[Haworth co-indexing entry note]: "Choices in the Paradigm Shift: Where Next for Libraries?" Phipps, Shelley E., and Krisellen Maloney. Co-published simultaneously in *Internet Reference Services Quarterly* (The Haworth Information Press, an imprint of The Haworth Press, Inc.) Vol. 10, No. 3/4, 2005, pp. 103-115; and: *Libraries and Google®* (ed: William Miller, and Rita M. Pellen) The Haworth Information Press, an imprint of The Haworth Press, Inc., 2005, pp. 103-115. Single or multiple copies of this article are available for a fee from The Haworth Document Delivery Service [1-800-HAWORTH, 9:00 a.m. - 5:00 p.m. (EST). E-mail address: docdelivery@haworthpress.com].

Available online at http://www.haworthpress.com/web/IRSQ
© 2005 by The Haworth Press, Inc. All rights reserved.
doi:10.1300/J136v10n03_10

KEYWORDS. Future role of libraries, competition from Google, collaboration, leveraging capacity

INTRODUCTION:
THE PARADIGM SHIFT IN HIGHER EDUCATION
AND ACADEMIC LIBRARIES

In a 1996 *Educom Review* article, Stan Davis (a former professor at Harvard Business School, Columbia, and Boston University), noted the transition of responsibility for higher education from the Church to the state over the last centuries. He then predicted, "the mantle of responsibility for articulating and dominating the new way of learning is going to pass to yet another institution . . . business. Because the old system is usually incapable of turning itself around, the new approach begins to gain market share."[1]

There are several indications that the passing of the mantle is now underway as many for-profit businesses devote themselves to achieving the goals that not-for-profit higher education set for itself. Private, for-profit institutions have become part of the higher education landscape. Publishers are creating and selling complete online courses that can be used by faculty or made available in independent learning environments. These gradual changes have occurred over the last decade and, at this point in time, compliment rather than replace the offerings of state-run institutions, providing a wider range of options for students as well as faculty.

The changes in academic libraries are more disruptive. It was inevitable that the capital markets would discover the profit to be made in making information transfer ubiquitous and easy. Google and others in the soft sector of the information market have developed new approaches to simplify information discovery and are becoming the first stop for many of our customers who are engaged in research and learning. Google and other Internet search engines are disregarding the concepts of precision and recall that are the established benchmarks of successful searching and are providing a more intuitive means to connect customers to ideas, opinions, data, research results, and previous learning.

Libraries have played a distinct and unique role in world cultures. Academic libraries have been identified with a wide range of activities and responsibilities. They have been steadfast in their commitment to the importance of serving the learning process, by collecting and organizing information content. They have also been strong in their commitment to preserve the printed, audio, and visual cultural heritage of their communities, and to make it available to future generations. They have been the standard bearers for freedom of access to information and for enabling "free" access–with the support of the government and stakeholder institutions. However, recently the primary focus of many academic libraries has been devoted to the role of providing a gateway to content.

It is the role of gateway that is most challenged by the competition of Internet search engines. As these new tools disrupt the view of libraries as information gateways it will be important to evaluate and redefine our core purpose. The paradigm is shifting and to be successful libraries must clearly identify their unique roles and then make strategic and timely decisions to maximize resources and leverage capacity within the information marketplace to provide value-added services to student, faculty and other customer groups.

THE LIBRARY AS GATEWAY: THE SHIFT FROM PURPOSE TO ARTIFACT

There was a time in the not too distant past when access to everything that was owned or licensed by the library was controlled by the library. The library was a funnel through which important information transactions occurred. Libraries were designed based on the premise that users would pass through the doors and that library staff, or at least appropriate signage developed by library staff, would connect them with the information that they needed to be successful. Libraries were able to view the gatekeeper role as central to their mission.

The push for automation, the transition to e-content, followed by the rapid adoption of the Internet caused several simultaneous changes in how libraries select, organize, and provide access to information. Libraries did not have the luxury of stepping back and considering how they might design systems and organize content to meet the changing expectations of users; instead they moved forward, automating existing processes and making online content available whenever possible. The role of gatekeeping, though only one means to an end, was never questioned and was presumed to remain valid in the virtual library environment. The complexity of systems, the lack of a cohesive path from index citation to full-text article and an array of different complex proprietary search techniques for information resources had reinforced the view of the library as gatekeeper. The means had, for most libraries, been framed as the "end" purpose.

The supposition was that users in the virtual environment would access the library via the library Website and that cleverly labeled Web pages would provide the signage necessary for users to navigate the profusion of information resources ranging from abstracting and index-ing databases to full-text collections. Since libraries were unable to re-duce the complexity of search systems and decrease the many steps involved in the discovery process, libraries developed additional ser-vices to train those who needed access but could not independently find their way through the systems.

Google significantly changed this picture. Its mission is "to organize the world's information and make it universally accessible and useful."[2] It has created the first truly useful way to bypass the library as a gateway to discovery. In the information-based economy, we can expect new en-trants to this market, offering new tools for vertical search, for evalua-tion of sources, for delivery of image, video, audio, and print. The Library as "gateway" is fast becoming an artifact. It is essential to reframe the purpose of academic libraries separate from the schemes and systems that were created as means to an end in a different time. The purpose of libraries was not to be a gatekeeper, but rather to provide the content and tools necessary to support research and learning.

TRANSFORMATION IN THE PARADIGM SHIFT: FINDING THE UNIQUE ROLE FOR LIBRARIES

The first step in the change process will be to clearly understand the unique role of libraries. The past decade has led us to tie our identity to connecting users to varied information resources. We did not design many of the search interfaces; instead we selected a wide variety of search and discovery tools that each optimized a specific type of discov-ery task. We created systems that provided good signage to help users select among the wide variety of tools and created instruction to explain the complexities of search to users. Now, with a wide array of Internet search engines that provide broad discovery of information, much of the search process is out of our control. What beyond the search and discov-ery process will libraries do to truly add value to the research and learn-ing processes?

In re-evaluating the purpose of libraries, it will be useful to examine the business sector to determine if strategies in the for-profit world might also be relevant within the not-for-profit world of education. Li-braries are becoming accustomed to planning based on the needs of cus-tomers, both the actual users and non-users who recognize the library as supporting their activities or the activities of the organization. In addi-tion, it is becoming more widely acknowledged that the expectations of stakeholders, those who fund "not-for-profit" enterprises similar to shareholders in the private sector, must also be satisfied in order to achieve sustainability. This is to say that customers must recognize that libraries enable them to do whatever they do–better. And, similarly, stakeholders need to recognize an explicit return on investment, or know that their investment is of value to the total enterprise.

In this kind of customer/stakeholder driven environment, one of the most important abilities for an organization is to be clear about and aware of the surrounding realities–what is actually happening–what competitors can achieve, how customers will respond, what is "true" about events and predictions, what the competitors' intent and capability are, and what is possible given the nature of business and product development. This analysis is difficult in all situations but within the context of a paradigm shift it is especially difficult. Many of our past assumptions and beliefs about the world may no longer be valid but they are then a lens through which we interpret and organize the external information that we use in planning and decision making. It is important to question deeply held, current beliefs and assumptions so the actual reality beyond our personal and well-shaped view of them becomes clearer and clearer. Senge and others refer to this as the practicing the discipline of "mental models."[3] A clear view of the present reality demands that we focus on our transformability–"a willingness to be open to new understanding and changing to become a different organization."[4] Transformability is a metamorphosis, and unlike adaptability, requires creative, non-linear approaches; there are no structured steps to follow. Some theories for this metamorphosis are being investigated–building on tacit and explicit knowledge in the organization, incorporating strategies that lead to understanding as well as action, using scenarios as a means of assessing possible consequences of little known future changes, and forming strategic alliances.[5]

As we remove our fuzzy, inwardly focused, professional glasses, and recognize the revolution in for-profit, corporate provision of search and discover to our customers, we can begin to experiment with these and other strategies. Deeply examining new roles and questioning our assumptions about our current beliefs are not yet comfortable for many in academic libraries. We must look at our environment to determine where we can play a significant role. Understanding our role in this larger system, practicing the discipline of systems thinking as described by Senge, is now of the utmost importance.

By clearly understanding our evolving purpose, we can refocus the enterprise on new or enhanced alternative products or services that will likely prove the most fruitful. Reports such as the National Science Foundation Revolutionizing Science and Engineering Through Cyber-infrastructure[6] have called on libraries to think more broadly and provide services that will transform e-Science. To do this, libraries will have to consider how they might contribute to the preservation and access of the scholarly record. This will include considering providing access and preservation for information that supports the new collaborative work patterns within the sciences. This might include support for experimental datasets and shared knowledge bases. It might also include new tools to support communication, collaboration, and timely sharing of information among the research community. It will be necessary to think creatively about what services a gateway to information might provide to the research community and redefine our role so that we meet the evolving needs. Support for teaching and learning is also changing in this new environment. A recent white paper released on behalf of the IMS Global Learning Consortium and the Coalition for Networked Information[7] calls for collaboration among those involved in developing tools to support instruction and libraries so that we can become more efficient and effective in providing reusable modules to support scalable delivery of instruction that will be essential in the future. This will involve developing a common and general understanding and definition of library services so that we have a firm foundation for deep collaboration.

As we move in these new directions, libraries need to know whether customers will value these new services/products enough to sustain the enterprise. Understanding how research is being accomplished, understanding how learning is achieved, the habits and preferences of researchers and learners, and what outcomes they desire as well as what the requirements of the processes they use will be critical if we are to play a value-added role in these processes. What these new, value-added services or products will be should be the focus of strategic planning and innovative strategy development. After creation, customers must fully understand what the new product or service enables them to do or be. Fine-tuned needs assessment should lead to value-added services. Marketing skills are also critical to success in this new environment.

If libraries are going to continue to play a significant role in the future of the research and learning processes, preservation of the cultural record, the protection of the freedom of access and support of ubiquitous access to information, that is so important to an educated and democratic society, then libraries will have to prove Stan Davis wrong, when he posits that we will be unable to turn ourselves around. As the paradigm shifts, those who can build on and create capacity to move with the shift, adapting and changing with the market and with primary customers, will ultimately survive.

Once our direction is clear, it will be essential to evaluate how we build the necessary capacity to meet customer expectations. Our role is not defined by a single service (e.g., simple search), but rather by a broader purpose (e.g., improving the quality of research and learning within our organization). We can look at our current situation and use an analytical approach to determine how best to develop a collection of products and services that will fulfill our purpose. The information marketplace is large and complex and there are a variety of products and services available to meet the needs of our customers. Some of these products we have developed (e.g., federated searching tools) and they now have for-profit competitors within the marketplace (e.g., Google). When we evaluate the market position of products that we have developed relative to competitors we can decide to retreat from the market, compete (if we can produce the same or better product at the same or lower cost), collaborate, when there is potential for mutual benefit, or leverage the competitors' product to create new capacity or enhance our existing capability.

FIRST REACTIONS TO THE PARADIGM SHIFT: COMPETITION

When evaluating how we provide search and discovery capability, it is essential to determine if competing with Google would be in our best interest. The concept of simple information discovery tools such as the one offered by Google is not new to libraries. Single-search interfaces such as federated searching and metasearching have been at the heart of many forward-thinking library projects. Library vendors have developed software to enable cross-data base searches; some academic libraries have partnered to build products.

While libraries struggled to convince their customers that precise, well-structured searches were in their best interest, Google quietly stepped in under the cloak of an advertising-based corporate entity seemingly unrelated to education and developed "simple search," based on keyword, that usually got users to what they needed, or at least started to, in an intuition-based, personally-controlled discovery mode. Even as customers began moving to the Internet as a first source of information, many librarians argued that Google was too imprecise to be useful, too focused on the unorganized "popular" and uncontrolled Web, in effect discounting its place as a viable tool in an academic environment. This disbelief and denial of the value of a new model that displaces current technology is often one of the first reactions in a paradigm shift. Arguments pointing to the shortcomings of the "competition" deny and ultimately overlook its potential significance. Diminishing the importance of the recent entrant into a market diverts the focus from true evaluation of the impact and realistic assessment of potential opportunities presented. Resistance to accept the competitor as providing value to our customers slows down strategic thinking.

As Google continued to work in the public marketplace, federated searching or meta-searching was seen as a possible alternative product that academic libraries could develop to provide a simplified search interface to locally-controlled scholarly literature. Metasearching allows single-search access of multiple information resources. On the surface it appears similar to Google and other Internet search engines, but behind the scenes the technologies as well as the economic incentives for adoption by information resource vendors are quite different.

Metasearching is accomplished by a software suite that coordinates several simultaneous real-time searches that each execute independently over the network. Results are returned to the software so that they can be further processed (e.g., sorted and de-duplicated) for the user. There are several drawbacks to this federated searching methodology. First, the network and the overhead of contacting and establishing a connection with an information resource provider can be slow and unreliable. The search is completed when the slowest provider has responded. In practice, this can take several minutes–far longer than the typical customer is willing to wait. Technical strategies which seemingly shorten this wait time by beginning to display results before all information resources have completed returning information are typically employed by metasearching software to hide the response delay from the user. Unfortunately, because all results have not been received and the result set is incomplete, these strategies limit the utility of many of the typical result-set management features, such as relevancy ranking and other sorting, that users have come to expect. Google, on the other hand, builds an index of all searchable content and the index becomes the source of the search, so searching is instantaneous and powerful algorithms can be used to completely sort the result set so that the probability of relevant information being close to the top of the list is high.

Another major problem with metasearching is related to the information marketplace and the willingness of information resource providers to support the full range of features available within the metasearching standards. The lack of support comes in both the search functionality and the completeness of metadata. Typically the Z39.50 protocol is used to support the functionality of searching. This is a well-established and rich protocol that has been designed to support a wide range of searching requirements. It is, however, rare to find an information resource vendor that supports the rich features available within Z39.50. It is more typical to find vendors that support only the most basic features. The minimal support for the standard's features reduces the effectiveness of the search. Metadata is also meagerly supported in the returned result set. The MARC format is usually used to return the results to the user. The MARC format was not established to describe information at the article level so important information, such as volume and issue, are not returned in a standard format. The limited functionality of the search combined with non-uniform metadata reduces the effectiveness of the metasearching framework. The searches are over-simplified and the results are difficult to interpret. Google, on the other hand, creates an index based on information that is derived from the full text of the materials. This index provides a rich foundation for searching (both very simple and complex) and also provides uniform and easy to interpret result sets.

Information resource vendors have been slow to support metasearching. A possible explanation for the slow adoption may be that metasearching offers them no competitive advantage in the information marketplace. It simply provides a "back door" for users who are already permitted to access their resources which bypasses the vendor's branding and other product features. On the other hand, the lure of new customers provides information resource vendors with incentive to allow Google to index their information. The simple Web search on Google, combined with pay-per-view technologies, provides a potential new market for publishers.

THE PARADIGM SHIFT: COMPETITION v. COLLABORATION

Competing with Google for single-search discovery of scholarly content utilized by researchers and students seems to be a futile effort for libraries. Google has a technical advantage and better market incentives to lure the participation of information resource providers. Some Google statistics are important to recognizing this fact: As of March 31,

2005, Google had a cash, cash equivalents and marketable securities balance of $2.507 billion. On a worldwide basis, Google employed 3,482 full time employees as of March 31, 2005, up from 3,021 as of December 31, 2004. Total assets add up to $3.8 billion; Total liabilities add up to $393 million. It is a publicly traded company with $3.4 billion in stockholders equity.[8]

There is little possibility of libraries to successfully play David to this Goliath. Collaboration seems a much more viable strategy. To be successful in the future, libraries will have to work *with* Google to ensure that users don't pay for information that we have licensed on their behalf.

Google is actively pursuing the academic market. It is currently beta testing Google Scholar which indexes only scholarly materials (only articles at this point). The relevancy ranking algorithms have changed to reflect the differences that scholars have in determining relevancy. Publishers have been quick to respond and make information available within Google Scholar.

Google has actively engaged libraries by providing mechanisms to have our customers' affiliations known as they link through to content. Google recognizes the IP address range of many universities and provides specialized links to catalogs and OpenURL Resolvers. In addition, they have a configuration tool that allows a browser session to be associated with a university. An off-campus customer will be passed through the associated OpenURL Resolver for authentication and then access to content will be seamless. By collaborating with Google and leveraging their capabilities, libraries have the opportunity to fulfill one of their most important roles–assisting users in discovering relevant information.

Google Print is another large-scale effort to expose what has formerly been the "hidden Web." Google is partnering with publishers and libraries to digitize books and make more content available. There are, of course, legal issues that must be resolved so only information that is out of copyright will be initially available in full-text format. Google is pushing, along with libraries, for legislation that will allow items that are no longer in print to be considered orphaned works and also made available. Google does not appear to be immediately interested in providing access to full content and it claims that only simple, limited views of content will be available. Google's primary interest appears to continue to be making content discoverable. The digital availability of full text, which it is pursuing in partnership with several libraries and publishers, is used to create a useful index of the world's information–a means to a specific end–the success of the search and discover process. Libraries have always embraced this means to their ultimate goal of supporting research and learning, however limited their ability, up to now, to provide this level of comprehensive access.

In addition to the products mentioned above, it has a suite of products they are testing and/or offering to a variety of types of customers–the general public, library users, advertisers. It has products for the wireless, hand-held tech users and for the desktop PC users. It is not afraid to fail in order to ultimately achieve success. It has the financial backing and cash flow to do research and development and the stockholder expectation for a return on investment. It has thus far exceeded shareholders' expectations. It has identified its revenue stream as coming from advertising, not directly from users and customers. The company has the business sense to understand that users will experience "free" access when using Google Search because users are acculturated to free TV and radio that is commercially sponsored.

Google understands users' Web-based behavior and has successfully built the capacity to succeed in the search and discover market. It, along with Amazon.com and a few other companies with deep business knowledge, was quick to market with Web-related value-added services that demonstrated the power of the Web and a deep understanding of its transforming capability. It was not first to market. But it has overtaken "search" and is implementing a global strategy.[9] It is important for libraries to discover how best to leverage this burgeoning capability to serve their core purpose.[10]

BUILDING ON OUR CAPACITY:
LEVERAGING THE CAPABILITY OF OTHERS

Libraries have multiple strengths to build on–knowledge of information organization, experience with technologies, adaptability, commitment to the value of information in society, a strong service commitment, organizational leadership and management skills, and a growing ability to work as a business. Our local holdings and preservation values are strengths. Our growing knowledge of digitization, imaging, metadata, electronic archival processing and repository storage are new capabilities, preparing us for new directions. Our knowledge of information literacy enables us to assist users with the invisible challenge of relevancy in retrieval strategies. Our experiments with physical and virtual information commons open up possibilities for a new role in the evolving learner-centered environments. The real estate we occupy has vast potential for serving communities of learners. In the past, libraries were very successful, valued, central to the research and learning process. Our product, the library, is well branded.

Libraries have value beyond the discovery of information. By leveraging the capability of Google to provide one of our services, libraries can focus greater attention on the broader goal of improving the quality of research and education. Effort previously used for creating virtual signage, "how-to" manuals, and search guides can be used to create the infrastructure for e-learning and e-science.

We don't know the future, but we can be sure that elements of the future are with us now. With our internally focused fuzzy glasses, Google looks like the Wolf in the Red Riding Hood story–dressed like our grandmothers, but with all too apparent large teeth that seemingly could gobble us up with little or no feelings of guilt. With our externally fuzzy glasses on, Google looks to us like a giant, colorful Teddy Bear come to rescue us from our complex dilemma of how to expand search and discover with the little capitalization we receive from our individual stakeholders. It offers to make our materials more available, quicker, delivered to the desktop or the hand-held screen. It offers to connect us easily to what we don't own but what our users need. It offers to do it free, and to partner with us so we can enhance our own value. It offers to provide us the opportunity to leverage their strength and our capability.

Google intends to organize the world's information and make it accessible and useful. Formerly, libraries believed that singly and in loosely connected consortial relationships, they would achieve this goal. We were ingenious at developing local and national catalogs and inter-library loan systems to fill in the gaps in our service delivery. We adopted and adapted technology; we learned process improvement; we moved from a largely passive, internal focus to an external customer focus. And now all of these attempts seem thwarted in the face of the gargantuan Google. All we really know is, if we could have, we would have invented it. This is evident in our ability to quickly incorporate it into our library services and to respond positively to their requests to partner in beta tests and content digitization. It is this identity and this capability that will enable us to transform and play our part in the evolving information environment.

REFERENCES

1. Davis, Stan. 1996. "Slicing the Learning Pie," in *Educom Review*, September/October, pp. 32-38.

2. Google Web site: <http://www.google.com/intl/en/corporate/index.html>.

3. Senge, Peter, *The Fifth Discipline: the Art and Practice of the Learning Organization*, NY, Doubleday,1990.

4. Chaharbaghi, Kazem, Andy Adcroft and Robert Willis. "Organisations, transformability and the dynamics of strategy." In *Management Decision*, 43 (1) 2005, p. 4.

5. Chaharbaghi, pp. 6-12.

6. Atkins, D. E., K. K. Droegemeier et al. (2003). Revolutionizing Science and Engineering Through Cyberinfrastructure: Report of the National Science Foundation Blue Ribbon Advisory Panel on Cyberinfrastructure: 84.

7. McLean, N., and Clifford Lynch (2004). Interoperability between Library Information Services and Learning Environments – Bridging the Gaps: *A Joint White Paper on behalf of the IMS Global Learning Consortium and the Coalition for Networked Information* <http://www.imsglobal.org/digitalrepositories/CNIandIMS_2004.pdf>.

8. Google Press Web site page announcing "Record Revenues for the First Quarter of Fiscal 2005" <http://www.google.com/intl/en/press/pressrel/revenues_q105.html>.

9. Technology news story from <www.stuff.co.nz>: "Google steps up fight for the Chinese market, "12 May 2005.

10. Hagel, John III and John Seeley Brown. *The Only Sustainable Edge: Why Business Strategy Depends on Productive Friction and Dynamic Specialization*, Cambridge, Harvard Business School Press, 2005.

Calling the Scholars Home:
Google Scholar as a Tool
for Rediscovering the Academic Library

Maurice C. York

SUMMARY. Library guides to Google Scholar reveal the concerns and fears of librarians as they watch their users slip further and further outside of their domain of influence. Comparing these fears against data from recent surveys and studies of students and faculty suggests that a profound change in the role of the library in relation to how users search for and discover information has been underway for some time, and that Google Scholar is only the most recent and visible manifestation of that revolution. *[Article copies available for a fee from The Haworth Document Delivery Service: 1-800-HAWORTH. E-mail address: <docdelivery@haworthpress. com> Website: <http://www.HaworthPress.com> © 2005 by The Haworth Press, Inc. All rights reserved.]*

KEYWORDS. Google Scholar, search behavior, academic libraries, search engines, library instruction, link resolvers, scholarly research, online databases, information discovery and retrieval

---

Maurice C. York is Librarian and Team Leader, Circulation and Reserves, Woodruff Library, Emory University, 540 Asbury Circle, Atlanta, GA 30322 (E-mail: mcyork@ emory.edu).

Google® is a Registered Service Mark of Google, Inc., Mountain View, California. *Libraries and Google®* is an independent publication offered by The Haworth Press, Inc., Binghamton, New York, and is not affiliated with, nor has it been authorized, sponsored, endorsed, licensed, or otherwise approved by, Google, Inc.

[Haworth co-indexing entry note]: "Calling the Scholars Home: Google Scholar as a Tool for Rediscovering the Academic Library." York, Maurice C. Co-published simultaneously in *Internet Reference Services Quarterly* (The Haworth Information Press, an imprint of The Haworth Press, Inc.) Vol. 10, No. 3/4, 2005, pp. 117-133; and: *Libraries and Google®* (ed: William Miller, and Rita M. Pellen) The Haworth Information Press, an imprint of The Haworth Press, Inc., 2005, pp. 117-133. Single or multiple copies of this article are available for a fee from The Haworth Document Delivery Service [1-800-HAWORTH, 9:00 a.m. - 5:00 p.m. (EST). E-mail address: docdelivery@haworthpress.com].

Available online at http://www.haworthpress.com/web/IRSQ
© 2005 by The Haworth Press, Inc. All rights reserved.
doi:10.1300/J136v10n03_11

INTRODUCTION

The advent of Google Scholar has divided librarians, roughly, into two camps: those who wish to protect their constituent users from the deceptive, scrubbed interface that masks redundant and gap-ridden content that can't possibly be used for real scholarship; and those who, if they don't outright embrace Google Scholar, are in some way trying to come to terms with the new 800-pound dragon in their living room by introducing their users to it in a neighborly, if sometimes cautious, manner that attempts to tie Schoogle, as it is affectionately called, back into the library's resources. The former group tends to predict the sudden erosion of the quality of scholarship in higher education as students flee the orderly and reliable world of the library's resources to be left to the unstable and chaotic whim of Scholar's algorithms and hit-or-miss content; they are also, to a greater or lesser extent, vaguely suspicious that Google will cost them their jobs one day. The latter group is for the most part uncertain what the future holds, but is fairly confident that users want the clean, honest lines of Google, whether or not it's good for them, and that attempting to turn the tide at this stage would be little better than an exercise in futility; some even see Scholar as a timely tool to help connect with users and encourage their constituents to explore what it can do for them. This bare division is somewhat artificial, of course; there is a range of opinion on either side with varying tints, shades, and tones. Yet the distinction generally holds well and is useful for investigating the phenomenon of Google Scholar in the academic library.

Among research and instruction librarians, the question invariably arises in conversation, What do you do about Google and/or Google Scholar, and how do you explain it to your students? The discussion often turns to metaphor at this point, with comparisons of Google to network television, public transportation, or Wal-Mart, and library databases to cable TV, limousines, and boutique shops. Pointed class stratifications aside, these metaphors tend to be only skin-deep and skirt the real heart of the issue: is Google a legitimate tool in the world of search and discovery, and if so, what is its relation to the other tools that we work so hard to promote to our users? The rise of Google Scholar, which boldly places one large foot squarely inside the territorial boundaries of "scholarly" resources that–before November of 2004–were firmly in the domain of librarians, makes this question even more poignant. The fundamental question is, what do we know about what our users desire and appreciate in their search for information, and given that knowledge, how do we aid them in that search in the way that best fits their needs? As long as we are in the realm of metaphor, there is one that may be useful to consider for this article: if the library's resources are an orderly and fortified castle on the wind-swept plains of information, do we call the populace within the walls and bar the gates to protect them from the Googlezon (or Amazoogle) monster, or do we organize an escort to accompany them as they venture beyond the walls? And if they venture too far, can we ever call them home again?

SCHOOGLE CHALLENGES, LIBRARIANS RESPOND

Google Scholar appeared so suddenly and with such fanfare that librarians who create online guides to resources had to respond quickly in an attempt to shape searchers' view and usage of the new apparent panacea before they went too far afield. The approach to Scholar was by no means unified or even relatively consistent as many libraries posted pages off-the-cuff, and the range of tone that characterizes the Scholar library guides, from wildly defensive to surprisingly embracive, often reveals the unvarnished fears and hopes of librarians as they took their first look at this new player.

Among those who took a defensive posture was the University of North Florida, which added Google Scholar to its Internet Search Engine Guide. The page gives tips on how to use numerous popular search engines, including Teoma, Ask Jeeves, Yahoo!, and Google itself, all of which have anchors labeled "Search Tips," which link down to helpful commentary. Google Scholar's anchor, however, is labeled "Info and Caution," and the descriptive text is not so much helpful as vaguely sardonic. The guide suggests that Google Scholar is "wonderful for those *who do not have access*" (emphasis theirs) to the library's databases; it points out that the library's databases have "many more options" and "much more depth;" and proceeds to provide a bulleted list of "things you can do with library databases *that you can't do with Google Scholar*" (emphasis theirs). Interestingly enough, Google Scholar's is the only search engine description on the page that ends with the enthusiastic line, "Need more information? Ask a Librarian!" (notably without any link to contact information for the fabled librarian). The apparent implication is that a librarian would be able to provide even more reasons not to use Google Scholar. Commonwealth College at UMass Amherst struck up a similar tone with a page entitled "Library Databases versus Google" that pointed out three decisive advantages of library databases over Google and Google Scholar: library databases are more efficient, free, and ethical rather than popular. The page offers no further guidance to using Google or Scholar.

Both of these pages demonstrate a certain overtone of information-seeking class distinction between the privileged "haves" (the members of the academic community) who get access to "the good stuff" and the pedestrian "have nots" (everyone else) who have to make do with Google Scholar. Students of history and literature will recognize this time-honored technique at once: the gatekeepers of the palace keep the royal family safely within the walls by reminding them how beautiful life is inside and telling them there is no reason to expose themselves to the seamy underbelly of life that lies beyond. This warning also echoes in the favorite lowest common denominator metaphors for Google Scholar: network television is cheap tin-pan entertainment for the masses; public transportation is dirty, crowded, and loud; and Wal-Mart is, well, Wal-Mart.

A LITTLE GOOGLE, BUT NOT TOO MUCH

A number of colleges and universities took a middling approach, neither dismissing Scholar nor endorsing it. Syracuse University has posted a guide that is fairly neutral overall, but is clearly pursuing an agenda of pointing users towards library databases and away from Google Scholar. This being a library Web page, there is little to fault in that bias, yet the overall content tone of the page reveals an underlying fear that users might leave the library site and not come back, offering users the blanket advice that "All researchers may find it easier to locate the text of articles through some of the Library's general databases and electronic journals." The guide lists numerous caveats to Scholar, including the fact that it contains materials that are not scholarly and has enormous gaps in coverage, not to mention "irrelevant and redundant" material and less comprehensive search options than library databases. Links back to library databases and subject librarians are prominent as well as to the catalog and interlibrary loan. The general message seems to be, you can try this, but it's really not a good idea without a librarian at your side.

The Music and Dramatic Arts library at the University of Connecticut takes a somewhat different approach on its "Google Scholar" page, providing tips on using Scholar but still discouraging its use through a pointed "FAQ." The page offers a "Consider this when using Google

Scholar" section that lists possible user statements in favor of Scholar such as "It's great that I can find journal articles and link to the full text." Every question is followed by a mildly condescending "Yes, but . . . " lead-in and a list of reasons why the statement is misleading, inaccurate, or just plain thick. For example, for the statement "Google Scholar is so easy. Just type and go," the comeback is, "While Google Scholar is attractive in its simplicity, it currently offers no way to focus your search. Ultimately, this wastes your time and keeps you from finding material most suited to your needs. Library databases such as RILM, Music Index, JSTOR, and HOMER (the library catalog) have sophisticated features that allow more precise searching." The library is trying to be genuinely compelling in its arguments for directing users back to library databases, but there is a certain inescapable irony in responding to users' appreciation of a clean, uncluttered interface by directing them to a series of databases with complex presentation and "sophisticated features." The library's message is only further complicated by the fact that the left-hand navigation for the page is a bewildering maze of ten drop-down menus that mask over a hundred links to library information and resources.

UConn's page was inspired by one at Oberlin and provides a link to it. Oberlin's guide is not overly negative about Scholar, but typifies the "gatekeeper" mentality, providing numerous references back to more sophisticated, "comprehensive, highly developed subject databases," such as LexisNexis, JSTOR, SciFinder Scholar, Inspec, and others that are billed as what a researcher wants to use when he or she wants "reliable access" and "sophisticated search techniques." The title of the page itself is indicative of the library's tone: "Google Scholar vs. Library Databases." It is a gamble on Oberlin's part that where librarians read "comprehensive" and "sophisticated," users will not read "ponderous" and "obtuse." Oberlin's page also offers the daunting proposition that "Rigorous academic research requires thorough searching across databases, varying your search strategy to include synonyms and alternate spellings of keywords, utilizing appropriate subject headings supplied by the database, and understanding the breadth and depth of literature indexed by each database."

Library guides to Google Scholar such as UConn's and Oberlin's draw fuel from and find comfort in articles such as Peter Jasco's review of Scholar in his Digital Reference Shelf column. Soon after Scholar was released, Jasco (2004) conducted a thorough and conscientious investigation of the boundaries and limitations of Google Scholar, ultimately coming up with an unfavorable comparison of Google Scholar to other free citation and abstracting services, such as CiteBase, Research Index, and RePEc/LogEc, as well as subscription databases such as Scopus, Web of Science, CSA, and EBSCO. Jasco's dissection of Google Scholar has a great deal to recommend it and there is credit to his observations, but he seems to take a certain glee in every error and omission he discovers. In expressing his dissatisfaction with Google's disclosure (or lack thereof) for the sources and span of coverage in Scholar, Jasco describes the Scholar FAQ as "more like the scripted questions in infomercials that let the inventor impress the carefully selected audience with the invention's capability to meet all the needs that the average customer will never have." Jasco's criticism of Scholar's handling of citations is unsparing and even a little giddy: "Google's approach is like mixing in a gigantic bowl the appetizer, soup, entree, salad, dessert and coffee. It is not exactly a mouth-watering potpourri, even though there are many delicious ingredients in the bowl." Jasco's conclusion is that Scholar can't be used for serious scholarship, pointing out that "the combination of the total lack of information about source coverage and the shallowness of coverage can hit the serious users and/or their employees hard."

Another highly linked supporting document is Andrew Goodman's post to the "Traffick: Internet Search Enlightenment" blog entitled "Google Scholar vs. Real Scholarship." Goodman (2004), posting the same day Scholar was released, again pointed to the incomplete results in Google Scholar and mused that the best way to get research done was still to go to the library, pull a pile of journals and books, and settle in for an all-nighter. Goodman admitted that Scholar might push online discovery to a new level sometime down the road, but concluded that "for the foreseeable future, you're going to get a lot farther, faster, by talking to a professor or librarian who can help you figure out where to look for the actual material you need."

GO FORTH AND SCHOOGLE

A third cohort of Google Scholar guides made a more expansive and open gesture towards the new service for their user community. A number of universities, either satisfied that Google Scholar was "good enough" or simply accepting of the fact that their students and faculty were going to go out and plunge in, tried to provide ways for users to take the library with them, to whatever extent possible, when they went to Scholar. The University of Texas at Austin set up Google Scholar on its proxy server and created a guide that encourages users to link into Google Scholar from the library Web site so that they can gain access to articles discovered in Scholar that were available under library subscriptions. The guide also takes the time to explain how to bring a citation back from Scholar and plug it in to the library's link resolver. UT Austin's Page doesn't come out for or against Scholar, but remains fairly neutral and provides helpful tips assuming users will go to Scholar at some point. Similarly, the University of Oregon provides a short blurb on Scholar on its "Searching the Web" guide, placing it conspicuously under its own category heading of "Scholarly Search Engines." U of O provides a link into Google Scholar with the library's institutional identifier tacked on to the end so that searchers will be able to take advantage of direct links to U of O's link resolver from its Google Scholar search results. While noting that Google Scholar is a "big deal" and linking to the Google Scholar blog, the guide emphasizes that Scholar is a *supplement* to the library's databases, not a *replacement*.

Duke University and Georgia State University took their Google Scholar guides a step further by integrating the Scholar search box directly into their sites. Duke includes some caveats up front–the by-now familiar disclaimers that Scholar searches a subset of scholarly literature, that the materials are not always scholarly, and that some material is only indexed in library databases. But then the Duke guide proceeds with detailed information on how to search Scholar, how to read Scholar's results, how to use Duke's citation linker from the Scholar interface, and how to use Open WorldCat results through Scholar. Beyond just information on Google Scholar, Duke provides a two-step Schoogle interface that has a search box allowing users to search Scholar directly from Duke's site, then provides search boxes below it for Duke's citation linker and library catalog.

Georgia State University offers searchers a similar 1-2-3 interface for querying Scholar directly from the library site, looking for citations in journals and books, and following up with subject librarians if more help is needed. GSU's Scholar FAQ provides detailed but not overwhelming answers to typical questions in a genuinely helpful manner. Rather than direct users to library databases up front, GSU respectfully places links to full-text library databases at the bottom of the FAQ under the heading "I'm not finding the information I need. Where else can I search for online full text documents?" In a refreshing departure from the heavy-handedness of many other Google Scholar guides, the GSU library actually encourages users to give it a try, and throws in an unobtrusive plug for library databases: "While we encourage you to try Google Scholar, keep in mind that this software is 'in Beta.' Beta status indicates that Google Scholar is still in development, and you may therefore encounter some inconsistencies or peculiarities. You may wish to supplement your research by searching some of the many other databases found on the Find Articles page."

CHALLENGES, CONCERNS, ISSUES, CHALLENGES

The examples of library Google Scholar guides cited above are, of course, only a small sample, but they typify the range of ways in which libraries are presenting Scholar to their stakeholders and highlight some of the common fears and concerns that libraries hold in common when it comes to the Google brand and how users respond to it. These concerns can be summarized in roughly four statements. First, users will abandon library databases and the library catalog as they come to use Google Scholar exclusively for their research, a concern that seems to be most often addressed by providing copious links to library databases and billing Scholar as incomplete and redundant, while library databases are sophisticated, comprehensive, and reliable. Second, users will come to think of librarians as irrelevant now that they have easy access to a powerful and simple (if deceptive) tool like Google Scholar; the typical solution to prevent this erosion is to provide numerous links and pointers to "Ask a Librarian." Third is the fear that users will be led astray into a world of incomplete and redundant content that will water down scholarship and dilute the quality of academic work. Unable to distinguish quality sources from those of a lower grade, users will become simple and unsophisticated as they become accustomed to using only that single, clean, tempting search box. The most common approach to this concern is to point out how many advanced narrowing and filtering options the library databases have. Finally, libraries appear to be greatly concerned that users will be tricked into paying for content the library already subscribes to.

Perhaps chief among these fears is that students and faculty will flock to Google Scholar and abandon the library altogether. The message that "Scholar is nice, but you still need us and our comprehensive databases" is pervasive throughout the majority of the library guides as well as many of the articles that bolster the viewpoint of the guides by providing them with verifiable outside opinions to link to. Even the articles that are positive about the potential of Google Scholar confirm this fear, as do Kennedy and Price (2004) in their observation that "What most of these folks really want is to quickly download an appropriate article and beat feet out of the library. And if they think they can get what they need from Google, the odds are slim that they will bother with library resources at all. College students AND professors might not know that library databases exist, but they sure know Google." It is this chilling vision of reality that lies at the root of the other cardinal fears–that librarians will become irrelevant and that the quality of scholarship in higher education will steadily erode. There is little solace to be found in affirmations such as Roy Tennant's (2001) oft-quoted formulation that only librarians like to search, everyone else likes to find, or in pieces such as Todd Miller's (2005) recent article in criticism of elaborate "nuclear" search engines and "In defense of stupid users."

WHAT DO SEARCHERS WANT? WHERE ARE THEY GOING?

A number of recent studies have investigated the expectations, desires, and behavior of students and researchers as they search for information and use online resources. It is worthwhile to investigate this research for insights into the fundamental assumptions that underpin such fears and concerns. The first assumption is that users are flocking to Google and prefer it to searching library databases or otherwise utilizing the library Web site, an assumption that is readily confirmed in a number of studies. The LibQUAL+ data for 2004 show that search has become predominant for both students and faculty as a mode of investigation, with over 90% using a search engine on a daily or weekly basis. The comparison of those who use search on a daily basis to those who use the library Web site on a daily basis shows a statistical cliff: six times higher among undergraduates, twice as high among grad students, and a third higher for faculty (Lippincott, 2004). Cornell University's 2003 LibQUAL+ data confirm the overall trend: daily use of search engines by faculty and students was in the 70th percentile range, while daily use of online library resources was in the 30th percentile range (Poland, 2004). The Contextual Resource Evaluation Environment (CREE) project, a research endeavor in the UK attempting to assess user requirements for searching native interfaces and for mediating searches through portal applications, discovered much the same thing: in a broad survey of over 4,500 instructors, students, and university staff, the study found that Google was by far the favored method of search, used by over 90% of the respondents (Awre, 2005); Google was also usually the first choice of place for starting research. In a less scientific survey, Regazzi asked librarians and scientific researchers to name the top medical research resources that they were aware of. The top databases named by librarians were Science Direct, ISI Web of Science, and Medline; the scientists' list topped out with Google, Yahoo!, and PubMed, in that order (Regazzi, 2004).

So far the data seem to confirm the basis for librarians' fears. The assumption that naturally follows is that researchers, having discovered this fast and easy online world of information, are coming to the library less regularly and consulting with librarians less frequently. With less contact with the library, users are generally unaware of the high quality of library resources and are satisfied with whatever they find on the Internet. Studies again generally confirm the fact that students are coming to the library less frequently. At Cornell University, the number of respondents to the LibQUAL+ survey who used the library daily dropped from 35% in 2001 to 27% in 2003, while the number of questions at the reference desk plummeted over the same period (Poland, 2004). Yet the notion that students are lost in a sea of poor-quality resources and don't seem to mind as long as they can get the paper turned in on time isn't entirely solid. Both students and faculty seem well aware that the library is a source of quality content and wish they could get greater amounts of that content more easily. In the Cornell LibQUAL+ results, the top request was for greater availability of online resources. It stands to reason that the pervasiveness of this request is more an indication of obfuscation and complexity in the library's maze of online tools than actual lack of content. The resources users want are indeed online and available through the library; they just can't discover them. The Google Scholar guides posted by numerous libraries strongly suggest to researchers that if they simply ask a librarian, they will be much more satisfied with their search and less frustrated in general. This proposition is true, to a certain extent. Satisfaction with personal interactions with librarians is high, but satisfaction with the library catalog and remote access to databases is very low; "Indeed, the librarian search engine, without the librarian, seems to be the desire of many respondents" (Poland, 2004).

LET US TRAIN YOU

Librarians, of course, have been observing this trend towards greater use of online resources and decreasing interactions with reference staff and subject specialists for several of years, and have been working with a number of different solutions to address the change in search habits. One of the major areas of focus has been on information literacy, especially the direct instruction of searchers in how to use databases and evaluate and use the information retrieved from them. This fundamental concept stands at the heart of the creation of instructional pages on Google Scholar, particularly those that give an overview of what Scholar is and then direct readers to ask a librarian for more information or attend a class that will teach them more. One of the basic assumptions underlying this approach, particularly in the case of the Google Scholar guides, is that user attitudes towards library resources and their usage of them can be changed or enhanced through one-on-one instruction and interactions with librarians.

A large-scale global study conducted by Elsevier in 2002 sought to explore this very assumption. The Elsevier study surveyed over 800 librarians in 20 countries and more than 4,200 users in 80 countries to discover how they search, whether training influences their search behavior, and whether the design of the search interface makes a difference in the experience and perception of databases. While 92% of librarians said they gave instruction in online resources, only 17% of users reported ever having such instruction (Elsevier, 2003). Librarians who participated in the study were clearly intent on having an impact on users' search habits and effectiveness through instruction, yet the study "found little evidence that librarian training for users had an effect on usage." Less than a fifth of users had been to a librarian-led training course in online resources, and most would ask a friend or colleague for help with online resources before a librarian (Elsevier, 2003). The LibQUAL+ data are not much more encouraging than the Elsevier study. Undergraduates give a very low rating to the library in terms of keeping them informed of useful services, and both faculty and undergraduates score the library quite low for helping "distinguish between trustworthy and untrustworthy information" (Lippincott, 2004). The library guides that steer users away from Google Scholar feature prominent links to "ask a librarian" services as the solution for users bewildered by the array of library resources and options available to them, yet LibQUAL+ indicates that only 21% of undergraduates ask librarians for help with their research.

The primary aim of instruction in the finer points of library databases is, naturally, to enable researchers to find high quality sources and raise the level of their scholarly output accordingly. Much of the urgency that comes across in the Google Scholar guides stems from a desire to let users know in no uncertain terms that if they rely on Google Scholar alone, the quality of their work may be in jeopardy. Herein lives the desire to alert the populace to danger and call them to safety within the walls of the library, be they virtual or physical. An effective call to return to the castle, of course, requires a clear-ringing trumpet, a compelling reason to break the routine of the day and head for the gate. The bet of Google Scholar guides such as those at UConn and Oberlin is that, given an explanation of how specialized databases are superior for refining and filtering searches for better results, users will realize that they are better off using these resources in their research rather than the shotgun, un-filterable, un-narrowable, often redundant and misleading search engine that is Google Scholar.

Yet the evidence suggests that libraries should pause for a moment before promoting the amazing powers of their super search engines too heavily. The Elsevier study discovered that the most desirable attributes of online search services for users were simplicity, ease of use, and intuitive design, with specialized search capabilities ranking at or near the bottom of attractive features. Interactions with numerous databases showed trends among users to avoid advanced search functionality and shy away from complex platforms that require an investment of time and effort to learn the interface (Elsevier, 2003). The focus groups of students and instructors for the CREE project revealed that "the almost exclusive use of Google" had less to do with the type or quality of results, but rather "mainly related to [the search engine's] simple format" (Ingram, 2004). Even more telling for library guides that provide a host of links to numerous specialized databases as alternatives to Google Scholar is the insight that "students raise differing designs across search engines as the most confusing factor in using these, and they felt frustrated with having to learn a new interface each time a new database or search engine is used" (Ingram, 2004).

THE KNOWN AND THE UNKNOWN
(OR, THE RIGHT TOOL FOR THE RIGHT JOB)

The news, so far, seems gloomy for libraries. We see ourselves as the proper home for scholarly research, but users are online more, they are in the library less, they seem almost allergic to the kinds of powerful interfaces that we know will give them what is best for their needs, and training has little overall impact on their usage of databases. Yet, again, libraries have seen this coming for some time now, which begs the question, why the sudden and sometimes shrill reaction to Google Scholar? The ultimate unspoken fear appears to be that once users succumb to the notion that they can get scholarly materials through Google's search engine, they won't return to use the library's resources at all. However, the data, which from a certain perspective read very poorly for the responsiveness of libraries to the new age of research and scholarship, don't support this conclusion at all. One of the standout highlights of the 2004 LibQUAL+ results is the rise in popularity of document delivery services–users do not want to come to the library, they want library materials to come to them (Poland, 2004).

Indeed, the increasing demand for document delivery services, combined with the ease of online request and account management services, has led to suggestions that the traditional Access Services triad of Circulation, Interlibrary Loan, and Reserves be reorganized into cross-functional Item Delivery and Course Support Departments, the latter being an integrated collaboration with traditional reference departments and IT staff to combine course material digitization and distribution, bibliographic instruction, and instructional technology (Hersey, 2004). This expectation that the library function as a safe and reliable entity for the location and delivery of quality content extends into the online realm of databases as well. In the CREE survey, Google topped all other search engines for frequency of use and first preference, but subject-specific resources were second in popularity to Google (Ingram, 2005). Students and instructors were highly aware of subject-specific resources and chose their tool according to their need, depending on the purpose of their search. The CREE focus groups found that for more cursory class assignments, the "anything at all" approach of Google was favored, while subject-specific resources were the tool of choice for more in-depth research.

A CREE focus group of students at the University of Hull, which cut across a wide variety of academic disciplines, showed that they had a good command of subject-specific databases and journals offered by the library, but simply preferred Google for initial discovery. In some cases students would search Amazon for books, then turn to the library catalog to see if the library owned a copy. The study also found that users tended to search multiple engines at the same time with multiple windows open, alternating between them according to the needs of their search. Once users discovered a reference to a source online, "all the students . . . would check the library before looking for it online" (Ingram, 2005).

The concept that Google is preferred for discovery while the library is trusted for locating and gaining access to materials has profound implications for the way that libraries view themselves and their role in the scholarly community. This concept does not stand alone: it is paired closely with the self-reliant and adventuresome nature of searchers, their desire to explore and survey information using simple and powerful tools while having the extensive and trusted resources of the library at their side. Google Scholar, for all of its birth pangs and youthful inadequacies, promises remarkable potential to provide searchers with exactly that, if libraries can partner with Google to develop a seamless and elegant balance between discovery and delivery. Link resolvers are not great discovery tools–and neither, apparently, are library catalogs–but both are excellent at locating known content, the major weakness of Google Scholar. A partnership between Google and libraries has the potential to enhance the visibility and value of library resources to researchers by bringing together two worlds: what researchers perceive as their universe of readily available resources, and what librarians perceive as the best sources of materials for researchers. The library guides to Google Scholar that have taken a stance of encouraging their users to give Scholar a try, who have taken the proactive stance to integrate Scholar into the Web site into library services, are taking important steps in taking the library out to the world of the researcher rather than cajoling the researcher to come into the fortress of the library.

A POSSIBLE FUTURE

The intelligent integration of Google Scholar with OpenURL and other location and authentication technologies is a combination that appeals directly to researchers' preferred methods of search, discovery, and access. Google Scholar's Institutional Access for libraries is the foundation for such services. From the fledgling pilot group of twenty or thirty libraries that exposed their link resolvers to Google Scholar, the number of participating colleges and universities has grown to over one hundred and fifty. Institutions participating in the program (which is now open to any institution that has a link resolver and is a member of the OCLC Open WorldCat program) give Google the location of their link resolver, and in return users searching Scholar from within the institution's IP range (or who set the institution as their location in Scholar's preferences) are able to locate and access content discovered in Scholar by clicking on the institutional link. Not all content in Google

Scholar is OpenURL compliant, and access through a link resolver is only as good as the link resolver implementation, but this early phase of link resolver integration has increased the value of Google Scholar immeasurably and has hinted at vast opportunities for libraries that would otherwise wait beyond the horizon.

OpenURL is only the first stage in opening the gates, and it still stands in its early phase of integration, since searchers must still pirouette through a small maze of links and interfaces before arriving at the content itself. The opportunities and possibilities for collaboration and partnership between Google and libraries are numerous. Libraries are in a position to lobby publishers to include subscription content in Google Scholar's index. The Open Access movement can receive a significant boost in exposure and use if libraries work with Google to ensure that the Scholar engine is crawling institutional repositories and Open Access directories. The emerging Shibboleth authentication scheme can be brought to bear to break down the cumbersome walls of IP authentication and proxy servers so that users can anonymously carry their access credentials with them wherever their exploration takes them. A new and innovative tool from the Windsor-Alberta-Georgia Google Scholar Localization Project or WAG the Dog project is the WAGger Web content localizer which scans a Web page for citation information and then throws the whole page against a link resolver to "localize" what the searcher is seeing according to what he or she has access to through the library, can be used to further enhance the presence of the library at the searcher's side in order to assist in locating and exposing content discovered through Google Scholar and other search engines (Singer, 2005). Google and Google Scholar can be integrated into library portal applications through the use of Google APIs and Web services, such as the CREE project is experimenting with, so that keywords and search terms can be passed directly into Scholar for discovery and then parsed out into available library resources that provide access to electronic content and request mechanisms for delivery of physical materials.

Libraries have been searching for the right hook to call the scholars home as they wander further afield and into the untamed territory of Google's world wide Web. The irony is, as the data from our own studies and surveys show us, that to truly bring the scholars home, we must abandon the walls and go to them. The walls, in fact, have already disappeared around us even as we stolidly stood guard at the gate. This shift in the library's culture and service, to go out and meet the student and researcher where they are rather than beckoning them to come inside, is set to take place not only in the online world, but in the library itself. Just as Hersey (2004) sees the transformation of Access Services into Item Delivery and Course Support departments, so does Poland (2004) draw the conclusion that subject librarians must leave their traditional roles and become "field librarians" who go out to the offices and labs of their constituents, who hold office hours on site and make themselves indispensable as experts in computer configuration and Internet/database access. The scholars are ready. The opportunity is ours to lose.

REFERENCES

Awre, C. (2005). The CREE project Web site. Retrieved June 11, 2005, from <http://www.hull.ac.uk/esig/cree/>.

Awre, C. (2005). How do users search? Examining user behavior and testing innovative possibilities within the CREE project. Paper presented at the CNI Spring Meeting, Washington, D.C. Retrieved June 11, 2005 <http://www.cni.org/tfms/2005a.spring/abstracts/presentations/CNI_awre_how.pdf>.

Commonwealth College: Library databases versus Google. Retrieved June 11, 2005, from <http://www.comcol.umass.edu/deansbook/research_2.asp>.

Duke University Libraries: Google Scholar. Retrieved June 11, 2005, from <http://www.lib.duke.edu/reference/schoogle/>.

Elsevier. (2003). Usability drives value of bibliographic databases. Retrieved June 11, 2005, from <http://www.info.sciencedirect.com/content_coverage/databases/sd_bdwhitepaper.pdf>.

Georgia State University Library: Using Google scholar at GSU library. Retrieved June 11, 2005, from <http://www.library.gsu.edu/googlescholar/>.

Goodman, A. (2004). Google Scholar vs. Real scholarship. Retrieved June 11, 2005, from <http://www.traffick.com/2004/11/google-scholar-vs-real-scholarship.asp>.

Hersey, D. P. (2004). The future of access services: Should there be one? Journal of Access Services, 2(4).

Ingram, C., Awre, C., Arora, V., Brett, T., & Hanganu, G. (April 2004). CREE focus groups: Results and comment: University of Hull. Retrieved June 11, 2005, from <http://www.hull.ac.uk/esig/cree/downloads/CREEfocusgroupreport.pdf>.

Jasco, P. (2004). Google Scholar beta. Peter's Digital Reference Shelf–December, Retrieved June 11, 2005, from <http://www.galegroup.com/servlet/HTMLFileServlet?imprint=9999&region=7&fileName=/reference/archive/200412/googlescholar.html>.

Jasco, P. (2005). Google Scholar (redux). Peter's Digital Reference Shelf–June, Retrieved June 11, 2005, from <http://www.gale.com/free_resources/reference/peter/current.htm#google>.

Kennedy, S., & Price, G. (2004). Big news: "Google Scholar" is born. ResourceShelf Retrieved June 11, 2005, from <http://www.resourceshelf.com/2004/11/wow-its-google-scholar.html>.

Lippincott, S., & Kyrillidou, M. (October 2004). How ARL university communities access information: Highlights from LibQUAL+™. ARL (236), 7-8.

Miller, T. (2005). In defense of stupid users. *Library Journal*, 130 (5), 58.

Music And Dramatic Arts Library, University of Connecticut: Google scholar. Retrieved June 11, 2005, from <http://www.lib.uconn.edu/online/research/speclib/music/schoogle.html>.

Oberlin College Library: Google scholar vs. Library databases. Retrieved June 11, 2005, from <http://www.oberlin.edu/library/science/google_tips.html>.

Poland, J. (2004). Adapting to changing user expectations. Paper presented at the 25th Annual IATUL Conference, "Library Management in Changing Environment." The Library of Cracow University of Technology, Krakow, Poland. Retrieved June 11, 2005 from <http://www.iatul.org/conference/proceedings/vol14/fulltexts/Jean%20Poland.pdf>.

Regazzi, J. J. (2004, February 23, 2004). The battle for mindshare: A battle beyond access and retrieval. Paper presented at the 46th NFAIS Annual Conference. Retrieved June 11, 2005, from <http://www.nfais.org/publications/mc_lecture_2004.htm>.

Singer, R. (2005). Google Scholar and the dawn of web localization. Retrieved June 11, 2005, from <http://rsinger.library.gatech.edu/papers/WebLocalizing.html>.

Syracuse University Library: What is Google Scholar? Retrieved June 11, 2005, from <http://libwww.syr.edu/instruction/questions/Google-Scholar.htm>.

University of North Florida internet search engine guide: Google Scholar. Retrieved June 11, 2005, from <http://www.unf.edu/library/guides/search.html#googlescholar>.

University of Oregon Libraries: Searching the web. Retrieved June 11, 2005, from <http://libweb.uoregon.edu/guides/searchweb/>.

University of Texas Libraries: Google scholar. Retrieved June 11, 2005, from <http://www.lib.utexas.edu/indexes/titles.html?id=161>.

Checking Under the Hood:
Evaluating Google Scholar
for Reference Use

Janice Adlington
Chris Benda

SUMMARY. Since the unveiling of Google Scholar (GS), academic libraries have struggled with the question of how and where (and in some cases, whether) to integrate GS into the suite of research resources they present to their users. This paper presents a critical evaluation of GS, examining its arrangement, authority, content, comparability with traditional indexing services, creation and currency, and usability, and offers tentative conclusions about its "fit." *[Article copies available for a fee from The Haworth Document Delivery Service: 1-800-HAWORTH. E-mail address: <docdelivery@haworthpress.com> Website: <http://www.HaworthPress.com> © 2005 by The Haworth Press, Inc. All rights reserved.]*

KEYWORDS. Google, Google Scholar, research databases, reference tools, evaluation, college and university libraries

Janice Adlington is Bibliographer for Classics, Philosophy and Psychology, Central Library (E-mail: Janice.adlington@vanderbilt.edu); and Chris Benda is Library Associate, Peabody Library (E-mail: chris.benda@vanderbilt.edu), both at Vanderbilt University, Nashville, TN 37203.

[Haworth co-indexing entry note]: "Checking Under the Hood: Evaluating Google Scholar for Reference Use." Adlington, Janice, and Chris Benda. Co-published simultaneously in *Internet Reference Services Quarterly* (The Haworth Information Press, an imprint of The Haworth Press, Inc.) Vol. 10, No. 3/4, 2005, pp. 135-148; and: *Libraries and Google*® (ed: William Miller, and Rita M. Pellen) The Haworth Information Press, an imprint of The Haworth Press, Inc., 2005, pp. 135-148. Single or multiple copies of this article are available for a fee from The Haworth Document Delivery Service [1-800-HAWORTH, 9:00 a.m. - 5:00 p.m. (EST). E-mail address: docdelivery@haworthpress.com].

Available online at http://www.haworthpress.com/web/IRSQ
© 2005 by The Haworth Press, Inc. All rights reserved.
doi:10.1300/J136v10n03_12

INTRODUCTION

It is indicative of the high esteem, grudging respect, strategic acceptance, or mounting fear with which Google is held in libraries that one of its recent products, Google Scholar (GS), is garnering so much attention only months after its release–and while it is still at the beta, or testing, level.[1] From articles in *Library Journal* to announcements on the home pages of library Web sites, from evaluative analyses of GS results to sessions at library conferences, GS is very much on the minds of the library (particularly the academic library) world.[2] In fact, at least two librarians, one in the United States and one in Canada, have blogs devoted to GS (Sondermann 2005; Giustini 2005).

Discussions of GS have already pointed out many of its advantages and shortcomings. On the positive side, many reviewers have remarked on its speed and usability, and the ease with which it links forward to more recent citing articles; its interdisciplinary scope; and its potential for resource discovery. Negatives include uncertainty about its coverage; its currency; its conception of what is "scholarly"; its lack of authority control and controlled vocabulary; and its unabashed generation of faulty citations, as artefacts of automated extraction. Like many librarians, we are struggling with the question of whether and how to incorporate GS into the suite of services the library presents, while recognizing that the Google business model is very different from that of our traditional database providers, and that Google is not obligated to respond to our questions or enhancement requests. To our students and faculty, the library and its databases may be only one among many possible sources of information. We strive to "compete," to make the library our users' first choice, by selecting and highlighting the highest quality sources, sharing what we know of their strengths and uses through library instruction and outreach, and providing knowledgeable one-to-one assistance. Before we feel comfortable recommending GS to our users, whether at a reference desk or through a Web page, we need to have some confidence that we know its strengths and weaknesses, and the contexts in which it is most likely to reward the researcher.

In this paper, we go "under the hood" with a traditional database evaluation of GS (as of May 2005), compare GS with selected alternate databases, and report anecdotally on uses with questions at a humanities/social sciences reference desk. Of course, GS is a work in progress, and though its rate of evolution is unknown, it is changing, sometimes rather abruptly. Unless Google abandons this beta, as it has apparently done with at least one other product,[3] the details of our analysis may rapidly be superseded. Our intention–and our hope–is that this discussion of GS will be both timely and indicative of the larger issues raised by such services.

WHERE DOES GOOGLE SCHOLAR (BETA) FIT?

Immediately following Google's initial announcement of the GS beta, many academic libraries produced Web pages to contextualize the service, identify its limitations, and publicize their databases as alternatives. These pages appeared as FAQs (e.g., the University of Nevada, Las Vegas), stepped instructions for searching GS and locating the materials (e.g., Georgia State University Library), and oppositional weightings of GS against the library databases or federated search services (e.g., "Google Scholar vs. Library Databases," Oberlin College Library; "Scholarsportal vs. Google Scholar," University of Windsor). Librarians wished to both help their users understand the new service, and take some ownership of a resource that could very easily be regarded as sitting outside and competing with the library. Google has further encouraged libraries to feature GS by establishing preferences, allowing users to identify themselves as affiliated with particular institutions, and working with link resolver vendors, so that users are directly connected to the appropriate copies–the ones subscribed to by their library–from the list of search results. This both helps the user and provides a form of co-branding for the library.

We know that many students start their research with Google. One of the most frequent comments we hear from faculty is that (some) students do not select appropriate sources for their papers, whether through lack of knowledge about scholarly practice in their fields, or satisficing, settling for the sources they can get quickly. At this point, GS perhaps most closely resembles our large aggregating databases, ProQuest, InfoTrac, or Ebsco, in their immediate provision of some full text, their mix of sources identified as "scholarly," and our uncertainty about precisely what is in the databases (although the commercial vendors provide title lists, their licensed full text content changes with some frequency). GS certainly eliminates much of the incidental material retrieved by Google, and for some subjects is as productive as the aggregators as a starting or gateway database.

Google's unwillingness to name the publishers or services which have cooperated in the creation of the GS database is an unacknowledged but significant barrier to serious researchers, who tend to know their sources well and who may have sophisticated (or sceptical) views of the uses of web search engines. What we know about these collaborations comes from industry insiders (Ingenta), press releases (CrossRef, MUSE), and deduction. Of course, faculty's initial judgment of GS will depend on how completely it covers their own publications, and for now they may view omissions as no more than a reflection of a transitional or growth phase. However, for GS to become a "professional" database, a trusted resource, these omissions must either be rectified or explained.

EVALUATING GOOGLE SCHOLAR

Electronic reference resources can be evaluated in a number of ways. J. Rettig (1996) and Rettig and LaGuardia (1999) provide lists to guide such evaluations; we shall be combining and adapting those lists to carry out our analysis of GS.[4] Our list includes the following items:[5]

- *Arrangement:* how is the material in the resource structured? is it indexed, and, if so, how? how well does the search feature work?
- *Authority:* what is the expertise of those who have created the resource?
- *Content:* what makes up the resource? what is its scope?
- *Comparability:* how does this resource compare with similar resources?
- *Creation and currency:* when was the resource created, how frequently is it updated, and how up-to-date is it?
- *Usability:* can users find what they need without difficulty?

Arrangement

Since Google has made its name with searching, it is not surprising that access to what GS has indexed largely involves searching (and not, for example, browsing). Limits are available–Boolean ANDs, ORs, and NOTs, phrase searches, and the choice to look for search terms only in the article title or in the full text–and users can also search by author, publication, and date. Caveats for the last three types of searches appear on the Advanced Scholar Search Tips page, and they revolve around two basic problems: the varying amounts and the varying forms of information that GS receives from the sources it indexes. For example, a source may not have a publication date included in the data that GS indexes, so searching by publication date may result in passing over otherwise relevant materials that do not happen to provide the requisite information. On the other hand, search results limited to particular years may find many items that were not published during those years, since GS seems at times incorrectly to consider other dates in the source information as publication dates. One can see this by doing an Advanced Scholar Search, filling in each of the date fields with 1800, and observing how many of the items retrieved were not published in 1800.

Related to the problems of variant information in the source material is GS's lack of authority control. This is a significant problem for faculty or graduate students who frequently search by name and expect to retrieve a bibliography of the author's research. Actually, authority control is a problem for many research tools; GS is not the only offender. However, some databases attempt to address this problem by providing author indexes, so that a user has a reasonable chance of finding all of the items by an author in that database simply by doing a search for the last name in the author index and pulling up the variant names next to one another. Of course, in practice this does not always work–for various reasons, including poor data entry–but it is probably the next best thing to authority control and is far better than guessing at the variants on one's own. Search tips counsel the user to try to guess at the variants ("Advanced Scholar Search Tips," 2005), and provide no assistance for distinguishing among individuals with common names.

Results are returned in relevancy order, though the specifics of that ranking are not public knowledge. According to GS's "About" page, "This relevance ranking takes into account the full text of each article as well as the article's author, the publication in which the article appeared and how often it has been cited in scholarly literature" (2005). There is not much detail here, although GS is far from being the only research database that employs relevance ranking without explaining precisely how it is done. However, these other databases typically allow users to re-sort results by other criteria, including author, title, and date. The ability to view or limit to the most recent research is particularly important in the sciences, although given the problems noted above with the year delimiter, it is understandable why GS does not currently include this option. Thus, users of GS are limited to looking at a relevancy ranked list of results, with a ranking based on algorithms that they hope are as useful in GS as they are in Google.

Users are also provided no assistance, in the form of suggested additional search terms or linked subjects, once they've received an initial set of results. GS does have a citation feature which allows users to find items related by subject. Since the citation link does not appear with every search result, however, this particular means of subject linking is somewhat limited. Lack of controlled vocabulary is not particularly surprising; after all, GS could not be quickly compiled or freely distributed if human intervention were required to analyze and standardize the intellectual content. But beyond this practical issue, we can see a convergence of Google's more general approach to indexing material and the manner by which users search for this material. On the one hand, GS is an expression of faith in the power of raw full text searching. On the other, any librarian who has watched students rush to JSTOR knows that students are quite happy to search full text rather than surrogate records–particularly when such searches guarantee full articles.

This penchant for full text on the part of both Google and many users, along with the difficulties that many users have with controlled vocabulary, tend to result in the de-emphasis of such vocabulary. This is unfortunate, since controlled vocabulary provides a means of discovering materials related to items already determined to be relevant–a means partially available through citation linking, but only partially so. It is also unfortunate because use of controlled vocabulary does not have to be difficult. For example, if suggested subject terms are both prominent and clickable, and are derived from the user's initial search (as in ProQuest), many students will use them and find them helpful in focusing on the intended domain.

One of the great strengths of the Web–in fact, arguably its backbone–is the ability to link material together easily. GS, through its links to citing items, provides one means of entry into a Web of related literature. The hyperlinked controlled vocabulary of library databases serves as another powerful method of moving from known to new items, one that reaches beyond the insularity sometimes apparent in reference lists. The ideal search engine–unlikely to be GS, unless Google purchases existing indexing sources–would facilitate both techniques of resource discovery.

Authority

Authority encompasses aspects of a resource such as the qualifications, reputation, or experience of those who created and/or published it. Reputation seems to be crucial for getting people to try GS in the first place–users turn to the product because of the Google name–but GS's real authority, like that of Google itself, derives instead from the seeming accuracy of its results and the undeniable speed with which it delivers them. By saying it this way, however, perhaps we are conflating reputation as judged by typical users of GS and reputation as judged by information professionals. GS actually makes that conflation easy, since Google has a de facto authority even among reference providers, and some of that authority may be bleeding over to GS. It should be said–though it almost goes without saying–that Google's reputation is generally well-deserved, as long as one keeps in mind where it excels and where it is limited. The danger is that GS may obtain a spurious (or, perhaps, merely premature) authority: just as Google's failure to find a Web site can lead users to conclude that it does not exist, students may make similar assumptions concerning omissions from GS.

We have noted above that GS does not provide a list of what material it is using to "compile" its results, as subscription-based–and some free–electronic resources typically do. This is an issue of scope, but it also relates to the authority of the resource–in two ways in particular. GS may link to multiple versions of a work, in preprint, postprint, and publication form. Although an industry standard for tagging and identifying versions is rumoured to be under development, until or unless this is established, the reader is on his or her own to determine the status of the linked materials. It is also the case that results may include items that are not particularly scholarly, though the degree to which GS features this kind of material is probably less than some think (see more on this below). Both of these matters raise questions about the degree to which one can use the results that GS provides without careful scrutiny.

Content

According to the "About Google Scholar" (2005) page,

> Google Scholar enables you to search specifically for scholarly literature, including peer-reviewed papers, theses, books, preprints, abstracts and technical reports from all broad areas of research. Use Google Scholar to find articles from a wide variety of academic publishers, professional societies, preprint repositories and universities, as well as scholarly articles available across the Web.

This statement of purpose gives a vague sense of the scope of GS: its intention is to be multidisciplinary, index various kinds of materials, and focus on scholarly sources. A number of reviewers have done "probing tests" (as Jascó [2004] calls them) which show that GS is, to some extent, a multidisciplinary resource, though heavily weighted in the direction of the sciences.[6] It is also clear from these probes that GS does index various kinds of material (journal articles and books, of course, but also preprints, working papers, newsletters, government documents, and so on). Unfortunately, Google cannot or will not produce the same type of source list that many database providers make available to their customers–lists that present exactly what journals are indexed in the database, their dates of coverage, and so on. Information about the specific material that GS indexes comes from publishers who have agreed to open their content to Google's spiders; from the participants in the CrossRef pilot project; from the probes conducted by GS reviewers mentioned above–but not from Google. Lack of such information about sources, or inability to generate such a list of sources in GS, is probably not a matter of great concern to users of GS who are simply interested in retrieving a few good items for their research. But reference providers have somewhat higher expectations for reference sources that they recommend for use.

With regard to the scholarly focus of GS, many of those who have examined GS have pointed out that it is not entirely clear what GS means by "scholarly literature." GS does give examples of such literature ("peer-reviewed papers," etc.), among which are items likely to be accepted as scholarly by reference providers ("books," however, is a relatively broad classification which may include "nonscholarly" treatments of topics). GS has been found to contain items which are not particularly scholarly (Wleklinski 2005 gives some examples),[7] but undergraduate research databases like ProQuest and InfoTrac index and provide full text for magazines like *People* and *Sports Illustrated*, which are not typically regarded as scholarly sources. Indeed, some professional databases cover items that may be useful for scholarly work but which, again, are not in themselves scholarly: for example, ERIC, the premier database for education-related topics, indexes lesson plans. Our own probes–admittedly, far from comprehensive–suggest that GS's content is probably at least as scholarly as the content that one would find by doing searches for peer-reviewed material in ProQuest or InfoTrac. Thus, while concerns can be raised over exactly what GS includes, we think the quality of those contents is probably at least as good as what is found in two of the major aggregating databases.

Comparability

Reports of comparisons between GS and individual indexes and abstracting databases are trickling out on preprint servers, blogs, and listservs. Conclusions tend to be impressionistic, drawn from relatively small numbers of arbitrarily selected searches. The results are nonetheless already impressive in some fields. For example, in December 2004, Malcolm Getz compared GS with EconLit by searching for 64 known items drawn from the reference lists of two economics articles from the *Journal of Economic Perspectives*, Summer 2004. GS returned valid hits for 80% of the items; by contrast, only 34% of the citations appeared in EconLit. The subscription database missed early works and recent working papers, and interdisciplinary works that were beyond the indexing scope of the database. However, Getz does go on to note that the subject limitations of EconLit are a strength when searching general concepts.

We wondered whether the striking success of GS might be nothing more than a function of the manner in which the database was compiled: if GS has indexed the original article, might we not expect all its references to be included? Is Getz's methodology a valid means of testing the database, and, if we started with articles which are not themselves in GS, would we instead report large gaps in coverage? To initially explore this question, we searched the reference list of a 2004 article from the Elsevier journal *Neuropsychologia*, which, as of January 2005, was not present in GS as either a citation or a link to full text. Contrary to expectations, we found 43 of its 45 references to be present in GS (with the two missing citations being a conference presentation, and, oddly, a Medline abstract). On our campus, 31 of these references further linked through to full text articles, as compared to 20 such links from within ScienceDirect; students would (in this instance) have a higher rate of instant gratification using GS than Elsevier's flagship journal collection.

Comparisons between GS and traditional databases tend to be based on known items, for the very good reason that subject searches of GS's full text will always return many more hits than are found in the short records of indexing and abstracting databases. For students, the experience may be similar to searching PsycINFO, then journals@Ovid, or the MLA and then JSTOR: the full text searches will appear to be very productive, although many of the items may be only passingly relevant. To capture the difference between GS and traditional databases, we performed a number of searches on "greebles," a recently coined term with the great advantage of appearing in only one context in the scholarly literature. *Greebles* are novel objects similar to faces used in experiments of object recognition: reports appear in the psychological or medical literature.

Greebles search, March 7, 2005:

PsycINFO	10
PubMed	12
Web of Science	10
ScienceDirect	6
Journals@Ovid	17
Google Scholar	107
Scirus	285 total (33 journal articles, 252 Web results)
Google	4,310 matches: includes gaming shareware and children's stories

When we first compared GS and PsycINFO, GS had many more hits, but missed half (5) of the articles PsycINFO identified. However, after the GS database was refreshed (April 18-19, 2005), GS omitted only one of these citations, to a book chapter. Articles on this topic only appear in the recent literature (since 1996), in a discipline that is well supported by electronic publishing: if these conditions are met, students may have more success finding materials using GS than the professional databases, with minimal omissions. These omissions should remain of concern to serious researchers, however: GS, like all databases, is not complete, although its lengthy lists of results on scientific topics may initially conceal that fact.

We were also interested in GS's citation features. In April 2005, Belew compared the performance of GS and ISI's citation indexes on 203 publications from 6 authors to determine the degree to which the two services corresponded in measuring "impact." He found that the two services roughly agreed in terms of numbers of citations, although GS and ISI found citations from different sources. GS seemed competitive with ISI for materials published within the past 20 years; however, GS identified more citations from books and conference papers, which are minimally covered by ISI, while ISI was stronger for journal articles. In our exploratory comparison of GS and ISI (again, focusing on the limited topic of *greebles*), we also found the raw number of citations to roughly match, suggesting that GS is already doing a reasonable job in identifying highly cited or significant articles. However, the actual citations were very different, with GS referencing many more Web sites and pre-publication versions, and randomly missing citations in journal articles. To track citations, both GS and ISI should be searched.

GS is particularly helpful when searching multidisciplinary topics, where the source journals can reasonably be expected to span multiple subjects and be indexed in multiple databases. It can also help a reference provider by suggesting databases or journal aggregators that he/ she would not initially have considered. For example, although GS's coverage in the area of Classics is currently minimal (particularly when compared with the core database, *L'Année Philologique*), PubMed unearths useful English-language material when there are medical aspects to the question (e.g., dissection in ancient Greece). Although GS is not sufficient for research, it, like Google itself, can sometimes provide an otherwise elusive starting point that will generate further ideas.

Creation and Currency

GS is a new service, having appeared as a beta in November 2004. Searches appear to run against a static database, which is updated with unknown frequency. Between the end of January and April 18, 2005, our test searches remained unchanged; between April 19 and May 31, we have similarly seen no updates. To test the currency of the database, we performed advanced searches of GS intended to find only items published in 2005. On April 14, 2005, this search turned up 501 items.[8] When this same search was repeated on May 4, 2005, the number of 2005 results had increased to 54,200; this number has not changed during the course of the month. Research database providers typically communicate changes to their content to those who subscribe to their products and, in most cases, updates are carried out on a predictable schedule. This is not the case for Google, and is cause for concern.

Related to the issue of the unpredictability of updates is the currency of content. In February 2005, R. Vine compared a search of PubMed records indexed by GS (site:ncbi.nlm.nih.gov), limited to items from 2004-2005, with a search of PubMed's native interface, and came up with starkly different results: 29,500 records in GS, 658,000 in PubMed. Her additional searches lead her to believe that GS had not updated their PubMed content after February-March 2004. We did a similar search, limiting to 2005 in GS and 1 January 2005-29 May 2005 in PubMed. GS presented 20,700 results on May 29, 2005, while PubMed returned 249,680 results on the same day. While GS appears now to be indexing some of the 2005 content of PubMed, the amount is less than one-tenth of what one would get by going directly to PubMed. The problem of broken links is also a currency-related issue, something that reference resources that link to Web pages always face. Frequent updating of the resource would ameliorate this problem but not eliminate it entirely (unless the updating were extremely frequent).

Usability

Jascó (2004) has probably commented most extensively on GS's usability; generally speaking, he is not pleased with its "discombobulated" results display. His specific criticisms include the following: possible confusion about labels that are associated with results (particularly the PS, or PostScript, label); repetition of what seems to be the same article–but is really different forms of it–throughout the results; lack of clarity about how citedness scores are related to relevancy ranking; the appearance of multiple links–typically simply URLs–associated with a single result; and the intermixing of "primary" sources with items which only cite those sources, all in a single display. Jascó's points are well-taken, and should give us pause as we contemplate adding GS to the set of tools that we use to help people with their research. It may be useful to set Jascó's comments into perspective, however. Like other multidisciplinary databases and like federated searching, GS provides a search and retrieval experience of comparatively greater ease than when searching multiple databases serially. It may suffer in other ways–including some of the ways we have enumerated above–but it does have going for it a familiar, minimalist interface. Another way to put it is that GS is about as easy to use–and frequently, as frustrating–as Google's search engine.

CONCLUSIONS

How then shall we view GS? Is it ready to be integrated into the suite of services that reference providers recommend to users, or would it be better to wait until it is further developed? Our review of the product is somewhat mixed. We are in agreement with those who have critiqued GS's lack of authority control, lack of choices for sorting results, lack of controlled vocabulary, and lack of version control; Google's unwillingness to specify what exactly GS indexes; the currency and completeness of its contents; and the uncertainty regarding the frequency with which it is updated. On the other hand, we were impressed by the degree to which GS manages to weed out non-scholarly materials, by its potential for resource discovery, by the quality and number of relevant results generated by GS in comparison with results generated in some research databases (for certain topics), and by its usability. Even if Google were to do nothing further with the database, we know it will be popular with our students and faculty. Our best role at present may be to promote its strengths, warn of its weaknesses–and to continue testing.

NOTES

1. See Price (2005) for remarks on the popularity of betas at Google.

2. A *very* selective list attesting to this library interest, many items of which were discovered on the GS blogs: Oder (2005); Tenopir, "Google" (2005); Tenopir, "Duplication" (2005) (*Library Journal*); UNC Chapel Hill Libraries (2005) (library home page); Jascó (2004); Vine (2005) (evaluative analyses); Lederman (2005) (library conference).

3. Google Catalogs is that instance (see Sullivan [2005] for more discussion).

4. The list in Rettig (1996) includes accuracy, appropriateness, arrangement, authority, bibliography, comparability, completeness, content, distinction, documentation, ease-of-use, illustrations, index, level, reliability, revisions, uniqueness. Rettig and LaGuardia (1999) list parentage and provenance, authority, audience, content, creation and currency, design, usability, and medium. It seems to us that some of the items in the Rettig list overlap with one another, and of course there is overlap between the two lists. We have selected items that seem most applicable to evaluating GS.

5. Jascó (2004) has already done a similar evaluation, and we rely on his (and others') observations in what follows.

6. E.G., Wleklinski (2005). On the humanities/social sciences side, Project MUSE is included in GS results, but JSTOR is not.

7. Jascó (2004) notes that "Google Scholar also includes a large number of pages that are not scholarly by any stretch of the imagination."

8. See above, however, for caveats on limiting results by year.

WORKS CONSULTED

Banks, M. A. 2005. The excitement of Google Scholar, the worry of Google Print. *Biomedical Digital Libraries* 2, no. 2 (March 22), doi: 10.1186/1742-5581-2-2. Viewed April 11, 2005.

Belew, R. K. 2005. Scientific impact quantity and quality: Analysis of two sources of bibliographic data. Cognitive Science Dept., Univ. of California, San Diego, preprint (arXiv:cs.IR/0504036v1). Viewed April 11, 2005.

Getz, M. 2005. Three frontiers in open-access scholarship. Cornell D-Space, preprint. http://dspace.library.cornell.edu/bitstream/1813/307/1/MGetz13Jan05Cornell.pdf. Viewed January 29, 2005.

Giustini, D. 2005. UBC Google Scholar blog. http://careo.elearning.ubc.ca/weblogs/googlescholar/. Viewed May 2, 2005.

Google Scholar. 2005. About Google Scholar. http://scholar.google.com/scholar/about.html#about. Viewed May 2, 2005.

_____. 2005. Advanced Scholar Search Tips. http://scholar.google.com/scholar/refinesearch.html. Viewed May 22, 2005.

Hamaker, C., and B. Spry. 2005. Key issue: Google Scholar. *Serials* 18, no. 1 (March): 70-72. http://serials.uksg.org/openurl.asp?genre=article&issn=0953-0460&volume=18&issue=1&spage=70. Viewed May 15, 2005.

Jascó, P. 2004. Review of Google Scholar Beta. Péter's Digital Reference Shelf. http://www.galegroup.com/servlet/HTMLFileServlet?imprint=9999&region=7& fileName=/reference/archive/200412/googlescholar.html. Viewed May 2, 2005.

Kennedy, B. 2004. Googlizers vs. Resisters. *Library Journal*, December 15, 2004.

Miller, T. 2005. In defense of stupid users. *Library Journal*, March 15, 2005.

Myhill, M. 2005. The Advisor reviews . . . Google Scholar. *Charleston Advisor* 6, no. 4 (April). http://www.charlestonco.com/review.cfm?id=225. Viewed May 8, 2005.

Lederman, D. 2005. Google: Friend or foe? Inside Higher Ed. http://www.insidehighered. com/news/2005/04/11/google. Viewed May 2, 2005.

Oder, N. 2005. Google Scholar links with libs. *Library Journal*, April 15, 2005. http://www.libraryjournal.com/article/CA516043?display=NewsNews&industry= News&industryid=1986&verticalid=151. Viewed May 2, 2005.

Price, G. 2005. Google and its betas. Search Engine Watch Blog. http://blog. searchenginewatch.com/blog/050211-110853. Viewed May 2, 2005.

Rettig, J. 1996. Beyond "cool": Analog models for reviewing digital resources. *Online* (September/October): 53-64. http://proquest.umi.com/.

Rettig, J., and C. LaGuardia. 1999. Beyond "beyond cool": Reviewing Web resources. *Online* (July/August): 51-55. http://proquest.umi.com/.

Sondermann, T. J. 2005. On Google Scholar. http://schoogle.blogspot.com/. Viewed May 2, 2005.

Sullivan, D. 2005. NYT on Yahoo's US gains & Google's endless betas. Search Engine Watch Blog. http://blog.searchenginewatch.com/blog/050131-131318. Viewed May 2, 2005.

Tenopir, C. 2005. Duplication is ubiquitous–online databases. *Library Journal*, April 1, http://www.libraryjournal.com/article/CA512212?display=Online+Dbs News&industry=Online+Dbs&industryid=3761&verticalid=151. Viewed May 2, 2005.

———. 2005. Google in the academic library. *Library Journal*, February 1, 2005. http://www.libraryjournal.com/article/CA498868?display=Online%20DbsNews& industry=Online%20Dbs&industryid=3761&verticalid=151. Viewed May 2, 2005.

UNC Chapel Hill Libraries. 2005. Home page. http://www.lib.unc.edu/index.html. Viewed May 2, 2005.

Vine, R. 2005. Google Scholar is a full year late indexing Pubmed content. SiteLines– Ideas About Web Searching. http://www.workingfaster.com/sitelines/archives/2005_ 02.html#000282. Viewed May 2, 2005.

Wleklinski, J. M. 2005. Studying Google Scholar: Wall to wall coverage? *Online* (May/June): 22-26. http://proquest.umi.com/.

Running with the Devil:
Accessing Library-Licensed Full Text Holdings Through Google Scholar

Rebecca Donlan
Rachel Cooke

SUMMARY. Linking full-text proprietary databases with Google Scholar revealed three significant limitations in terms of precision (no subject heading search), transparency (no listing of information sources), and visibility (Google Scholar details are hard to find). Google Scholar is not a "one stop shopping" search engine that retrieves all relevant data from a library's licensed content. Despite these shortcomings, Google Scholar is a worthwhile search option for students, which may steer them away from Web resources, and towards the library's catalog and databases. *[Article copies available for a fee from The Haworth Document Delivery Service: 1-800-HAWORTH. E-mail address: <docdelivery@haworthpress.com> Website: <http://www.HaworthPress.com> © 2005 by The Haworth Press, Inc. All rights reserved.]*

Rebecca Donlan is Head of Library Collections & Technical Services (E-mail: rdonlan@fgcu.edu); and Rachel Cooke is Arts & Humanities Librarian (E-mail: rcooke@fgcu.edu), both at Florida Gulf Coast University, Fort Myers, FL.

Google® is a Registered Service Mark of Google, Inc., Mountain View, California. *Libraries and Google®* is an independent publication offered by The Haworth Press, Inc., Binghamton, New York, and is not affiliated with, nor has it been authorized, sponsored, endorsed, licensed, or otherwise approved by, Google, Inc.

[Haworth co-indexing entry note]: "Running with the Devil: Accessing Library-Licensed Full Text Holdings Through Google Scholar." Donlan, Rebecca, and Rachel Cooke. Co-published simultaneously in *Internet Reference Services Quarterly* (The Haworth Information Press, an imprint of The Haworth Press, Inc.) Vol. 10. No. 3/4, 2005, pp. 149-157; and: *Libraries and Google®* (ed: William Miller, and Rita M. Pellen) The Haworth Information Press, an imprint of The Haworth Press, Inc., 2005, pp. 149-157. Single or multiple copies of this article are available for a fee from The Haworth Document Delivery Service [1-800-HAWORTH, 9:00 a.m. - 5:00 p.m. (EST). E-mail address: docdelivery@haworthpress.com].

KEYWORDS. Google, Google Scholar, Open URL resolvers, link resolvers, full text

Florida Gulf Coast University was invited in the spring of 2005 to participate in a beta test linking our licensed full-text databases with Google Scholar. Some librarians, including a few at our institution, see Google as the antithesis of the sort of intellectual access librarians create to materials that have been carefully selected for scholarly work. The mere mention of student reliance on Google provokes exasperated sighs and calls of condemnation from many librarians and instructors. Given the popularity of Google among our students and faculty, however, we thought it was an excellent idea. Why not run with the devil and use Google for our own purposes: leading our students to all the content we select and pay for? As Stanley Wilder points out in his article "Information Literacy Makes All the Wrong Assumptions,"

> [The] real threat of the Internet altogether . . . is that it is now sufficiently simple and powerful that students can graduate without ever using the library. That is unfortunate because, for all its strengths, the Internet cannot give students the high-quality scholarly information that is available only through subscription, license, or purchase.[1]

We have certainly seen the truth of this in our work with students. We like Google, and use it frequently, but as librarians, we know that it is just one source among many. Many of the students we serve at the reference desk report that they "already looked for articles in Google but couldn't really find anything." It isn't that these students find nothing; it's that they get too many hits and too few pertinent items, spread among pages and pages of irrelevancies. Presumably many of their classmates have done the same in their dorms or at home and either decided they had good enough information or assumed that there was nothing available on their topic. Those students who come to us are delighted to learn that a proprietary database usually has much more, and more useful, information than they were able to retrieve on their own.

So, when offered the opportunity to link the popularity of the Google search interface to the depth and breadth of our licensed content, we jumped. Serials Solutions, with whom we have worked for many years, was testing Google Scholar as a referring source in its Article Linker open URL resolver service, to which we subscribe. Serials Solutions already has a list of all our licensed full-text databases, so all we had to do was permit it to share our IP ranges with Google Scholar. It seemed that this might prove to be a simple, elegant solution to a complex problem.

Before we talk about our experience, it is important to know how Google Scholar works. Google Scholar searches the same content as the primary Google Web crawler, but narrows down the results to scholarly literature, defined by Google as "peer-reviewed papers, theses, books, preprints, abstracts and technical reports from all broad areas of research."[2] Shirl Kennedy and Gary Price report that the search algorithm is designed to "make a calculated guess at *what it thinks* is scholarly content mined from the open Web . . . [but] precisely what makes something 'scholarly' enough to be included in Google Scholar, Google will not say."[3]

Users can limit searches by author, date range, and publication. Google Scholar does not, however, provide a list of the journals it indexes. Database aggregators like Cambridge Scientific Abstracts, EBSCO, or ProQuest do provide such lists, an important feature for the knowledgeable searcher. If you know a particular journal is pertinent, you want to search the database that indexes it and not waste your time on an index that does not. Google Scholar's search results are ranked by relevancy, defined by Google to include the full text of each article, the article's author, the publication in which the article appears, and how often it has been cited, but without knowing how any of these factors are weighted, it is difficult to know why articles are ranked as they are. One can limit a search by a few factors, but cannot then sort the result set by date, author, publication, or citation rank. Adding such sorting capability is an important enhancement we hope Google will consider.

Google Scholar does offer some features, however, that many proprietary databases do not. Citations in Google Scholar can date back well before those available in typical full-text databases, leading to important or seminal articles on various topics, though of course, full text of these is not likely to be available online, either for a cost or for free. Search results include books as well as articles, offering a better reflection of the types of materials available on any given topic. Perhaps best of all, Google Scholar offers citation linking, which is an especially useful service considering the typical cost of citation indexes.

So far, Google Scholar seems to be working without technical difficulties for our on- and off-campus users, but linking to full-text content through Google Scholar is not necessarily simple. Often database interfaces are fairly easy to intuit. Google Scholar is not. It is important to read the "About Google Scholar" pages in order to understand results. Below are three sample results from a search on "sandhill crane" that illustrate some of these interpretive peculiarities.

Sample 1: [CITATION] Effectiveness of marking powerlines to reduce sandhill crane collisions/AE Morkill, SH Anderson - Wildl. Soc. Bull, 1991
Cited by 6 - Web Search - Resources @ FGCU Library - Library Search

The notation "[CITATION]" in front of this entry is cryptic. All Google Scholar search results are citations. Why do only some results merit the label? The answer is in the "About Google Scholar" page, which explains, "Google automatically analyzes and extracts citations and presents them as separate results, even if the documents they refer to are not online."[4] Informed searchers from, say, the scientific community might understand this, or might be more motivated to go to the "about" pages for the explanation. Undergraduate students will most likely click on the citation and wonder why there is no full text. Changing the label to [CITATION ONLY] would be clearer.

If the item is a monograph, the "Library Search" link appears. Clicking this link searches for the item in OCLC's WorldCat. This particular item, though, happens to be a monographic serial, so the "Resources @ FGCU Library" link is also displayed, which is described in the next example. This isn't a fault of the Google search engine so much as an example of how items can be monographs and serials at the same time. Users may be confused, but fortunately Google Scholar offers multiple options for retrieving content. Redundancy in this case is a good thing and users do not much care about the difference between serial versus monographic publication.

Sample 2: Fusarium mycotoxins from peanuts suspected as a cause of sandhill crane mortality; RM Windingstad, RJ Cole, PE Nelson, TJ Roffe, RR . . . - Journal of Wildlife Diseases, 1989 - jwildlifedis.org
Cited by 4 - Web Search - ncbi.nlm.nih.gov - Resources @ FGCU Library

Google Scholar can distinguish between types of citations (i.e., journal articles versus monographs). Whenever Google Scholar finds a journal article that FGCU does not have in its online full-text collection, the "Resources @ FGCU Library" link appears. To the average user (librarians included), this link implies that FGCU does have full text online, so when one clicks on the "Resources @ FGCU Library" link and gets the Article Linker search screen that repeats the citation and notes "Sorry, no full-text resources found," it is highly frustrating. Perhaps changing the link text to "Search your library's catalog" might help. Also, since the reason for bringing up the Article Linker screen is to offer the user the opportunity to search the FGCU library catalog for print availability or to request an article on interlibrary loan, why not include monographs in this category?

Another point of confusion arises when Google Scholar retrieves citations from proprietary databases to which your institution does not subscribe. If, for example, Google Scholar retrieves a citation from Project MUSE, and the user clicks on the citation title link rather than the "Resources at the FGCU Library" link, the user is prompted to enter a User ID or password to access this database. To our users, this appears to be the usual off-campus authentication process to which they are accustomed. But because we do not subscribe to Project MUSE, users will be puzzled after they enter their ID number to receive an "Access not authorized" notice. The *only* way to access FGCU's licensed full-text content is to click on the "Full-Text @ FGCU" link, described in the example below. Although Google Scholar's help pages clearly state that one must be affiliated with a library to retrieve licensed full-text resources, there is no explicit statement in the help pages about *which* link to click to get to these resources.[5]

> **Sample 3:** Demographics of a declining flock of greater sandhill cranes in Oregon - Full-Text @ FGCU Library / CD Littlefield - Wilson Bulletin, 1995 - elibrary.unm.edu
> Cited by 8 - View as HTML - Web Search

The "Full-Text @ FGCU Library" link opens the Serials Solutions' Article Linker interface to our licensed content. Article Linker's tables are populated with all the serial titles included in the full-text databases we have registered with Serials Solutions, so it "knows" that we have electronic full-text access to the *Wilson Bulletin* for the cited issue. The patron clicks, the Article Linker box with a link to the article appears, and the user clicks on the "article" link. At this point the proxy server is invoked for our off-campus users. This linking works quite well, although in this case, the article also happens to be reproduced on the open Web. But again, multiple avenues of access are better than one.

Here are some real-life searches that we fielded at our reference desk and used to test how well Google Scholar retrieves pertinent full text in FGCU's e-resources collection. Search types appear in parentheses next to the search string.

Search 1: "Robert Smithson" (Exact Phrase)

Hits: 277 total, of which 23 were full-text articles owned by FGCU. To find these 23 articles, users would have to scroll through 28 pages of hits to see them all. Two of these articles ended up not having full-text available after all. This is a general problem with open URL resolvers, attributable either to a change in provider content that Serials Solutions had not yet updated, or a peculiarity in the Open URL that was incompatible with the target database.

Search 2: "Uninsured motorist" (Exact Phrase)

Hits: 121 total, of which 9 were full-text available at FGCU. These articles were spread through 13 pages of hits. The user and librarian were looking for information on the social, economic, and health impacts of uninsured motorists, and had tried this search in ProQuest and Lexis/Nexis without much luck. The nine Google-retrieved hits were found at a variety of organizational Web sites, but it appeared that many of the journals in which the articles appeared were indexed in Wilson's OmniFile, another large multi-disciplinary full-text database held by FGCU. The student performed more searches directly in Wilson's OmniFile and retrieved 37 hits. This suggests that some licensed databases are quite strong in certain areas, and in fact offer quite a bit more than the free content searched by Google Scholar, but Google Scholar did provide a nice hint to speed up the search and make it more productive.

Search 3: "marijuana legalization medicine" (Keyword)

Hits: 357 total, of which 63 were FGCU full-text, spread through 36 pages of hits. Most were relevant, pertaining to the legalization of marijuana for medicinal use, and most hits came from such journals as *Annals of Internal Medicine* or *Pediatrics* (both in our large aggregations from EBSCO and ProQuest). In this instance, Google Scholar performed a good broadcast search across several different providers, and provided reliable, authoritative, and current content.

Search 4: "Star Wars" (Exact Phrase) and "symbolism" (Keyword)

Hits: 167 total, of which 22 were full-text at FGCU, none particularly relevant. Most were passing references to religious symbolism in science fiction movies, including *Star Wars*. The search string may not have been effective, but there is no way to limit one part of the search (Star Wars) to the title of the article and allow a full-text keyword search of the term "symbolism."

Search 5: "Physical therapy" and "patient attitudes" (Exact Phrase)

Hits: 39 total, of which 6 were full text at FGCU, over only 4 pages of hits. Most were fairly relevant, although a previous search of CINAHL retrieved 62 hits.

Search 6: "Elie Wiesel" (Exact Phrase) and "night criticism" (Keyword)

Hits: 183 total, of which 42 were FGCU full text, spread over 19 pages of hits. About half of these were relevant; most were very broad and discussed Wiesel's *Night* within the larger context of holocaust narrative. A similar search in Gale's Literature Resource Center retrieved 31 hits extracted from Gale's literary criticism collections alone, but only one pertinent article in the Gale interface to MLA. In this case, Google Scholar and the Gale Literature Resource Center complemented each other's results.

Search 7: "Definition of rhetoric" (Exact Phrase)

Hits: 129 total, of which 20 were FGCU full text, spread over 13 pages of hits. The student needed to know how a variety of philosophers have defined rhetoric. Several pertinent articles that summarized definitions of rhetoric from Aristotle and other philosophers were retrieved, including several from the open Web that would not have been retrieved through our proprietary databases. On the other hand, searching "rhetoric" in the *Encyclopaedia Britannica* online, to which FGCU subscribes, pulls up 649 hits in the EB, 52 hits in the *Britannica Student Encyclopedia*, links to online journal articles, and links to 21 selected Web sites on the topic. The *Britannica* display page is well organized with extracts from the leading articles. *Encyclopaedia Britannica* is not, however, a full-text journal source, and so is not in Article Linker as a referring source or target. In this case, the student would have benefited from the librarian's direction to the encyclopedia.

So, is Google Scholar the simple, elegant solution we hoped for? We found Google Scholar to be a good complement to our existing resources, but not the "one-stop shopping" that most users will expect. At present, we see three important problems with the service: precision, transparency, and visibility.

Google Scholar is, essentially, a free federated search engine. Federated search engines depend upon keyword searching, which in turn is only as good as the subject headings used in the databases that are included. All databases are not equal in this respect. Libraries must continue to support quality subject access in the databases to which we subscribe, and librarians must be able to explain why subject analysis is worth the cost. As Tina Gross and Arlene G. Taylor point out in their article "What Have We Got to Lose? The Effect of Controlled Vocabulary on Keyword Searching Results,"

> It was found that more than one-third of records retrieved by successful keyword searches would be lost if subject headings were not present, and many individual cases exist in which 80, 90, and even 100 percent of the retrieved records would not be retrieved in the absence of subject headings.[6]

We need to be able to explain and defend the added value of subject thesauri in the databases for which we pay a considerable percentage of our materials budgets. Otherwise, we cannot blame our funding agencies for thinking that Google is "just as good." The irony, of course, is that eventually, Google will not be "just as good" as those expensive proprietary databases if we stop paying for them.

The second concern we have with Google Scholar is a general lack of transparency. Google should be able to tell users which databases, online journals, institutional repositories, and so forth that it searches. We suspect that this secrecy stems partly from the sheer size of the data universe Google's Web crawlers search–who can list everything?–but also partly from a market-driven desire to stay competitive. There must be a reasonable compromise that would give users at least some idea of what they're searching.

Third, and probably the most critical issue, is visibility–or more specifically, Google Scholar's lack of visibility to the average user. The great appeal of Google Scholar to librarians is that it should help the naïve user by narrowing a result set to pertinent materials. "Scholar" is listed as one of the options like "Images" or "News" above the search bar, but if you want to link to full text, you need to go further, and click on "Set Scholar Preferences" to enter the name of your institution in a search box. Are most students likely to figure all this out by themselves? Probably not. Almost certainly, they will continue to do their Web searches from the Google home page. A useful enhancement from Google would be to add a link at the head of a results set asking, "Are you looking for scholarly articles?" that, when clicked, would repeat the search in Google Scholar.

All in all, it has been worthwhile for us to find a common purpose with this demon. We plan to keep working with Serials Solutions and Google Scholar to offer suggestions and refinements. At this point, Google Scholar is a good tool, but it does not provide simple, unified access to all available, relevant text on any given topic in a library's licensed content. Given the fundamental loss of precise subject retrieval inherent in any federated search engine, however, this may not be a goal worth attaining. We recommend that libraries partner with Google Scholar so that we can lend our insight and expertise to its development.

REFERENCES

1. Wilder, Stanley. "Information Literacy Makes All the Wrong Assumptions." *Chronicle of Higher Education* (online), January 7, 2005. http://proquest.umi.com. ezproxy.fgcu.edu/pqdweb?did=785485391&sid=1&Fmt=3&clientId=8631&RQT=309& VName=PQD.

2. About Google Scholar. http://scholar.google/com/scholar/about.html, retrieved 5/24/2005.

3. Kennedy, Shirl, and Gary Price. "Big News: 'Google Scholar' is Born." ResourceShelf, Thursday, November 18, 2004. http://www.resourceshelf.com/2004/11/wow-its-google-scholar.html.

4. About Google Scholar. (Ibid.)

5. Google Scholar Help: Accessing and Citing. http://scholar.google.com/scholar/help.html#access3, retrieved 6/7/05.

6. Gross, Tina, and Arlene G. Taylor. "What Have We Got to Lose? The Effect of Controlled Vocabulary on Keyword Searching Results." *College & Research Libraries* 66(3), May 2005, 212-230.

Directing Students
to New Information Types:
A New Role for Google
in Literature Searches?

Mike Thelwall

SUMMARY. Conducting a literature review is an important activity for postgraduates and many undergraduates. Librarians can play an important role, directing students to digital libraries, compiling online subject resource lists, and educating about the need to evaluate the quality of online resources. In order to conduct an effective literature search in a new area, however, in some subjects it is necessary to gain basic topic knowledge, including specialist vocabularies. Google's link-based page ranking algorithm makes this search engine an ideal tool for finding specialist topic introductory material, particularly in computer science, and so librarians should be teaching this as part of a strategic literature review approach. *[Article copies available for a fee from The Haworth Document Delivery Service: 1-800-HAWORTH. E-mail address: <docdelivery@haworthpress.com> Website: <http://www.HaworthPress.com> © 2005 by The Haworth Press, Inc. All rights reserved.]*

Mike Thelwall is affiliated with the School of Computing and Information Technology, University of Wolverhampton, Wulfruna Street, Wolverhampton WV1 1SB, UK (E-mail: m.thelwall@wlv.ac.uk).

Google® is a Registered Service Mark of Google, Inc., Mountain View, California. *Libraries and Google*® is an independent publication offered by The Haworth Press, Inc., Binghamton, New York, and is not affiliated with, nor has it been authorized, sponsored, endorsed, licensed, or otherwise approved by, Google, Inc.

[Haworth co-indexing entry note]: "Directing Students to New Information Types: A New Role for Google in Literature Searches?" Thelwall, Mike. Co-published simultaneously in *Internet Reference Services Quarterly* (The Haworth Information Press, an imprint of The Haworth Press, Inc.) Vol. 10, No. 3/4, 2005, pp. 159-166; and: *Libraries and Google*® (ed: William Miller, and Rita M. Pellen) The Haworth Information Press, an imprint of The Haworth Press, Inc., 2005, pp. 159-166. Single or multiple copies of this article are available for a fee from The Haworth Document Delivery Service [1-800-HAWORTH, 9:00 a.m. - 5:00 p.m. (EST). E-mail address: docdelivery@haworthpress.com].

Available online at http://www.haworthpress.com/web/IRSQ
© 2005 by The Haworth Press, Inc. All rights reserved.
doi:10.1300/J136v10n03_14

KEYWORDS. Information seeking, literature search, Google, search engines, specialist vocabularies, librarianship

INTRODUCTION

One of the defining features of academic research is its embedding in a recognized subject literature (Merton 1973). In a published paper, an explicit literature review section can achieve this embedding, depending upon the type of research and the field in which it is published. Literature review is also part of the scholarly process of learning a new field in some subjects. In some disciplines, such as sociology, literature searching is a skill expected of undergraduates even from their first year. In others, such as mathematics, literature reviews can be delayed to the postgraduate level. Whatever the subject differences, in a typical university there will be a considerable number of students that need to learn how to conduct an effective literature search using the available resources including books, journals, digital libraries, and the Web.

Two of the central issues that the Web has brought to the fore in education are the possibilities that it has created for dishonesty (Hinman 2002), and the need for effective evaluation of the quality of online sources (Cunningham 1997). Nevertheless, many students still extensively use the Web in an effective and honest way. Moreover, there is a need to ensure that we take full advantage of this vast new resource in every way possible (e.g., Thelwall 2004). Google is effective for one particular aspect of literature searching: the identification of relevant introductory material to enhance acquisition of background knowledge of a new topic.

PRECISION, RECALL, FILTERING, AND SPECIALIST VOCABULARIES

In the era of digital libraries, one of the key search skills is the mastery of keyword searches and interfaces (Marchionini 1995), but this may not be sufficient for an effective literature review. The problem is related to the issue of topic relevance. There are many different possible purposes for a literature search, including identifying useful methods, but a common task is to identify topic-relevant papers in a *new* subject area (Fry and Talja 2004; Talja and Maula 2003). In order to identify a large enough collection of topic-relevant papers, the searcher has to resolve two different issues, which will be described here with the information retrieval terms *precision* and *recall*.

The recall problem is designing a search strategy that will find enough relevant literature, whereas the precision problem is designing a query that will not return irrelevant literature. High recall but low precision is a typical problem caused by a search that is too general, and the solution is either to reformulate the query or to spend considerable time *filtering* the relevant literature from the larger set. In a typical successful search, a researcher may formulate a keyword query that produces a list containing many relevant documents in addition to some that are not relevant (balancing precision and recall), then proceed to inspect the list to pick out the genuinely relevant documents (filtering). Ideally, a search could be constructed that found the complete set of relevant documents without any unwanted extras, but this is probably a rare occurrence.

Searches can be conducted in many ways, such as browsing relevant journal contents lists and citation chaining (Bates 2002), but keyword searches will be discussed here primarily, because they are a logical starting point for a new field. Ignoring technical skills, such as interface mastery and Boolean search construction, topic-based keyword searching can be usefully split into three types: controlled vocabulary, specialist vocabulary, and natural vocabulary. The distinction arises because in some disciplines, particularly the hard sciences, new terms are coined and universally used with given field-specific meanings (Fuchs 1992). New researchers must thus expend considerable effort to understand the words that are used to describe and discuss the topic. As a result of this, learning the specialist vocabulary becomes a prerequisite to effective literature searches. Controlled vocabularies are an extreme case, with a fixed set of words with agreed meanings chosen and enforced upon scholars, for example in article keyword lists. An example is the ACM Computing Classification System <http://www.acm.org/class/1998/>, although ACM publications often require both official keywords and author-defined keywords.

In fields where a specialist vocabulary exists, learning the vocabulary is inseparable from learning to be competent to conduct searches with high recall. Filtering is also an issue if there are many unwanted results because the task of assessing the relevance of a paper implies some understanding of its content, even if only from the negative perspective of diagnosing that it is irrelevant. With a literature search for an unknown topic, however, the first step must be to learn sufficient specialist vocabulary to be able to conduct searches with sufficient recall. In some cases this may be straightforward; for example a controlled vocabulary would help by limiting the potential choices, although ambiguity is endemic to any classification system. In other cases this may be extremely difficult, possibly most often when there is a non-controlled specialist vocabu-lary. For example, a student wishing to find research about Web search engines in computer science would need to discover that Web Informa-tion Retrieval is the appropriate topic description to search for and few relevant papers contain the phrase "search engine" in their title. A litera-ture search without this knowledge could easily miss all the major re-search and find only social science discussions of search engines.

In areas without a controlled or specialist vocabulary, filtering may be less of an issue because articles will be more easily decipherable without specialist knowledge external to the topic, whereas recall can be a problem in a new way. Lacking a specialist vocabulary, authors will naturally adopt their own terms making high recall searches difficult or impossible to construct.

In summary, in some fields the need to learn a specialist vocabulary means that researchers conducting topic-based searches in unfamiliar fields will need to first learn its specialist vocabulary, which means gaining a basic topic understanding.

ITERATIVE LITERATURE SEARCH STRATEGIES

A traditional approach to literature search emphasizes its iterative na-ture, recognizing that researchers must go through some kind of learn-ing process in order to identify the most relevant literature (Kuhlthau 2004). The searcher must use traditional sources to repeatedly search for and read literature before getting a satisfactory result. This process will work, given sufficient subject knowledge to conduct the initial search, but risks completely missing the relevant literature or being in-efficient in finding it. An alternative is to begin with an initial explor-atory phase designed to learn some basic specialist vocabulary.

For a new topic literature search, then, the first step can be explor-atory research designed to gain an overview of content and vocabulary. There are many sources of information for this, including other schol-ars, subject encyclopedias, review articles, and undergraduate text-books. The Web is an additional source with the advantage that it is easily accessible and searchable. In emerging research fields, there might not be any textbooks or review articles and so the Web might be the only available source of introductory material.

In contrast to scholarly digital archives, the Web is not restricted to contributions aimed at academics: others are also aimed at a wider audi-ence. For example, there may be online course notes or presentation slides, subject gateways, and informational Web sites such as Wikis

(Guest 2003) and Blogs (Bar-Ilan 2004). In addition, research groups often have a Web site with a brief description of their research activities. All of these are potential sources of introductory material for academic topics. Moreover Web publishing seems most prevalent in the hard sciences (Thelwall et al. 2003) where such information is most needed for learning new topics and so there is a fortunate match between the need for information and its provision.

USING GOOGLE
TO FIND INTRODUCTORY TOPIC MATERIAL

Given the availability of introductory topic material on the Web, it is still necessary to find it, which is the same problem as digital library searching. Nevertheless, search engines like Google work in a way that makes introductory material particularly easy to find, even though it is hard to find high quality research papers with the standard Google (Jepsen et al. 2004). The reason is that hyperlinks are important in Google's ranking algorithm, and probably also in the ranking algorithms of other search engines, as described below.

When a searcher enters keywords in Google, its algorithm rapidly identifies the matching set of pages, but must then decide the order in which they should appear. Since most users only look at the first few results it is important for the most useful pages to be listed first. Google's algorithm for doing this is based upon the premise that the most useful Web pages will have many links to them (inlinks), because people are less likely to link to uninteresting pages. Google also weights inlinks by the importance of the link source page (Brin and Page 1998). As a result, the first few pages in Google's results tend to be those that are linked to most pages, and by the most important pages. These should be the most popular pages. Google also takes into account many other factors, such as the existence of link anchor text, so the match between links and ranking is not exact. Link anchor text is the text in the Web page that is clickable to activate the link. Often the link anchor text is blue and underlined. Previous research has shown that Google is particularly good at basic tasks such as identifying the Web sites of academic journals, tending to rank these highly in response to searches for their name (Thelwall 2002).

Topic introduction pages seem likely to be popular because they are useful to a wide audience including those learning a new field and people external to it that wish to find out about it. In the logic of Google, such pages should therefore tend to be highly ranked. They should also use non-specialist language, in addition to specialist language, if only using the former to explain the latter. Hence, it should normally be possible to use "natural language" queries in Google and similar pages to find topic-introductory material. The following factors are likely to influence this possibility.

- *Whether a Web topic introduction exists.* Some disciplines use the Web more than others (Kling and McKim 2000). For example, in computer science material should be available about most topics but there may well be many areas of the humanities that are not represented, with obvious exceptions like digital archiving.
- *Topic popularity.* Topics that are larger in terms of membership are more likely to have material published online, especially if they are part of taught courses. This popularity should also tend to extend to link creation.
- *Word frequency.* Topics will be most difficult to find when the words used to describe them are widely used, especially if they have multiple meanings. For example, the word "statistics" is widely used for the discipline as well as for all kinds of facts and figures and for Web server statistics. Hence the volume of pages containing the term "statistics" makes searches difficult or impossible (i.e., high recall and low precision make filtering impractical).

Given the difficulties mentioned above, such as searching for a topic describable by very common words like "video storage,"searchers should experiment with searches that use different words to describe their topic, in an attempt to find some that match introductory pages and rank them high enough that they can be found. Successful strategies are likely to vary by topic. For instance, in some cases it may be necessary to try rare synonyms in order to avoid getting too many search results. In the above example, a phrase like "video information retrieval" would be able to return many relevant matches from the computer science research into how video footage is stored and made searchable.

SUMMARY

Librarians and educators should consider suggesting to students that they start a topic-based literature search for a new topic by conducting an online search for a general topic introduction. This is especially important in fields with high specialist vocabularies and the absence of a universal controlled vocabulary, which probably covers most of the hard sciences. Librarians may need to help with the construction of effective Google searches, using Boolean logic or appropriate search strategies. Using this introductory material, students can learn some of the topic specialist vocabulary, which should help them to design future digital library searches. The knowledge should also help the searcher to better filter matching documents, hence improving their overall search efficiency. Literature review is still likely to be an iterative process, with repeated search-read cycles as the topic is more fully learned, but a solid initial stage should serve to give a foothold that might otherwise be difficult to gain from digital libraries alone.

REFERENCES

Bar-Ilan, J. 2004. Blogarians–A new breed of librarians. *Proceedings of the American Society for Information Science & Technology*.

Bates, M. 2002. Speculations on browsing, directed searching, and linking in relation to the Bradford distribution. In *Proceedings of the Fourth International Conference on Conceptions of Library and Information Science (CoLIS 4)*. edited by H. Bruce, R. Fidel, P. Ingwersen and P. Vakkari. Greenwood CO: Libraries Unlimited.

Brin, S. , and L. Page. 1998. The anatomy of a large scale hypertextual Web search engine. *Computer Networks and ISDN Systems* 30 (1-7):107-117.

Cunningham, Sally Jo. 1997. Teaching students to critically evaluate the quality of Internet research resources. *ACM SIGCSE Bulletin* 29 (2):31-38.

Fry, J., and S. Talja. 2004. The cultural shaping of scholarly communication: Explaining e-journal use within and across academic fields. Paper read at ASIST 2004: Proceedings of the 67th ASIST Annual Meeting.

Fuchs, S. 1992. *The professional quest for truth: A social theory of science and knowledge*. Albany, NY: SUNY Press.

Guest, D.G. 2003. Four futures for scientific and medical publishing–It's a wiki wiki world. *British Medical Journal* 326 (932-933).

Hinman, L. M. 2002. Academic integrity and the World Wide Web. *ACM SIGCAS Computers and Society* 32 (1):33-42.

Jepsen, E.T., P. Seiden, P. Ingwersen, and L. Björneborn. 2004. Characteristics of scientific Web publications: Preliminary data gathering and analysis. *Journal of the American Society for Information Science and Technology* 55 (14):1239-1249.

Kling, R. , and G. McKim. 2000. Not just a matter of time: Field differences and the shaping of electronic media in supporting scientific communication. *Journal of the American Society for Information Science* 51 (14):1306-1320.

Kuhlthau, C. C. 2004. *Seeking meaning: A process approach to library and information services, 2nd Ed.* Wesport, CT: Libraries Unlimited.

Marchionini, G. 1995. *Information seeking in electronic environments.* Cambridge: Cambridge University Press.

Merton, R. K. 1973. *The sociology of science. Theoretical and empirical investigations.* Chicago: University of Chicago Press.

Talja, S., and H. Maula. 2003. Reasons for the use and non-use of electronic journals and databases: A domain analytic study in four scholarly disciplines. *Journal of Documentation* 59 (6):673-691.

Thelwall, M. 2002. In praise of Google: Finding law journal Web sites. *Online Information Review* 26 (4):271-272.

_____. 2004. Will digital libraries generate a new need for multi-disciplinary research skills? *LIBRES* 14 (2):Retrieved April 18 from: <http://libres.curtin.edu.au/libres14n2/index.htm>.

Thelwall, M., L. Vaughan, V. Cothey, X. Li, and A. G. Smith. 2003. Which academic subjects have most online impact? A pilot study and a new classification process. *Online Information Review* 27 (5):333-343.

Evaluating Google Scholar
as a Tool for Information Literacy

Rachael Cathcart
Amanda Roberts

SUMMARY. There are a growing number of articles on the juncture of Google Scholar and libraries; this article seeks to address the ability of this resource to meet the information needs of students and researchers using the ACRL Information Literacy Standards. Each standard is applied to Google Scholar in this examination, and recommendations for how librarians might respond are offered. *[Article copies available for a fee from The Haworth Document Delivery Service: 1-800-HAWORTH. E-mail address: <docdelivery@haworthpress.com> Website: <http://www.HaworthPress.com> © 2005 by The Haworth Press, Inc. All rights reserved.]*

KEYWORDS. Information literacy, Google Scholar, federated searching, bibliographic instruction to undergraduates

---

Rachael Cathcart is Reference Librarian, Florida Atlantic University, S. E. Wimberly Library, 777 Glades Road, Boca Raton, FL 33431 (E-mail: cathcart@fau.edu). Amanda Roberts is ALA NMRT President-Elect for 2005-06 (E-mail: palmanda1@yahoo.com).

[Haworth co-indexing entry note]: "Evaluating Google Scholar as a Tool for Information Literacy." Cathcart, Rachael, and Amanda Roberts. Co-published simultaneously in *Internet Reference Services Quarterly* (The Haworth Information Press, an imprint of The Haworth Press, Inc.) Vol. 10, No. 3/4, 2005, pp. 167-176; and: *Libraries and Google®* (ed: William Miller, and Rita M. Pellen) The Haworth Information Press, an imprint of The Haworth Press, Inc., 2005, pp. 167-176. Single or multiple copies of this article are available for a fee from The Haworth Document Delivery Service [1-800-HAWORTH, 9:00 a.m. - 5:00 p.m. (EST). E-mail address: docdelivery@haworthpress.com].

Available online at http://www.haworthpress.com/web/IRSQ
© 2005 by The Haworth Press, Inc. All rights reserved.
doi:10.1300/J136v10n03_15

On its Web site, Google boldly declares that its mission is to "organize the world's information and make it universally accessible and useful," describing itself as one of the world's "best-known brands" that owes its ubiquity to the "word of mouth of satisfied users." Enter the latest development in the Googlized world, a new search service geared to the academic research community called Google Scholar. Google has partnered with various publishers, such as IEEE and ACM, to index scholarly publications that previously were available only through fee-based subscription services. Because of these partnerships, Google Scholar theoretically allows students and researchers to search a familiar and highly popular interface, and retrieve research articles and citations that are far more reliable and scholarly than what is typically offered by the original Google and other search engines.

To some librarians, Google Scholar may seem to be a positive answer to the problem of students' overuse of the World Wide Web. While students are still relying on a search engine instead of library resources, they reason, at least students are searching reliable material, as opposed to apocryphal, dubious Web pages, and despite the many technical problems of Google Scholar, at least students can use it to find a few articles that are good enough. On the surface, this is an attractive argument. However, the goals of academic librarians are more sophisticated than helping patrons find answers to reference questions. Instead, educating users to understand the structure of the world of information is seen as a necessity for promoting students' independence as citizens of a complex information universe. This is one of the basic tenets of the ACRL Information Literacy Standards.

GOOGLE SCHOLAR AND INFORMATION LITERACY

With the advent of Google Scholar and the continuing evolution of the online information environment, the way librarians go about educating students–in both the classroom and at the reference desk–will need to evolve as well. In order to facilitate that evolution, it is useful to examine Google Scholar in terms of how well it meets the ACRL Information Literacy Standards. To briefly define or summarize, the standards roughly state that the information literate student ought to be skilled in how to "identify an information need, access that information, critically evaluate the information found, apply it to the real world (or, at least to the assignment), and put the information into the context of larger societal and ethical issues." In this examination, one will find that while Google Scholar has some useful and redeeming qualities, its ultimate value in meeting these standards is limited.

Identify the Information Need

In order to demonstrate the ability to "identify the information need," a student should be able to articulate a research question, thesis, or problem, use general reference sources to gain a better understanding of the topic, identify key terms, determine the potential types of resources for information on the topic, and show an awareness of the time and availability constraints (i.e., the need for Interlibrary Loan) of the various information resources available to be employed. This set of skills is learned and developed over time through repeated encounters with research materials, databases, the reference desk, and in some cases, information literacy classes.

Due to the varying nature of the infinite variety of possible sources, identifying the information need can be an overwhelmingly complex and unnecessarily time-consuming process for the neophyte. Of course, when students seek the help of a librarian, information seeking becomes less painful. In many a reference interview, a student is found to have entered the entire research question or thesis into the search field of the catalog or a database, including many extraneous words (e.g., *in*, *the*, *to*, or *with*). In the name of encouraging the student to break down the research question into its primary key terms, a reference librarian urges him to eschew all but those core terms. The librarian might also recommend looking at a thesaurus or encyclopedia in a related discipline, or introduce the library's interlibrary loan service if it seems that time will permit.

To its credit, Google Scholar does attempt to assist with the problem of the lengthy, poorly constructed search query. Should an entire research question be entered–extraneous words and all–a message will appear above the results stating, "The following words are very common and were not included in your search." Following this message is a link to a brief explanation that could, theoretically, serve to help a student integrate the need to focus more on the core terms of a search. However, this is not offset by the fact that Google Scholar does not offer the services of a librarian, link to any "Ask-A-Librarian" service, or provide course-related instruction.

While the Google term suggestion technology may be beneficial at a specific point of need, it does not, and cannot, proactively teach a student the *why* and *how* of constructing a complex query so that he is able create an improved search on another topic in another interface. Instilling research independence in students is clearly a goal of information literacy, but Google Scholar does nothing to instill this independence–at least not an independence based in the kinds of skills that will truly meet their information needs. In fact, due to the popularity of Google's name as well as students' already established dependence on the Google search engine, Google Scholar may lure even more students away from library sources.

Access the Needed Information

With regard to accessing information, students should know how to select appropriate resources and information retrieval systems, construct and implement effectively designed search strategies, locate information in both online and print formats, and refine search strategies when necessary. In terms of promoting the ability to choose from an appropriate range of resources and information retrieval systems, Google Scholar, by the nature of its very existence, falls short. It represents one database as opposed to the hundreds available at a university library; and at that, one which is incomplete in scope and in how it is indexed, secretive about what is included, and lacks a controlled vocabulary. In "Google Scholar: the pros and cons," Peter Jacso elaborates briefly on these shortcomings. On its secrecy, he remarks:

> The underlying problem with Google Scholar is that Google is as secretive about its coverage as the North Korean government about the famine in the country. There is no information about the publishers whose archive Google is allowed to search, let alone about the specific journals and the host sites covered by Google Scholar. (Jacso, 2005)

Google Scholar appears to show promise by at least introducing the user to some basic search capabilities. In Google Scholar's advanced search screen, advanced search tips, and "scholar help" page, one finds the embryonic makings of the kind of database librarians have become accustomed to–or at least the training wheels from which students might graduate to library databases. Specifically, the advanced search screen allows users to limit by:

- Publication title (full or abbreviated journal title)
- Date range
- Author
- Keywords in the text or title

Features not included in Google Scholar's advanced search:

- A way to limit to certain types of documents (i.e., peer-reviewed, refereed journals)
- A time-saving way to sort the hundreds of results

In the advanced search tips, users are told how to perform these limits and given examples, along with some rudimentary Boolean-type operators. If the Google Scholar searcher is independently motivated, he can access the "Scholar Help" page, which answers questions about searching, indexing, accessing, and citing. The inevitable questions related to accessing full text, the need to seek out the holdings of a library one is affiliated with, and the need for proxy authentication are also addressed. However, while the help page mentions that users may sometimes be prompted to purchase articles, there is no direct or overt effort to explain that library access often renders such purchases needless. The user is left to make that connection on his own. Of course, this assumes that the user takes the extra steps to read the help section. The end result is that many students who do not realize what the library has to offer will be bypassing materials free to them.

Unlike information literacy instruction and reference services, Google Scholar doesn't give students a clearly constructed opportunity to learn the basic information literacy skill of accessing materials. Because of the trust and search ease associated with its brand name, Google Scholar may actually promote the idea that most information on the World Wide Web is online, full text, and free–an idea that is already frustrating for all educators. This is especially problematic because Google Scholar does not, and cannot due to copyright restrictions, offer most of the documents in its search results for free. At best, Google Scholar supports the notion that your next door neighbor's Web page about Springer Spaniel behavior is not as reliable as a research study found in a library index; at worst, we lose more students and scholars to the World Wide Web because they are under the misguided assumption that Google indexes everything.

Evaluate the Information Found

Activities indicating competency would include the ability to summarize the main ideas of the resources found, determine the quality and credibility of a source, compare new information with past knowledge and incorporate into one's knowledge base, and determine whether further research into similar or new topics is called for. At face value, Google Scholar is not appreciably better or worse than a library's resources, aside from the general lack of comparable variety and scope in what is offered. While the user's initial experience of searching may be more pleasant than searching a library database, Google Scholar does not offer a mechanism for managing the large number of retrieved results. Without being able to e-mail results or immediately connect to a database through article linking technology, access can become time-consuming and confusing, leaving little time for content evaluation.

Apply Knowledge Gained to a Specific Purpose

In a practical sense, this could be conceived of as not only applying new knowledge to an assignment, but also applying it to real world problems that go beyond the assignment (i.e., global warming, school bullying) and topics of personal relevance to the student (i.e., popular music, fashion, health or social conditions they've had personal experience with). Presuming the likelihood that students using Google Scholar are already familiar with the Google interface and have used Google for personal information needs, students who use Google Scholar may be more inclined to develop an approach to research that makes a direct, integrated connection between the personal information-seeking and academic information-seeking. This connection may actually help the information literacy movement if it is recognized and appropriately channeled into a constructive learning experience.

Put the Information into the Context of Larger Societal and Ethical Issues

In the most immediate and specific of terms, this could be interpreted to mean that the student is proficient in properly referencing all resources without plagiarism, has an understanding of copyright and other issues related to privacy, security, free vs. fee-based information services, intellectual property, copyright, fair use, and Netiquette. While Google Scholar does attempt to regurgitate the records of publishers, because of its automated technology and lack of meta-tagged records, some citations in results lists are not complete. For those students who use Google Scholar and bypass library databases and reference services, there is no mediating force that can advise or correct a citation that may be incomplete or inaccurate. For those students who do not have an understanding of the importance of documentation, Google Scholar does not offer an opportunity for them to learn proper documentation format.

Many subscription-based library databases offer suggestions on preparing bibliographies or offer automated citation formatting. These databases have an established history of partnerships with libraries and do listen and respond to the needs of their customers. Google Inc., on the other hand, has not proven its incentive to truly meet the information literacy needs of students.

RECOMMENDATIONS

Google is a powerful, publicly traded company. As with all business ventures, Google's ultimate focus is not providing a service that truly meets the needs of researchers for comprehensive, quality information, but its bottom line. Librarians have complained about the rising costs of journal publications for years, and these complaints are directed at publishers with which libraries have had a historical relationship. Librarians have already experienced conflict with for-profit information providers. The potential for further conflict with Google, which would seem to have even less incentive to truly be after the hearts and minds of librarians, appears inevitable. Furthermore, we already know that we have a problem with student overuse of Google. Why encourage it, particularly when Google Scholar's attempt to match the comprehensiveness of what virtually any university library provides falls so short of what the academic community needs?

Yet–whether we like it or not–the "Googlized" world is upon us. Students and researchers, emboldened by the autonomy that the World Wide Web has provided, are increasingly less dependent on libraries alone for their research. Librarians and educators may shudder at the assumptions this empowerment allows to perpetuate and flourish about how information is provided, but there is a new driving force that we must adapt to. If we are able to meet this challenge, we will be in a better position ultimately to instill the values of information literacy and critical thinking–perhaps more effectively than ever before. With these ideas in mind, two primary and allied recommendations are offered: the exploration and embracing of federated and meta-searching technologies, and a co-occurring large-scale marketing and branding effort to counter and capitalize upon the Google Scholar phenomenon.

Federated and Meta-Searching

In Martin Myhill's review of Google Scholar in the April 2005 issue of *The Charleston Advisor*, he adeptly and effectively eradicates any doubt as to whether libraries have a viable and superior alternative to Google Scholar in terms of serving the information needs the academically minded community. In the likes of MetaLib, MetaFind, and MuseGlobal, Google Scholar has "much to be jealous of." In MetaFind, Myhill explains, a patron is allowed to "search a number of information sources simultaneously with one interface . . . using relatively sophisticated search criteria" and the results can be "sorted, further limited and deduplicated if required." Compare that with Google Scholar, where claims of digitizing "the contents of five of the world's most important academic institutions" are deflated when further investigation reveals significant limits in what is actually to be made available. The projects, instead of reflecting even a majority of what the libraries contain, comprise noteworthy contributions that nonetheless are just a fraction of what each library owns. It seems Google Scholar is succeeding mightily at perpetuating the "online lies" that William Miller wrote of in 1997.

Beat Them at Their Own Game

In "'Google Scholar' Is Born," Shirl Kennedy and Gary Price present a challenge to the library community. They urge us to capitalize on the opportunity that Google Scholar affords us, and to remind our user community of the invaluable nature of what the library offers. Based on the past, they also express doubt as to whether we are up to this challenge. Yet, the consequences of such resignation are an ever increasing number of students, higher education administrators, and legislators mired in the heady myths about online information that entities like Google are all too ready to promote. These are stakeholders with misguided influence over our budgets, our policies, and our services.

Thus, Google Scholar signals a need for information professionals to be ever more adaptive, creative, and unceasingly vigilant in making our stakeholders aware of our role in the electronic world of information. We want students who are information literate; students want convenience. We fear that students who are catered to at the expense of quality information will fail to gain the necessary skills for thriving in the evolving information climate. While the changes taking place may leave a bitter taste in the collective library mouth, we have a choice:

cling fiercely to the belief that students must become information literate *our* way, or find adaptive ways to accomplish the same goals. This does not mean having to give up on our ideals, or that no student will ever again learn to appreciate the value of a properly-designed advanced search screen. It simply means that we're willing to see the grey area of the issues we're faced with.

In the spirit of applying the desire to respond adaptively, we make the following recommendations: the extensive use of branding, turn Google Scholar into an information literacy ally, and seek to approach the issue with an appreciation for the grey areas.

Employ the Extensive Use of Branding

Particularly with meta-search technologies, branding should be utilized to capitalize upon and counter the name recognition of Google and Google Scholar. Once a meta-search technology has been implemented at your library, make use of the logo in places such as your library's homepage, in campus and classroom portal systems, in information literacy instruction sessions, on flyers posted in the library and around campus, in the library's campus newsletter, and the school newspaper. Make reference to Google or Google Scholar to give context and show that the library has something better.

Turn Google Scholar into an Information Literacy Ally

While Google as a search engine was an entirely different animal from a library database, Google Scholar resembles one enough to more readily be used for comparison. Because it offers the familiarity of Google, yet introduces the user to scholarly articles and the concept of a citation index, it could serve as a bridge to the more reliable, comprehensive resources offered by libraries. Side-by-side searches will reveal the gaps in Google Scholar coverage as compared with more thorough offerings in library-based databases. Hence, one response to this resource and its flaws would be to use it in information literacy instruction–however carefully and sparingly–as a tool for connecting students with the resources and concepts that will better meet their information needs.

Approach Information Literacy Overall with Continued Creativity and Adaptability

Not all of us are in favor of federated searching technology. We don't want Google Scholar forcing us to compromise and we don't want the drive among students for convenience to result in the dilution of what is expected of them. That is an understandable position. Yet, approaching it as a black and white issue is not effective. If we continue to seek ways of appealing to their drive for convenience and their familiarity with Google Scholar, we may be able to turn these new technologies into allies.

REFERENCES

Information Literacy Competency Standards for Higher Education. Retrieved May 11, 2005, from the Association of College & Research Libraries Web site: <http://www.ala.org/ala/acrl/acrlstandards/informationliteracycompetency.htm>.

Jacso, Peter. Peter's Digital Reference Shelf: Google Scholar Beta. (2004, December). Retrieved June 1, 2005, from the Thompson Gale Web site: <http://www.galegroup.com/servlet/HTMLFileServlet?imprint=9999&region=7&fileName=/reference/archive/200412/googlescholar.html>.

Jacso, Peter. Peter's Digital Reference Shelf: Google Scholar Redux. (2005, June) Retrieved June 2, 2005, from the Thompson Gale Web site: <http://www.galegroup.com/servlet/HTMLFileServlet?imprint=9999&region=7&fileName=/reference/archive/200506/google.html>.

Kennedy, S. and Price, G. Big news: "Google Scholar" is born. (2004, November 18). Retrieved March 29, 2005 from the Resource Shelf Web site: <http://www.resourceshelf.com/2004/11/wow-its-google-scholar.html>.

Miller, W. (1997). Online lies we'd better face. *Education Digest,* 63: 29-31.

Sullivan, Danny (2004). Google Scholar Offers Access to Academic Information. (2004 November 18) Retrieved June 26, 2005, from the Search Engine Watch Web site: <http://searchenginewatch.com/searchday/article.php/3437471>.

Tenopir, Carol (2005). Google in the academic library. *Library Journal,* 130(2):32.

Optimising Publications for Google Users

Alan Dawson

SUMMARY. Librarians should think explicitly about Google users whenever they publish on the Web, and should update their policies and procedures accordingly. The article describes procedures that libraries can adopt to ensure that their publications are optimised for access by users of Google and other Web search engines. The aim of these procedures is to enhance resource discovery and information retrieval, and to enhance the reputation of libraries as valued custodians of published information, as well as exemplars of good practice in information management. *[Article copies available for a fee from The Haworth Document Delivery Service: 1-800-HAWORTH. E-mail address: <docdelivery@haworthpress.com> Website: <http://www.HaworthPress.com> © 2005 by The Haworth Press, Inc. All rights reserved.]*

KEYWORDS. Digital libraries, metadata, search engines, optimization, electronic publishing

THE RISE OF GOOGLE

The development of Google from search engine to multinational corporation reached a new stage in June 2005, when it became the world's

Alan Dawson is affiliated with the Centre for Digital Library Research, Department of Computer and Information Sciences, University of Strathclyde, Glasgow G1 1XH, Scotland (E-mail: alan.dawson@strath.ac.uk).

Google® is a Registered Service Mark of Google, Inc., Mountain View, California. *Libraries and Google®* is an independent publication offered by The Haworth Press, Inc., Binghamton, New York, and is not affiliated with, nor has it been authorized, sponsored, endorsed, licensed, or otherwise approved by, Google, Inc.

[Haworth co-indexing entry note]: "Optimising Publications for Google Users." Dawson, Alan. Co-published simultaneously in *Internet Reference Services Quarterly* (The Haworth Information Press, an imprint of The Haworth Press, Inc.) Vol. 10, No. 3/4, 2005, pp. 177-194; and: *Libraries and Google®* (ed: William Miller, and Rita M. Pellen) The Haworth Information Press, an imprint of The Haworth Press, Inc., 2005, pp. 177-194. Single or multiple copies of this article are available for a fee from The Haworth Document Delivery Service [1-800-HAWORTH, 9:00 a.m. - 5:00 p.m. (EST). E-mail address: docdelivery@haworthpress.com].

Available online at http://www.haworthpress.com/web/IRSQ
© 2005 by The Haworth Press, Inc. All rights reserved.
doi:10.1300/J136v10n03_16

biggest media company, measured by stock market value. The Google brand name is now familiar to millions of people who have never even used the Web. Yet as Google introduces further innovations and extensions to searching, such as Google Print and Google Scholar, there is increasing concern about the impact that habitual Google use amongst students has on education in general and on information literacy in particular (Devine & Egger-Sider, 2004; Markland, 2005).

In most discussions of the effects of Google on libraries, librarians are usually seen as consumers and information seekers, whether for themselves or on behalf of students and other library users. In contrast, this article focuses on the role of libraries as online information providers, in view of the fact that so many people now depend on Google as their primary means of access to digital information.

While most librarians probably use the Web and Google routinely in their work, the impact of the ubiquitous use of Google on librarians is still unclear. It is tempting to conclude that the universal availability of fast and easy access to online information is devaluing, and perhaps undermining, the traditional role of librarians as intermediaries. Yet, as Becker (2003), Bundy (2004), Rumsey (2005), and others have shown, there is still a great need for librarians as educators, to help guide information seekers to relevant sources and to interpret search results. The main difficulty for librarians in promoting information literacy is comparable to Rumsfeld's (2002) perceptive observations about unknown unknowns; if users don't know there are things they don't know about Internet searching, then they may not perceive any need for librarians to help them. This principle may also be applied to librarians; if they don't know there are things they don't know about online publishing, they may not perceive any need for guidance. This article therefore aims to change some "unknown unknowns" about the publishing process to "known knowns."

THE RESPONSIBILITY OF LIBRARIANS

Traditional values associated with librarians include precision, discipline, attention to detail, and helpfulness. They may be seen as curators or custodians of books and other sources of information, but librarians are not usually regarded as publishers of information. Yet almost all libraries do publish, on a small scale at least. For some libraries this may amount to little more than details of opening hours and location posted on a Web site. For many others it will extend to making available their catalogue of holdings online, along with guidance notes, while an increasing number of libraries are digitising some of their collections and publishing them online.

Digital publishing involves responsibilities that are often overlooked. While most libraries will think about issues such as accuracy, design and accessibility while publishing information for users via their own Web sites, they may be less aware that they are also (potentially) publishing information via Google. As yet "publishing via Google" is not a common expression. Google is seen as a search engine, not a means of publication. Yet, as Dempsey (2004) points out, increasingly "on Web" means "available via Google." Online publishing can therefore be seen as a two-stage process: adding content to a Web site is merely the first stage of publishing. The second stage is getting that content successfully indexed by Google. This second stage is arguably more important, as it vastly increases the likelihood of the published material being discovered and used. However, for librarians it should not be simply a question of ensuring that their material is "published via Google." Librarians should aim to set a good example as digital curators (who else is better placed?). This means taking the necessary steps to ensure that the indexing and retrieval process works as well as possible, given the inherent limitations of Google. The remainder of this paper aims to describe and explain these steps so that Google users are well served by librarians and by other responsible online publishers such as museums, universities, and public institutions. In short, it shows how and why to optimise online publications for Google. As well as producing benefits for those carrying out the optimisation, by making their content easier to maintain and discover, in the long term the cumulative effects of more widespread optimisation will benefit everyone.

THE PUBLISHING PROCESS

The principles for publishing specifically with Google in mind are largely the same as the principles for sound information management and publishing practice; there is no inherent conflict. Table 1 summarises these principles and the reasons why they matter for publishing via Google.

A simple example may serve to illustrate the consequences of not following the above guidance. Searching Google for "Journal of Internet Cataloging" (in June 2005) produced about 7,200 hits. Top of the list of search results was the *Journal of Internet Cataloging* home

TABLE 1

What	Why
Allocate concise identifiers to publications according to a consistent scheme.	In conjunction with the domain name, the file name (or other identifier) will form the URL of a publication that will uniquely identify it in on the Web. Ideally this will not be changed, so the naming scheme should allow for internal reorganisation or policy changes. A combination of prefix, letters, and numbers may be more robust than long, readable item names.
Ensure that every published document is owned by a specific person.	Specifying who is responsible for every published document makes it less likely that documents will be duplicated, overlooked, or become obsolete. Fostering a culture of digital curation can have intrinsic benefits for any organisation, and will also enhance the currency and value of Google indexing and searching.
Keep publications current.	It is always good practice and helpful to delete or archive old versions of documents, just as old notices should be removed from noticeboards. It is particularly important that they are removed from publicly accessible Web directories, so that they are not found and indexed by Google, thereby cluttering search results and confusing users.
Use XHTML rather than proprietary formats where possible.	Although Google can index PDF and Word documents, these formats are less desirable because they are proprietary rather than open, they require additional software or plugins, and the documents are usually larger and slower to access. Research has shown that Google does not index large documents in full (Price, 2004). Several other disadvantages of PDF have been outlined by Dawson & Wallis (2005).
Comply with accessibility standards.	Keeping document formats relatively simple makes them easier to maintain, more likely to comply with Web accessibility guidelines (W3C, 2004), and more accessible to search engine robots. Relatively complex features of Web pages, such as frames, forms, scripts, animations, logins, and session identifiers, are deterrents to Google indexing as well as to people with disabilities, so should only be used if essential for a specific service or application. They are rarely required for routine publication. Use of meaningful ALT text in <img> tags will enhance indexing as well as promote accessibility (Calishain & Dornfest, 2003).
Use relative internal links, not absolute links.	To minimise the likelihood of broken links. Collections can be moved and all internal links will still work.
Use style sheets to control formatting.	Document design can easily be changed. Removing unnecessary markup, e.g., in font control tags, improves the content-to-markup ratio, making documents easier for the Google software robots to index and helping achieve a higher ranking in Google search results. Guidance on use of CSS is given by W3C (2005), while some examples of simple and sophisticated CSS usage are given by the Glasgow Digital Library ebook collection (http://gdl.cdlr.strath.ac.uk/gdlebooks.html) and the CSS Zen Garden (http://www.csszengarden.com/) respectively.

page (http://www.internetcataloging.com/) and second was its table of contents. The very high relevance of these first two results to the search term illustrates the foundation on which Google has built its formidable reputation. Why would anyone wish to look beyond those top two results?

Following either link provides access to the table of contents of the journal from Volume 1 Number 1 in 1997 to Volume 5 Number 1 in 2001. There are no later issues available. This may easily lead the casual searcher to conclude that the journal has ceased publication, or that it no longer published tables of contents online. Neither is true. In fact the journal is alive and well, and accessible via The Haworth Press Online Catalog, which appears at numbers 3, 4, and 5 in the search results.

These results are far from ideal, but the fault does not lie with Google, which is doing a good job in ranking the most relevant results so highly. The appearance of obsolete and duplicate information in the search results is the responsibility of the publishers, who have failed to clear up after moving the content to a new location. Even in the new location, there appear to be two home pages for the journal, offering different information. Of course it is better to have some duplication than no information at all, but this type of duplication and retention of obsolete information, though very common on the Web, would not be regarded as acceptable in a library catalogue, and goes against the well-established principles of precision in information management. Rather than criticise Google for its failings (in this case and most others it works rather well), it is surely the responsibility of librarians, cataloguers, and publishers, large and small, to take more care in managing their own online publications. By doing so both publishers and users will benefit, in ensuring that searchers can more easily locate current publications.

These principles and guidelines for good publishing practice, as summarised and advocated above, are already well known and widely accepted, though often poorly implemented. However, relatively little has been published about optimising metadata, about republishing documents, or about the fine tuning of indexing by Google. These topics are addressed below.

METADATA OPTIMISATION

It is widely known that Google (along with most other search engines) does not make use of information held in HTML <meta> tags when indexing and ranking documents (de Groat, 2002; Sullivan, 2002). However, this does not mean that metadata is irrelevant to Google. On the contrary, it increases the significance of the one metadata element that Google does use: the HTML <title> tag.

Title tags are important for three reasons: firstly, because the Google search algorithms give them significant weight; secondly, because users see title tag contents highlighted in their search results; and thirdly because title tags become the default names for bookmarks in Web browsers. It therefore follows that anyone who wishes to encourage access to their publications should use the title tag carefully and consistently. When publishing online, librarians should make sure that every document and every Web page contains a title tag that applies accurately and specifically to the contents. To pursue the above example of the *Journal of Internet Cataloging*, the main reason that Google search results were so relevant was because the publishers had helpfully ensured that the journal title appeared in the title tag (so they had done part of their job well). Some further guidance on use of the title tag to enhance Google searching is given by Dawson (2004).

One particularly important consideration for metadata optimisation is the way in which long documents are split into separate sections or pages for online access. Views and practices on this vary considerably. Many publishers make complete documents available as single large PDF files, whereas others aim to limit information to a single screen so that users do not have to scroll down a page to see all its content. For example, Wilson and Landoni (2002), in their guidelines for electronic textbook design, recommend the use of short pages as they can "increase users' intake of information." However, they were concerned only with the usability of e-books (where the benefits of chunking content into very short pages are arguable), and did not consider the effects of chunking on resource discovery. As well as causing an unwieldy proliferation of pages, such fine chunking makes it less likely that pages will be located via Google (as each one will have less content and fewer links) and also makes it more difficult to create accurate and meaningful title tags for each page. A better strategy is therefore to organise publications so that Web pages reflect the natural structure of the content. For example, a large ebook should be split into separate chapters, and perhaps into separate sections within chapters, but not divided further by paragraphs, and not organised by printed page, as paper pages usually represent an artifact of the printing process rather than inherent document structure. As well as enhancing usability and speed of access, chunking content by chapter or section allows title tags to be varied to include the titles of chapters or sections, along with the title of the overall work. This aspect of metadata optimisation is a significant aid to resource discovery via Google, as has been demonstrated by Dawson & Hamilton (2005). The process can be automated for large-scale publication of structured documents, so that it becomes highly cost-effective, although the mechanism for doing this varies according to context and is beyond the scope of this article.

THE REPUBLICATION PROCESS

The well-meaning slogan "cool URLs don't change" has not permeated far into the ranks of Webmasters and content managers. Reorganised Web sites and broken links seem as common as ever. Yet this is not surprising. There are often good reasons for moving documents and re-organising Web sites. Institutions change, people come and go, departments merge and split, and publications need to be updated to reflect new policies and realities. Most Web publishing is by nature volatile. However, this is bad news for Web searchers, as links to old locations persist in Google indexes long after the content has been moved or deleted. Solutions to the problem do exist but are often overlooked. A brief step-by-step guide to moving, renaming, or republishing document collections is therefore given below. This is intended to inform and encourage librarians and others to play their part in reducing the persistent problem of broken links, and thereby improving the value of search results. Note that this guidance applies *only if the documents are being re-named or restructured*. If the content is simply being updated, using the same file names and structure, then the problem of broken links does not arise and the guidance is not applicable.

Step 1. Publish the new collection to a new directory or folder on the Web server, while leaving the old version in place, so that there is temporary duplication.

Step 2. Add links to the publications in their new location, and remove all links to the old location, but leave the old collection in place on the Web server.

Step 3. Edit all the documents in the old folder to prevent them being indexed by Google, by inserting the relevant instructions to all Web crawlers (not just Google) into the <head> element of each Web page. This can be done by using any program that will do a global search-and-replace on all the files in a folder. For example, a simple macro could be used to locate

```
</head>
```

in every document and change it to:

```
<meta name="robots" content="noindex,nofollow">
</head>
```

Alternatively, if the documents are published via a content management system, then the relevant template needs to be changed to incorporate the new line, but it is important to ensure that the template only applies to the old documents.

This step will prevent all documents in the old folder from being indexed in future, but it does not remove references to them from the existing Google index. Searchers will therefore still be able to find the documents via Google, and links to them will still work. It is true that users will find the old versions, but *that is the only one available to Google users at this stage*, for second-stage publication of the new version has not yet occurred.

Step 4. Configure the Web server (e.g., IIS or Apache) so that any http connections to the old folder are redirected to the new one (this may require liaison with a Webmaster or system support personnel). It is possible to redirect all files within a folder to a single new location, or to redirect specific old files individually to specific new files. The latter option is more time-consuming but more helpful to users.

Step 5 (optional). In order to assess whether any individual redirection is required, use Google to find out which old pages are being linked to by external Web sites, by using the `link:` prefix in the search term, e.g. `link:gdl.cdlr.strath.ac.uk/redclyde`. The search results will display pages (internal and external) that link to the specified URL, and can be used to identify pages requiring individual redirection (although the results of using the `link:` prefix are not always comprehensive). An alternative strategy is to use a special-purpose program to automate individual redirection of old pages to new pages. This program will be server-dependent (for example, ISAPI_Rewrite for IIS or mod_rewrite for Apache) and will usually require the assistance of technical staff, but is worth considering if a large and heavily-used collection is being moved.

After carrying out step 4 or 5, users should be able to find the new documents via the old file locations, with no broken links. If implementation of redirects presents a problem, one solution is to use the PURL service (http://purl.oclc.org/) to maintain persistent identifiers and redirections.

Step 6. Search Google about once a week to see when the documents in the new location have been indexed, by typing in a relevant search term (e.g., a distinctive phrase from one of the documents) and noting the URLs displayed in search results. Once the indexing of new files has occurred then the old files can be removed, although the old folder and the redirections should be maintained for as long as links to old locations appear via Google.

Step 7. When it is clear that searching Google produces only links to the new publications, with none to the old versions, then the old folder, and the redirections, can be removed. However, this should only be done if there are no external links to the old collection. In practice, retaining long-term redirections should not cause any problems. The crucial issue is to maintain the link between the URL and the content, even if one or the other changes.

Although these procedures may sound complex, the whole process is conceptually fairly simple. This level of attention to detail should ensure that users do not get broken links when attempting to access the content, even after it has been moved. Rather than being frustrated by the inadequacies of Google and the preponderance of broken links, librarians can help the situation by taking greater responsibility for maintaining the effectiveness of Internet searching.

The above guidance draws on practical experience of reorganising, renaming, and republishing specific digital library collections, but it is not intended to be exhaustive, as there are different means of achieving the aims of persistent publishing. In practice, some types of republishing are simpler than others, and other issues not covered above may arise. A simple case study may serve to illustrate this. For example, owing to a change in policy as the Glasgow Digital Library expanded, it was decided to change the collection identifier prefix for the Springburn Virtual Museum from two characters ("sp") to six characters ("spring"). Applying the change was trivial–the collection identifier field in the database was changed manually, a global change was made to all the item identifiers in the database, and all the relevant image files (including backup copies) were renamed using a bulk renaming program. All the relevant documents were then recreated automatically from the database, with the new six-character prefix, and copied to the Web server. However, in this case the new files were copied to the same folder as the old files, so that *the main URL for the collection would be unchanged*. This was a simple case of renaming files within a single folder, with no content restructuring. The other steps outlined above were then followed, and the changeover occurred smoothly. A more common, and more complex, scenario involves the restructuring of large collections. In such cases it is advisable to keep the old and new collections separate rather than mix old and new files in the same folder structure.

CONTROLLING INDEXING BY GOOGLE

The guidance above recommends using:

```
<meta name="robots" content="noindex,nofollow">
```

tag to prevent old versions of Web pages from being indexed by search engine robots. This is a useful and effective tool for controlling publishing via Google, but its use is not limited to the republication process. Before describing how this tool may be used routinely in publishing, it is worth summarising the effects of the variations in syntax:

`<meta name="robots" content="index,follow">`	allows full robot access. This is the default, and is therefore redundant.
`<meta name="robots" content="noindex,follow">`	allows robots to follow links but not to index content. This allows precise control over indexing and can be very useful.
`<meta name="robots" content="index,nofollow">`	allows robots to index content but not follow links. This is less likely to be useful.
`<meta name="robots" content="noindex,nofollow">`	prevents robots from either indexing content or following links.

Use of these tags (especially the "noindex" option) is so simple and effective in controlling Web site indexing that the real difficulty is in deciding when to use them. The main value is in preventing unnecessary duplication, for if everything is indexed then duplication is likely, particularly where publishers try to be helpful by providing more than one route of access to the same content. However, it is not always obvious when to switch off indexing. The guidance offered below is therefore illustrative rather than prescriptive. The easiest way to illustrate the subtleties of controlling indexing is by using specific examples of handling different types of object within a digital library.

Example 1. Document text
Probable setting: index, follow
<http://gdl.cdlr.strath.ac.uk/100men/gm66.htm>

Normally, publishers will want the substantive content of any publication to be indexed, so that it can be readily located. The only reason for preventing indexing would be to limit access.

Example 2. Title pages
Probable setting: index, follow
<http://gdl.cdlr.strath.ac.uk/smihou/>

If all the text on a title page is repeated on substantive pages, then indexing both title page and text pages will produce duplication of search results. Despite this, indexing of title pages is recommended, because they are useful signposts to users, and because they attract more external links than other pages, so are likely to be ranked relatively highly in search results.

Example 3. Tables of contents
Probable setting: noindex, follow
<http://gdl.cdlr.strath.ac.uk/haynin/haynincontents.html>

If all the text on a table of contents page also appears in the full text of a document (or in the abstracts of journal articles), then there is no need for the table of contents to be indexed (users would prefer to go directly to the relevant text). However, if neither full text nor abstract are available online, then the table of contents should be indexed.

Example 4. Combined title and contents pages
Probable setting: index, follow
<http://gdl.cdlr.strath.ac.uk/minstr/>

If the same page serves as the title page and the table of contents page, then there are conflicting arguments. In such cases indexing is advisable, as a little duplication is better than no information.

Example 5. Chapter contents
Probable setting: index, follow
<http://gdl.cdlr.strath.ac.uk/keacam/keacam02.htm>

As well as a table of contents, some large documents, such as e-books, may have a contents page for each chapter or section. While the same argument against indexing can be applied as for the main table of contents, there is a subtle difference; the chapter itself may have a title. If the user's search term matches a word or phrase in the chapter title, then the best result is to display the chapter contents page, rather than any other occurrences of that term. It is also possible for the term to appear only in the chapter title but not in the text. Optimal results may not be possible in all cases, but it seems advisable to leave indexing on.

Example 6. Image wrapper pages
Probable setting: noindex,nofollow
<http://gdl.cdlr.strath.ac.uk/aspect/aspect2003/sld/a03sldgba01a.html>

Wrapper pages are commonly used to add branding and navigation to a collection of images. While Web browsers will happily display links to unwrapped jpegs or other image files, it is common practice to wrap such images inside a Web page offering a familiar identity and interface. If indexing is left on, such wrapper pages can add immensely to the clutter and duplication in search results. The problem is so well-known and long-standing (and so few people bother to control indexing) that Google has taken measures to counteract it by suppressing duplication in its search results (hence the common message *"In order to show you the most relevant results, we have omitted some entries very similar to [those] already displayed"*). While Google's deduplication is indeed helpful, a more robust and satisfactory solution is for information providers to prevent the problem arising by suppressing indexing of wrapper pages that have no unique text content.

Example 7. Back-of-book indexes
Probable setting: noindex,nofollow
<http://gdl.cdlr.strath.ac.uk/stecit/stecitindextopic.html>

Back-of-book indexes provide entry points and navigation for paper publications. They are not common in e-books or other online publications, and it may be thought that the prevalence of searching has rendered such indexes redundant. Yet research has shown that, where indexes exist, users both value them (Wilson & Landoni, 2002) and can find information more quickly using them than via searching (Barnum et al., 2004). But should the indexes themselves be indexed? Doing so does undoubtedly create redundancy, as most terms appearing in an index also appear in the full text. Yet one of the arts of manual indexing is to use index terms that do not appear in the text itself. If a user search term matches such an index term, and the index is not indexed, then no match will be found, even though the content is relevant. But indexes are designed for browsing, not searching. There are clearly arguments either way. On balance, perhaps it is not worth indexing indexes unless they are known to contain a significant proportion of terms that are not found in the full text. Judgment is best made after testing some illustrative search terms in specific cases.

Example 8. Subject indexes
Probable setting: index,nofollow
<http://gdl.cdlr.strath.ac.uk/subjects/gdlindexsubjects.html>

It is surprising that so few libraries or academic publishers provide access to their online publications via a controlled set of subject terms such as LCSH. Journal publishers routinely list issues in date order, and sometimes offer an author index, but rarely a subject index. Where a subject index does exist, the same considerations apply as to back-of-book indexes. However, the issue is not clear-cut. Preliminary evidence from the Glasgow Digital Library suggests that allowing subject indexes to be indexed by Google can increase the probability of relevant items being located via Google searches, even though the subject indexes are designed for browsing rather than searching. Again there is a balance to be struck between maximising resource discovery and minimising redundancy, and the best policy is not obvious. As controlled subject terms are less likely to appear in the full text than back-of-book index terms, there are probably stronger arguments for indexing subject indexes than back-of-book indexes.

Example 9. Multiple document formats
Probable setting: index,nofollow

If the same document is published in different formats, e.g., HTML and PDF or Word, it is hard to envisage any reason to index more than one version. However, the use of meta tags to suppress indexing will only work in HTML documents. An alternative method is therefore needed. One option is to include links to the alternative versions from the HTML version, along with the "nofollow" instruction to software robots. The disadvantage of this is that it will apply to all links, which may not be desirable. Another option is to store PDF and Word versions in a separate folder, and then prevent indexing of all documents in that folder by including the relevant instruction in a file called robots.txt at the top level of the Web server. For example, indexing of everything in a folder called "pdfs" could be suppressed by adding the two lines

```
User-agent: *
Disallow: /pdfs/
```

to the `robots.txt` file. This would require suitable access permissions and possible liaison with technical staff. Further information is available from <http://www.robotstxt.org/>.

PRINCIPLES OF INDEXING

The above examples show that once the mechanism for controlling indexing is understood, it becomes fairly simple to control. The difficulty lies in deciding what works best for users. In order to help decide what to index, some basic principles of Web indexing can be stated as follows:

- Any page that contains unique text content should be indexed.
- Duplication in search results should be avoided where possible.
- A little duplication is better than an empty result set.

In other words, while one match between search term and result might be optimal, two matches are better than none. These principles can then be applied to specific types of document as illustrated above. In a large collection it would be tedious to individually control indexing for every document, but this is not necessary. The main requirement is to be able to identify the distinct document types, and then to automate the process of index control. For example, if documents are automatically generated from a database or content management system, the program or template that controls output needs to be able to identify which type of document is being output, and to enable or suppress indexing in accordance with specific rules that reflect agreed indexing principles. This level of precision is perfectly achievable, but in practice requires some thought and testing to produce optimal results.

GOOGLE AS A LOCAL SEARCH ENGINE

The main point about "publishing via Google" is that it allows users to readily find relevant resources without having to know where to look (other than Google). However, having located a relevant Web site, users may wish to explore in more depth the resources available therein, by browsing or searching within a specific site. While this can be done from the Google home page, using the relevant syntax to restrict searching to a specific site, in practice few users do this. It therefore makes sense to consider using the facilities of Google to offer a local search service. Any Web site (or a section of a Web site) that is already indexed by Google can be made locally searchable by adding a search box and pre-limiting a Google search to a specific domain or folder. For example, adding the following markup to a Web page would limit all searches to the domain cdlr.strath.ac.uk:

```
<form method="get" action="http://www.google.com/search?">
<input type="text" name="q" size="30" maxlength="255" value="">
<input type="hidden" name="q" value="site:cdlr.strath.ac.uk">
<input type="submit" name="sa" value="Search">
</form>
```

Changing the third line to

```
<input type="hidden" name="q" value="inurl:cdlr.strath.ac.uk/pubs">
```

would restrict the search even further to the "pubs" folder of the same domain. (Much of the time, the `site:` and `inurl:` prefixes deliver the same result set, though Calishain & Dornfest (2003) assert that `inurl:` is generally more flexible.) This facility to restrict searches to specific folders is immensely useful, as it offers a simple means of making separate collections, or individual e-books, independently searchable. It does however require that the organisation of folders (directories) corresponds to the structure of collections.

While most large collections already have their own search facilities, these can be expensive to set up and maintain. In contrast, Google is quick and easy to set up as a local search service, it is easy to customise the display of search results, it is familiar to users, searches are very fast, and it is free. Furthermore, although Google makes no use of metadata other than titles, its relevance ranking usually works remarkably well, and the summaries are often useful. For example, searching the University of Strathclyde Web sites locally via Google for the very common word "library" (in 2005) produces over 18,000 matches, with the main university library top of the list and the next three being major library-related resources. The relevance ranking is excellent, and the result ordering is just what a collection manager or user might hope for. Google is evidently capable of performing effectively at a local level, despite the lack of metadata, just as it does on a global scale.

On the negative side, because Google does not use metadata, searches can not be limited to author, subject or date fields (it is possible to limit searches to titles, but relatively few users do this). While this may be acceptable for a large and irregular collection of documents and departments, such as a university, it is far less acceptable for a tightly-focused and well-catalogued collection such as a journal archive. Search options are limited to those provided by Google, so useful features such as stemming are not supported. And perhaps more critically, the indexing of content is irregular, with a time lag (usually up to one month) between publication and searchability. Perhaps the biggest disadvantage is that collection managers do not have full control of the search algorithms, but this may be a price worth paying for a highly cost-effective service.

Some of the other limitations can be overcome using a combination of ingenuity and diligence. For example, field searching can be simulated by ensuring that the field name appears next to the content (e.g., Author: Hovis Presley), and then embedding the field name in the search form, in the same way that domain names can be embedded in forms to restrict searching to a specific site. The results are not as precise as genuine field searching but may well be sufficient for most purposes.

If Google is used to provide a local search service, the issues of republication, metadata optimisation, and indexing control become even more important, because duplication, inaccuracies, and inconsistencies are far more noticeable in a small result set. Furthermore, users are more likely to judge these as being the responsibility of the local institution rather than an inevitable consequence of searching across the whole of the Web.

CONCLUSIONS

It is easy to criticise Google for not allowing the same precision as library catalogues and specialist databases, for returning too many results, with too much duplication, for including results that are out of date, irrelevant or superficial, and for failing to index the "invisible Web" (Sherman & Price, 2001). While these criticisms are valid up to a point, they are not so much criticisms of Google itself, which offers a superb large-scale service, as criticisms of those who publish carelessly on the Web, by leaving old or duplicate documents lying around for Google to find, by moving or deleting documents without leaving any redirection, or by discouraging Google software robots from indexing their content. Librarians and other information professionals must take their share of this criticism unless they follow sound procedures to optimise publication via Google. This article has outlined the issues and shown how the overall effectiveness of Google can be improved, not by making changes to search algorithms or metadata standards, but simply by behaving professionally and taking care to publish responsibly.

By improving their own practices in online publishing, and understanding how and why these affect the retrievability of publications via Google, librarians will eventually be in a better position to educate others to follow similar sound practices. They will therefore be developing a new role for themselves–that of disseminating good practice in information provision as well as in information retrieval–and will be contributing to the broad view of information literacy that incorporates information management and technological fluency, as advocated by writers such as Bundy (2004) and Warnken (2004).

In the long term, the increased precision of resource description and indexing that arise from enhanced online publishing will improve the match between search terms and search results, so will ultimately improve information retrieval on the Web. As more and more people become electronic publishers, there will be benefits for both information providers and information seekers in extending e-publishing literacy.

REFERENCES

Barnum, C., Henderson, E., Hood, A., Jordan, R. (2004). Index versus Full-text Search: A Usability Study of User Preference and Performance, *Technical Communication*, Vol. 51 No. 2, pp. 185-206.

Becker, N. J. (2003). Google in perspective: Understanding and enhancing student search skills, *New Review of Academic Librarianship*, Vol. 9, pp. 84-100.

Bundy, A. (2004). One essential direction: Information literacy, information technology fluency. *Journal of eLiteracy*, Vol. 1, pp 7-22.

Calishain, T. and Dornfest, R. (2003). *Google Hacks*, O'Reilly, Sebastopol, CA.

Dawson, A. (2004). Creating metadata that works for digital libraries and Google. *Library Review*, Vol. 53 No. 7, pp. 347-350. <http://cdlr.strath.ac.uk/pubs/dawsona/ad200402.htm>.

Dawson, A. and Hamilton, V. (2005). Optimising metadata to make high-value content more accessible to Google users. *Journal of Documentation*. In press.

Dawson, A. and Wallis, J. (2005). Twenty issues in ebook creation, *Against the Grain*, Vol. 17 No. 1, pp. 18-24.

De Groat, G. (2002). Perspectives on the Web and Google: Monika Henziger, Director of Research, Google, *Journal of Internet Cataloging*, Vol. 5 No. 1, pp. 17-28.

Dempsey. L. (2004). The three stages of library search. *Cilip Update*, November 2004. <http://www.cilip.org.uk/publications/updatemagazine/archive/archive2004/november/lorcan.htm>.

Devine, J. and Egger-Sider, F. (2004). Beyond Google: The invisible web in the academic library, *The Journal of Academic Librarianship*, Vol. 30 No. 4, pp. 265-269.

Markland, M. (2005). Does the student's love of the search engine mean that high quality online academic resources are being missed? *Performance Measurement and Metrics*, Vol. 6 No. 1, pp. 19-31.

Price, G. (2004). A couple of comments About Google. <http://www.pandia.com/post/020-2.html>.

Rumsey, S. (2005). Search interfaces for dummies? Paper presented at *LILAC 2005: Librarians Information Literacy Annual Conference*. <http://www.cilip.org.uk/groups/csg/csg%5Filg/Lilac05/Papers/rumsey.pdf>.

Rumsfeld, D. (2002). Briefing for United States Department of Defense, 12 Feb 2002.

Sherman, C. and Price, G. (2001). *The invisible web: Uncovering information sources search engines can't see*. CyberAge Books. <http://www.invisible-web.net/>.

Sullivan, D. (2002). *Search Engine Features for Webmasters*. <http://searchenginewatch.com/webmasters/article.php/2167891>.

W3C (2004). Web Content Accessibility Guidelines 2.0. <http://www.w3.org/TR/WCAG20/>.

W3C (2005). Cascading style sheets home page. <http://www.w3.org/Style/CSS/>.

Warnken, P. (2004). The impact of technology on information literacy education in libraries. *The Journal of Academic Librarianship*, Vol. 30 No. 2, pp. 151-156.

Wilson, R. and Landoni, M. (2002). *Electronic textbook design guidelines*. <http://ebooks.strath.ac.uk/eboni/guidelines/>.

Google and Privacy

Paul S. Piper

SUMMARY. Google has emerged as the preeminent Internet search engine, but more important, it has achieved an iconic status. It is solidly entrenched in our language and popular culture. But there is a darker side to Google. Google collects personal information about its users, and it aggregates third party information more effectively than many third world governments. While there has been no abuse (that we know of) by Google of personal information, that potential exists, and there are numerous instances of third parties using Google to aggregate personal information for dubious purposes. *[Article copies available for a fee from The Haworth Document Delivery Service: 1-800-HAWORTH. E-mail address: <docdelivery@haworthpress.com> Website: <http://www.HaworthPress.com> © 2005 by The Haworth Press, Inc. All rights reserved.]*

KEYWORDS. Google, privacy, Internet search engine

They know your name, your phone number, your address, your e-mail, your computer's IP. They know the structure of your family, their income, their age. They know that two weeks ago your hot-tub was being cleaned. They know you are concerned about colon cancer. They

Paul S. Piper is Reference Librarian, College of Arts and Sciences, Western Washington University, Bellingham, WA 98225 (E-mail: paul.piper@wwu.edu).

[Haworth co-indexing entry note]: "Google and Privacy." Piper, Paul S. Co-published simultaneously in *Internet Reference Services Quarterly* (The Haworth Information Press, an imprint of The Haworth Press, Inc.) Vol. 10, No. 3/4, 2005, pp. 195-203; and: *Libraries and Google®* (ed: William Miller, and Rita M. Pellen) The Haworth Information Press, an imprint of The Haworth Press, Inc., 2005, pp. 195-203. Single or multiple copies of this article are available for a fee from The Haworth Document Delivery Service [1-800-HAWORTH, 9:00 a.m. - 5:00 p.m. (EST). E-mail address: docdelivery@haworthpress.com].

Available online at http://www.haworthpress.com/web/IRSQ
doi:10.1300/J136v10n03_17

know you like jazz and alt country. They know you like wet T-shirt photos, and S&M. They know your credit rating. They know that you flew to Milwaukee last November, that your son plays soccer, and that your spouse drives a BMW. They know you favored Kerry over Bush, that you support leftist and environmental causes, that you're a member of Moveon.org. They like your blog. They have a silly name.

The above, of course, is fiction. Or is it? How much does Google know about you? Or perhaps, a more apt question is, how much could they know about you if they wanted, or needed to? Richard Smith, former chief technology officer of the Privacy Foundation (http://www.privacyfoundation.org) cited in a *Houston Chronicle* article (Jesdanun, 2004) said "Google makes it easy to connect all the dots. I think Google is the biggest privacy invader on the planet." Smith is not alone. Daniel Brandt of Public Information Research, Inc., and owner of the Web site Google Watch (www.google-watch.org/), is even more critical, nominating Google for the Big Brother award in 2003. Far more moderate in their assessment, many other people still question the issue of privacy with concern to Google. A phrase search in Google of "Google privacy" turns up around 13,800 hits, and this obviously doesn't include all the variations possible. Interestingly, the same search in Yahoo results in around 114,000 hits.

I first began thinking seriously about this issue several years ago. One slow evening at the Reference Desk, a librarian I worked with stepped back from her computer and told me that she was appalled. I asked her why. She said she had just learned that if you type a phone number into Google, and it is not an unlisted number, the search provides a name, address and maps to that person's house. In that particular case, she had just entered her own number, and was concerned about her own privacy. She didn't like the fact that anyone she gave her phone number to could locate her. It might be argued that standard reference tools like the Polk Directory can provide the same information. But obviously the Google feature is infinitely more powerful because of its ease and pervasiveness. And Google's service offers two features that the Polk Directory couldn't dream of offering–it provides satellite images and gives you a map.

When Google recently used its Keyhole acquisition to begin showing satellite photos of locations, a number of people reacted, some quite violently. The buzz on many blogs and Internet discussion groups, as well as in the mainstream press showed a high level of concerned interest. Face it, most people would rather not think about the fact that little spheres are arcing overhead photographing everything below them, some with remarkable clarity. Resolution of the Google product varies, and some locations don't reveal much but a blur, but a friend of mine swore he could see a wheelbarrow in his Capitol Hill yard. Obviously, a "service" such as this could be interpreted as an assault on privacy. But should it? As Google argues, these images are available other places (Mapquest and Microsoft's Terraserver). They are not secret. But again, it's a case of access. Google makes it ridiculously easy to find and use them.

There are a few scenarios we need to consider with regard to Google and privacy. The first is that Google is deliberately gathering extensive information about its users, which translates into many millions of people worldwide (150 million plus queries a day). We have to conjecture why this might be, and the choices range from marketing to product enhancement to unadulterated paranoia. I have witnessed enough of Google's corporate strategy, as well as had personal interactions, at conferences, with both Sergey Brin and Larry Page, to think that Google is legitimately attempting to offer the finest and most flexible Internet search product it can. But that's simply my opinion, and there exist some troubling questions.

Google amasses a vast array of personal information. As noted on www.google-watch.org/, "The privacy struggle, which includes both the old issue of consumer protection and this new issue of government surveillance, means that the question of how Google treats the data it collects from users becomes critical. Given that Google is so central to the web, whatever attitude it takes toward privacy has massive implications for the rest of the web in general, and for other search engines in particular."

When you search Google a cookie is placed on your hard drive. This cookie assigns a unique identification number to your computer. Unless you have disabled cookies, which in this case would render Google unworkable, for every search you do Google records and retains the unique identifier, the computer IP (Internet Protocol) address, the date and time of your search, your search terms, and the configuration of your browser. They retain this data indefinitely.

The Google Toolbar expands this ability. If installed on your PC, Google Toolbar records every Web site you actually visit, and sends that information back to Google, whether you are using the toolbar to search the Web or not. This information is used to supplement its page rank data, which is at the center of Google's search algorithm. And Google is certainly not alone in using spyware. According to WebRoot, the makers of SpySweeper, there are over 6,000 forms of spyware on the Internet today. Google warns you of this capability, and allows you to disable this feature, which is in the "Advanced Features," when you install the toolbar.

While there is no evidence that Google has ever attempted to match IP numbers to names, it is not difficult to do. And Google will not reveal if its records have ever been subpoenaed. The key question is, why does Google need this information, and what is it doing with it?

In its privacy statement (Google, 2005), Google claims to "recognize that privacy is an important issue, so we design and operate our services with the protection of your privacy in mind." It then lists all the types of information it gathers.

The "Information Sharing" section of this policy states that "We do not *rent or sell* your personally identifying information to other companies or individuals, unless we have your consent. We may *share* such information in any of the following limited circumstances [italics mine]:

- We have your consent.
- We provide such information to trusted businesses or persons for the sole purpose of processing personally identifying information on our behalf. When this is done, it is subject to agreements that oblige those parties to process such information only on our instructions and in compliance with this Privacy Policy and appropriate confidentiality and security measures.
- We conclude that we are required by law or have a good faith belief that access, preservation or disclosure of such information is reasonably necessary to protect the rights, property or safety of Google, its users or the public."

Note the key wording at the beginning of this disclosure–they don't "sell or rent," but they can "share" this information.

Two additional clauses are:

- "We take appropriate security measures to protect against unauthorized access to or unauthorized alteration, disclosure or destruction of data."
- "We restrict access to your personally identifying information to employees who need to know that information in order to operate, develop or improve our services."

But the statement does not say why Google collects this data, except to note: "We use this information to operate, develop and improve our services."

While the above statements give some people pause, Google is a free service, and certainly is not forcing anyone to use it. And in reality, many libraries collect information that could be construed as being equally, or more damaging. But libraries have always had a huge commitment to First Amendment rights. And there have been numerous cases where libraries have gone to court, and fought successfully to protect those individual rights. Google, on the other hand, is a private business, and while it may be well-intentioned, it has no altruistic or philosophical commitment to First Amendment and privacy issues. It is in business to make money.

What if Google decided to share this information with the government? Would you want your searching behavior known? What if the Department of Homeland Security asked Google to provide all it knows about certain persons? Or the IPs of every search that included certain terms? Would Google go to court to protect the user's rights? I don't think so.

Of course there are several obvious ways to evade this data-collection, including disabling cookies; using public computers at libraries, Internet cafes, etc., which make it much more difficult, if not impossible to trace use; using an anonymous proxy service; or using a different search engine. But who bothers, really. The serious criminals probably do, but the rest of us don't. And yet there have been numerous cases where searching behavior is used to prosecute people, usually in government or corporate settings where computer use is highly regulated.

Another Google technology that originally raised red flags with regard to privacy was Gmail. Take this quote, direct from the About Gmail page (http://gmail.google.com/gmail/help/about_privacy.html): "Google scans the text of Gmail messages in order to filter spam and detect viruses, just as all major webmail services do. Google also uses this scanning technology to deliver targeted text ads and other related information. This is completely automated and involves no humans."

While it may be true that other major webmail providers filter mail using text analysis (I couldn't find proof of this!), none of the other major free mail providers—Yahoo Mail and Hotmail—has anywhere near the arsenal of technology and content at its disposal that Google does.

An alternate way of looking at Google and privacy is to analyze one's (or Google's) ability to readily aggregate an array of information about someone in a very short time. This is accomplished by effectively searching the extraordinary warehouse of personal (and non-personal) information on the Internet. The content of the Internet, of course, is not

Google's triumph, nor its fault. Google simply does a very good job at finding and consolidating this information.

This morning's *Doonesbury* had Zonker stumbling onto Trump University while he was Googling Trump's latest wife. The habit of Googling individuals is now extremely widespread, and with many collegiate, and post-collegiate populations it's *de rigeur* after meeting a new friend. The array of material about people on the Internet is truly staggering, and runs the gamut from news stories, articles, personal Web sites, blog and newsgroup postings to prison records, medical information, and financial information, as well as the opinions of other people. The Internet made Paris Hilton a celebrity; it could also tell you your new boyfriend was a gay fetishist in San Francisco several years ago.

I remember one anecdote while teaching an Internet literacy class, which I do yearly. During the second class I had everyone Google themselves. The results were mixed. Some students found newspaper articles of sporting or debate triumphs, others found information about their parents or relatives that mentioned them, others found nothing. One woman gave a slight shriek, turned crimson, then closed the browser window. When I asked her a few minutes later what she'd found, she wouldn't say. I pursued the matter no further. But at the end of class, in a personal evaluation I had the students do, she commented on the extraordinary power of the Internet to never forget. She wrote that some people would like to forget things they have done.

Given the fact that Google caches Web pages, and that the Internet Archive, Memory Hole, and other sites deliberately archive Web pages, it is getting more difficult to get rid of information on the Web. Not that this is bad. Archiving Internet information is potentially as important as archiving any other information.

There was another case recently in Canada, where a man apparently forced his three-year-old daughter to drink water containing GHB, otherwise known as the date rape drug. The December 14, 2004 *Vancouver Sun*, incensed at the gag order the RCMP placed on the case, released specific details of the man, including that he had a resumé posted on the Internet. Bloggers began having a field day locating the man's true identity using Google (http://www.darrenbarefoot.com/archives/001521.html), and many succeeded.

In a recent telephone interview with John Soma, (Soma, 2005) a professor of law, and director of the Privacy Center at Denver University, Professor Soma made some excellent points concerning Google and privacy. His view was that the loss of individual privacy is a reality of contemporary technology, and Google simply does technology better. The current evolution of technology is so rapid that a parallel co-evolution of checks and balances is not keeping up.

Dr. Soma wonders whether Google has any responsibility for its content. Being a free Internet service, Google has deliberately tried to distance itself from discussions of this type, but it hasn't been entirely successful. It has acted to ban certain types of advertising (guns and Internet gambling, among others), remove egregious hate sites (jewwatch. com), and certain news sources (*National Zeitung*, a neo-Fascist newspaper). In a strongly worded statement in an Internetnews.com article, Google spokesman Steve Langdon stated: "Google News does not allow hate content. If we are made aware of articles that contain hate content, we will remove them" (Kuchinskas, 2005). One might be tempted to ask then, why the American Nazi Party, and many other white power sites, still appear in Google searches? Obviously, this is a huge can of worms that it is not in a rush to tip over.

Yet is it unreasonable to expect a service provider, even a free one, to enforce content standards? PubMed, the free Medline hosted by the National Library of Medicine has set exceedingly strict standards for its service. Database providers in Europe are often criminally responsible for wrongful information. Obviously, Google could limit its content to reputable sites, and in fact, it has done so to some extent by creating subsets of its database such as Google Scholar and Google Uncle Sam (assuming the government is neutral and authoritative). But if it attempted to do this with the primary index, it would no longer be Google, and it would quickly fall from the top of the search engine heap.

Privacy itself is a complex concept, and not immune from scrutiny. While many citizens are decrying the loss of personal privacy, many businesses and governments, in these post-Enron, post 9/11 days, are making sure their operations are more private. No one is successfully tracking the number of Web sites the Federal Government has removed or altered since 9/11. Yet the federal government has taken steps, via the Patriot Act and other legislation, to legally violate personal privacy.

Advocates for a truly open informational grid argue that as long as information is in restricted hands, egregious things can and will happen. Advocates of a more open system would say "you can watch me, but I can also watch you." An excellent article framing the debate between open information versus privacy, and the role of technology in both, is Sheldon Pascotti's "Are We Doomed Yet?" (Pascotti, 2003).

A demonstrative example of more open approach to privacy involves Google's new Keyhole satellite imaging feature. Some environmentalists are now turning this potential privacy violation around, and touting its potential to track illegal clearcutting and mining, oil spills, and other environmental catastrophes.

An irony of the Google era is the rush, often legislative, to suppress electronic versions of public documents. The Florida legislature, for example, passed a bill to close autopsy reports, which had previously been open in their paper form. Pennsylvania's Department of Transportation has reduced the amount of information it releases about traffic accidents, and Federal courts debate the issue of leaving open electronically filed court documents (the paper copies are still open) (Shields, 2001).

And even the Department of Health and Human Services patient privacy act, a well-supported means of curbing unauthorized sharing of patient medical records, has some unforeseen consequences. Several newspaper associations in Washington (Allied Daily Newspapers of Washington and the Washington Newspaper Publishers Association) filed an objection. Members claimed that in-depth investigative journalism, such as the *Seattle Times'* article examining deaths in an experimental cancer treatment program, would now be nearly impossible. Whether privacy is valid or restrictive often depends on point of view. The forces of open or transparent access, and those who would prefer to keep the prying eyes out, both have compelling arguments. And situated in the center is Google, a tool whose very structure and operation position it solidly in the center of the debate.

While the question of privacy is a complex and philosophical one, the fact remains that Google is both a direct harvester of sensitive personal information, and a comprehensive aggregator of personal information made accessible by third parties. The unification of these two extremely powerful functions into one entity creates a tool many totalitarian governments would envy. How Google chooses to use the information it gathers, and whether it chooses to claim responsibility over its content remain to be seen. As with numerous technological advances, once the cat is let out of the bag, it is virtually impossible to get it back in.

REFERENCES

"Google Privacy Policy" 07/01/2004 <http://www.google.com/privacy.html>.

Jesdanun, Anick. "In age of Google, privacy issues get lost in the search." *The Houston Chronicle* March 28, 2004, 8.

Kuchinskas, Susan. "Google Axes Hate News." *Internetnews.com* March 23, 2005. <http://www.internetnews.com/xSP/article.php/3492361>.

Pacotti, Sheldon. "Are We Doomed Yet?" *Salon.com* March 31, 2003. <http://www.salon.com/tech/feature/2003/03/31/knowledge/print.html>.

Shields, Todd. "Don't Go There." *Editor and Publisher* May 7, 2001, 13-16.

Soma, John. Personal Interview, 4/19/05.

Image:
Google's Most Important Product

Ron Force

SUMMARY. In a few short years, Google has become one of the world's best known brands. Its strategies to preserve the brand image pose a challenge for information professionals who attempt to present Google's capabilities in a factual manner. *[Article copies available for a fee from The Haworth Document Delivery Service: 1-800-HAWORTH. E-mail address: <docdelivery@haworthpress.com> Website: <http://www.HaworthPress.com> © 2005 by The Haworth Press, Inc. All rights reserved.]*

KEYWORDS. Google, brand image

In a few short years, Google has advanced from an interesting project by a couple of Stanford Electrical Engineering graduate students to a company with a larger capitalization than Time-Warner. Its popular image, as the "gatekeeper of the world's knowledge,"[1] poses a challenge to information professionals who are aware of the limitations of the medium and the true extent of the "world's knowledge." In order to deal with faculty and students who are "true believers," it's necessary to un-

Ron Force is Dean of Library Services, University of Idaho, P.O. Box 442350, Moscow, ID 83844 (E-mail: rforce@uidaho.edu).

[Haworth co-indexing entry note]: "Image: Google's Most Important Product." Force, Ron. Co-published simultaneously in *Internet Reference Services Quarterly* (The Haworth Information Press, an imprint of The Haworth Press, Inc.) Vol. 10, No. 3/4, 2005, pp. 205-209; and: *Libraries and Google®* (ed: William Miller, and Rita M. Pellen) The Haworth Information Press, an imprint of The Haworth Press, Inc., 2005, pp. 205-209. Single or multiple copies of this article are available for a fee from The Haworth Document Delivery Service [1-800-HAWORTH, 9:00 a.m. - 5:00 p.m. (EST). E-mail address: docdelivery@haworthpress.com].

Available online at http://www.haworthpress.com/web/IRSQ
© 2005 by The Haworth Press, Inc. All rights reserved.
doi:10.1300/J136v10n03_18

derstand how Google reached its status as a verb, and how it maintains its brand image. The image of the smart, offbeat, innocuous, and "cool" company is vital for a corporation that has potential access to unprecedented amounts of personal information,[2] and depends on public trust to continue its primary source of income: delivery of advertising.

Google was certainly not the first company to comprehensively crawl the Web. AltaVista[3] was well known in the middle '90s and was beloved by information professionals since its search interface had the familiar bells and whistles–Boolean search, date limitation, etc. Search results were relevance-ranked by the search criteria. Google, on the other hand, moved the search machinery behind the scenes. Instead of a busy search form with multiple options, an almost blank screen with just a whimsical logo and a plain entry box greeted the user. A few key words almost instantaneously returned a huge result set, and magically, what seemed to be the most relevant result appeared in the first few items, thanks to *V.C. PageRank*, the patented algorithm which ordered the search by the number of links to the page and other factors. Even information professionals waxed enthusiastic over the clean and uncluttered results.[4] The public soon made "Google" synonymous with "search," to the point that commercial library vendors were being urged to make their interfaces "more like Google."

Google's interface parallels the search strategies naturally adopted by the public. I first noticed this back in the '80s, when the first databases were being released on CD-ROM. Because our library had only one workstation, we were concerned to encourage efficient searches, so we had a mandatory course for those who wished to search, and taught the Venn diagram, Boolean logic, and the use of the thesaurus and descriptors. The public took the course, but when allowed to search independently, immediately abandoned all they'd been taught, entered one or two key words, and browsed the results for relevant articles. Google was a good fit for this instinctual searching, and the fact that something relevant almost always appeared on the first page immediately made other Internet search portals (with the possible exception of Yahoo) also-rans.

Venture capital adopted Google, and the new company began to spin out products: Froogle (sales catalog search), News (without selection by human hands), Google Toolbar, Mail, Scholar, all released as "betas" with a simple news release announcement. Unlike dot-com start-ups of five years before, the products just appeared, with no advance word-of-mouth and seemingly no commercial purpose. There were only a few stumbles, such as when it was revealed that the mail engine scanned messages to trigger appropriate advertising messages.

Still, Google seemed to be immune to the negative image that had over-taken Microsoft when it became dominant in operating systems.

Google carried the image into its initial public offering, shunning the usual offer through investment banks for an open auction format to allow ordinary investors to get a crack at what would ordinarily be restricted to the wealthy and connected. The founders did, however, retain "super shares" which keep decision-making in their hands to prevent the company's direction from being influenced by Wall Street.[5] Google continued its quirky image when meeting with investors, having the group addressed by their corporate chef instead of the Chief Financial Officer.

Up to this point librarians had a "love-hate" affair with Google. It became indispensable at the reference desk, while librarians tried to convince undergraduates that not everything worth knowing was indexed by Google. The relationship with the company was made even more ambivalent by two beta projects: Google Print and Google Scholar.

Google Print reached agreement with several publishers to produce a searchable database of full text books. Initially, Google had only a limited number of publishers, but in December 2004, announced working relationships with major research libraries to digitize their collections. This news was greeted by the general public and the news media as the answer to that often asked question "When can I access all the books in the Library of Congress?" Commentators speculated that local libraries would become obsolete. However, on further questioning of the library partners it became apparent that:

1. For the most part, only selected parts of the collections would be scanned,
2. Copyright would limit public full-text access to pre-1923 works and,
3. It would take at least ten years to complete.

By this time, the public had internalized the initial good news, and didn't want to hear from the killjoy librarians.

Google Scholar was introduced following a similar pattern, skipping the news release and relying on word of mouth (or blog) to let people know that they have an index to scholarly resources that includes citation indexing, a feature previously limited to expensive, proprietary indexes. Once again, the general (academic) public greeted it as the Second Coming, enthusing over its ease of use and the large number of citations it produced. One faculty member commented that it even offered one-click access to the full text! His enthusiasm wasn't curbed when I told him that the full text had nothing to do with Google, but with IP recognition and the large amount of money the library paid to publishers for online subscriptions.

As expert searchers began to review Google Scholar, it became apparent that there were huge gaps in the data, missing articles, even from partner publishers that had let Google crawl their data base.[6] The largest scientific publisher had chosen not to participate–not surprising, since it was selling a competing product. Searches turned up items that could hardly be described as "scholarly."[7] Google, of course, didn't reveal where the data came from, the extent of the database, or how it determined content. Further reviews after Google had added an advanced search turned up even more strange results, such as a search against a subset producing more hits than the same search against the entire database.[8]

Google has an image as a quirky company that's not like other corporations. Founder Sergy Brin's guiding principle, "Don't be evil," appears to set the company on a high moral plane. However, Google is also known throughout the industry for its secrecy. This secrecy and reluctance to publicize its methods and technology means that for users, Google becomes a *tabula rasa* upon which users can project their hopes and assumptions. And, because Google "isn't evil," they must be "the best." This leads to an officer of the university proposing to base evaluations of tenure candidates' research on the number of citations their articles received in Google Scholar. When the database's anomalies and omissions were pointed out, he replied that the results seemed still "pretty close," a bad example of the "good enough" syndrome. It's one thing for an undergraduate paper to miss some references, worse to lose a grant because of pertinent omissions, but to base an important career decision on deeply flawed data would be "evil."

This is not to imply that Google would deliberately misrepresent a defective product. However, the reality is that Google obtains 99% of its revenue from search advertising.[9] Products like Google Print and Google Scholar are designed to draw potential "click throughs" to their service. Constantly generating "cool" products, whether or not they generate revenue directly enhances the brand image, and keeps the stock price on an upward trajectory despite the already astronomical price-earnings ratio.

In the end, image *is* Google's most important product.

NOTES

1. "Google at the Gate." *American Libraries,* 36, no. 3 (March 2005), p. 41.

2. "Google Growth Yields Privacy Fear." *Wired News,* (July 17, 2005). <http://www.wired.com/news/archive/0,2618,2005-07-17,00.html>.

3. <http://www.altavista.com> (since changed to "look like Google").

4. Kirkpatrick, David. "What's a Google? A Great Search Engine, That's What." *Fortune,* 140, no. 9, (November 8, 1999), p. 298.

5. Webb, Cynthia, L. "Google Takes a Walk down Wall Street." *Washington Post,* April 30, 2004 (accessed via LexisNexis June 13, 2005).

6. Jacso, Peter. "Google Scholar Beta." *Peter's Digital Reference Shelf,* December 2004. <http://www.galegroup.com/free_resources/reference/peter>.

7. Wleklinski, Joann M. "Studying Google Scholar: Wall to Wall Coverage?" *Online,* 29, no. 3, (May/June 2005), p.22-26.

8. Jacso, Peter "Google Scholar (Redux). *Peter's Digital Reference Shelf,* June 2005. <http://www.galegroup.com/free_resources/reference/peter/>.

9. "MSN Draws Its Sword in Search Battle with Google." Yahoo! News, (February 14, 2005). <http://www.morevisibility.com/news_industry/2005/021005_Yahoo.html>.

Keeping Up with Google:
Resources and Strategies
for Staying Ahead of the Pack

Michael J. Krasulski
Steven J. Bell

SUMMARY. Librarians need to be the Google experts in their community since it enables librarians to be more competent in educating users. To keep up with the developments of Google the authors reviewed eleven Web sites and blogs and create a strategy for keeping up using these sites. Three are highly recommended for a keeping-up regimen. The authors also suggest that librarians either use search engine alerting services or RSS technology to deliver news feeds into a news aggregator in their keeping-up regimen. *[Article copies available for a fee from The Haworth Document Delivery Service: 1-800-HAWORTH. E-mail address: <docdelivery@haworthpress.com> Website: <http://www.HaworthPress.com> © 2005 by The Haworth Press, Inc. All rights reserved.]*

Michael J. Krasulski is Coordinator of Public Services (E-mail: krasulskim@philau.edu); and Steven J. Bell is Director of the Library (E-mail: bells@philau.edu), both at Philadelphia University, Paul J. Gutman Library, School House Lane and Henry Avenue, Philadelphia, PA 19144.

All the sites reviewed were accessed during the month of April 2005.

The authors appreciate the advice received from their colleague Gary Price.

Google® is a Registered Service Mark of Google, Inc., Mountain View, California. *Libraries and Google®* is an independent publication offered by The Haworth Press, Inc., Binghamton, New York, and is not affiliated with, nor has it been authorized, sponsored, endorsed, licensed, or otherwise approved by, Google, Inc.

[Haworth co-indexing entry note]: "Keeping Up with Google: Resources and Strategies for Staying Ahead of the Pack." Krasulski, Michael J., and Steven J. Bell. Co-published simultaneously in *Internet Reference Services Quarterly* (The Haworth Information Press, an imprint of The Haworth Press, Inc.) Vol. 10, No. 3/4, 2005, pp. 211-223; and: *Libraries and Google®* (ed: William Miller, and Rita M. Pellen) The Haworth Information Press, an imprint of The Haworth Press, Inc., 2005, pp. 211-223. Single or multiple copies of this article are available for a fee from The Haworth Document Delivery Service [1-800-HAWORTH, 9:00 a.m. - 5:00 p.m. (EST). E-mail address: docdelivery@haworthpress.com].

Available online at http://www.haworthpress.com/web/IRSQ
© 2005 by The Haworth Press, Inc. All rights reserved.
doi:10.1300/J136v10n03_19

KEYWORDS. Google, current awareness, blogs, keeping up, professional development

INTRODUCTION

Librarian perceptions of and attitudes towards Google, the search engine, are as diverse as the ever-growing number of products and services offered by Google, the company. Google-adoring librarians may support the complete and utter "Googlization" of library databases so that every search is a "Google experience." Other librarians choose to resist "Googlization" and instead favor keeping library database interfaces exactly as they are. However, the vast majority of librarians are schizophrenic about Google and librarians can shift their position on any given day. Because Google is so popular, and because it currently dominates the search engine landscape, the one position that none of us can afford to take is choosing to ignore altogether what Google is doing and plans to do. It is no exaggeration to suggest that librarians need to be Google experts.

Becoming a Google expert requires an appropriate strategy for keeping up with Google. This article examines a collection of resources and strategies that we think will enable any librarian to develop an effective regimen for a "Google Keep Up" strategy. The resources are reviewed, and the goal of this article is to identify the qualities of each so that librarians can choose those that best fit their needs and available time for keeping-up activity. We conclude by recommending a strategy that we believe would provide a good baseline for every librarian who can benefit from doing a better job of keeping up with Google. Of course, we hope many readers will choose to go beyond that level because if nothing else, for the foreseeable future, keeping up with Google is a necessary and fun way to spend a part of each day.

WHY KEEP UP WITH GOOGLE?

Regardless of what position a librarian takes on Google, it certainly is incumbent upon every library professional to achieve as high a level of expertise about Google as is possible. Why is that? We can think of four good reasons:

- To take full advantage of the search system
- To establish a position as campus or community expert
- To help keep colleagues alert to change and improvements
- To keep up with the competition

The more a searcher knows about any search system, the more effective he or she is at obtaining the best possible results. Even though Google is deceptively simple, it offers a range of advanced techniques that can enhance results. While Google adds new search features infrequently, those who follow the Google literature continue to discover previously unknown techniques. Not long ago one of the authors discovered that Google's search engine allows for a crude form of proximity searching (only up to within three words), a technique that receives no mention in Google's help page. Experts can pass on to readers of their articles and postings this information.

A January 2005 Pew Internet and American Life report on search engine users provides ample evidence that even though the vast majority of search engine users are naïve about search engines, they also report satisfaction with their search results (Fallows 2005). These findings emphasize the value of establishing oneself as the campus search engine expert, and proactively working to help the user community become more knowledgeable about search engines, Google in particular, and techniques for improving search results. Through our instruction sessions, newsletters, and interpersonal interactions, the library community needs to share information about improving search skills. However, this can be accomplished only if we know more about Google than our users.

Consider the introduction of Google Scholar or a new Google feature such as Desktop Search or Google History. On our campus, we find that faculty and students often fail to discover these new tools and techniques in a timely fashion. As we endeavor to increase awareness of existing features, such as those found on the Google advanced search screen, we also need to alert our colleagues to the new tools that Google introduces. While some, such as Google Scholar, are rarely missed by librarians because they are heavily publicized in our popular professional literature, there are those lesser-known features that librarians will only discover through an organized and systematic keeping-up regimen.

Whether Google represents competition for libraries or is simply a benign information option for our user community, it is incumbent upon our profession to keep up with Google, Inc. as a form of competitive intelligence. We need to know how its products and services compare to our own information resources and services. If our goal is to encourage our user communities to take full advantage of all available information options it is critical to be able to identify which resources do the best job for any given research task. It is important to be able to demonstrate when Google works best, or when a library database is the right choice.

Think of it as being able to show the competitive advantage of using library databases. We have probably all experienced a sales pitch from a library product vendor representative who was unaware that the competition already offers better features. Do we want to be in the same position when we engage in user education? Keeping up is a form of competitive intelligence. Knowing more about Google, especially future innovations and initiatives, simply enables us to be more competent in educating our user community.

RESOURCES FOR KEEPING UP WITH GOOGLE

There are primarily three types of resources for keeping up with Google. The first type includes electronic newsletters. E-newsletters are characterized by a regular weekly or monthly frequency, a more formal publication and distribution process, and the fact that they are delivered to an e-mail inbox. The second type includes blogs that use RSS (Rich Site Syndication) technology to allow for the distribution of daily or near-daily postings. Blog content is typically characterized by the blogger's personality and insights, and the reporting and writing styles are less formal than those of an e-newsletter. The third resource consists of news articles from a multitude of sources that are aggregated into a single source. Individuals now have the power to construct such customized searches for themselves using the RSS capabilities embedded in many news sources (e.g., Yahoo, Findory). Our methodology for identifying the best sources for keeping up with Google included our own experience as Google followers, conversations with experts such as Gary Price, and limiting inclusion to only those sources that are frequently (more than once a week) updated. To confirm that we missed nothing essential we consulted the resource lists provided by the various Google bloggers, as well as searching various engines with terms such as "google," "blogs," "resources."

To organize the Google Keep Up resources covered in this article we devised the following four categories as indicators of the quantity or extent of Google reporting:

- Nothin' But Google–those resources that are completely Google-centric.
- Lotsa' Google–those resources that primarily concentrate their content on Google, but are likely to report occasionally on peripheral topics.

- Sorta' Google–those resources that report on the search engine industry or that provide news and search tips for a broad range of search engines, but that do provide ample news about Google.
- Not-A-Lotta Google–rather than simply discard these sources because they report on Google less frequently than those sources in other categories, we find they have some value because they provide interesting commentary or insights the other sources may miss.

Nothin' But Google

Google Blog
<http://www.google.com/googleblog>

Google Blog is the official blog of Google, Inc. Google staff post news, information, and insights about Google. The blog is a fun read. Typical posts include Google Gossip, tips sent in by Google users, and new product announcements. Because Google Blog is clearly the best resource for keeping up with news about and activity at Google, Inc., it is naturally the primary news source for a host of Google bloggers. However, being the voice of Google negates this resource for any critical evaluation of its own products or activities. Think of it as going to a company's own Web site to get information about the company; you can expect some bias. Like the search engine itself, the blog is clutter free and easy to navigate. Google Blog is necessary in your Google regimen.

Topix Google News
<http://www.topix.net/com/google>

Topix, online since 2002, is by design a one-stop source for news and information about specific topics. It is organized into the following five sections: headline news; recent news; press releases; archives; and related news sources. This structure keeps the news about Google, Inc. well organized for rapid accessibility. According to Gary Price, search engine expert and creator of *ResourceShelf*, Topix is the most comprehensive site on the Web today for Google news. Now that Google has gone public, the reporting leans towards news about Google the corporation; expect to wade through stories about Google's stock performance.

Topix contains items from a broader range of unique source publications than any other Google resource we examined. Users are able to set up alerts for any new Topix postings containing Google news. From our perspective, the only drawback at Topix is its tendency to focus on the corporate side of Google. It's understandable, but of little interest to librarians. Even so, we force ourselves to monitor this news owing to its potential to report important advances or news from Google Labs, the research and development division of Google, Inc. News aggregator users will be pleased to know that Topix supplies an RSS feed for the Google, Inc. news page. Because it draws on thousands of sources for Google news, this site rivals Google's own for news and information, but provides it without any inherent bias.

UBC Google Scholar Blog
<http://careo.elearning.ubc.ca/weblogs/googlescholar>

Unlike the previous two resources, this one is a personal blog. Dean Giustini, a reference librarian at the University of British Columbia, Vancouver, Canada, maintains the University of British Columbia Google Scholar Blog. Online since April 2005, this blog is certainly the newest addition to the genre. Giustini pulls his news postings from the usual variety of sources including professional journals, blogs, newspapers, and resources mentioned elsewhere in this article. The blog is low on clutter, rather easy to navigate, and adds Giustini's own perspective to the reporting. Interestingly, Giustini promotes his blog as a site where Canadian librarians can keep up with Google Scholar. His postings, however, are primarily drawn from American sources. For that reason, his blog lacks an authentic Canadian perspective on Google. UBC Google Scholar Blog should be considered only a marginal resource for a Google keeping-up regimen.

Lotsa' Google

Google Weblog
<http://google.blogspace.com/>

Aaron Swartz maintains Google Weblog. He is a Stanford University student, and has been tracking Google since March 2002. While this blog primarily covers Google, there are occasional postings about other search engines. Research Buzz, Google Blog, and *The New York Times* look like his most common sources for content. He offers a streamlined blog that is easy to read and navigate. An RSS feed is provided for those desiring to capture the content in their news aggregator. His postings are usually brief and right to the point, but things can get interesting when he expounds his comments on Google innovations. For example, he offered insightful remarks on Google's plan to digitize Anglo-American libraries. Google Weblog does tend to duplicate other sources we mention, and as the work of a hobbyist, it will strike the reader as sometimes lacking in professionalism. It also includes advertisements but they are kept out of the way. Still, Google Weblog is worth considering, and we recommend giving it a try for a few months to determine if its occasional insights are of value, or if the news it provides is better obtained elsewhere.

InsideGoogle
<http://google.blognewschannel.com>

InsideGoogle is a part of the Blog News Channel maintained by Nathan Weinberg. Google is the focus of the blog, but as with some of these other resources, news about other engines creeps in as well. Unlike some of the other resources, Weinberg makes it a habit to cite the source of his information. The majority of his posts come from Searchenginewatch and even though he pulls heavily from it, he organizes the content well and adds original content about Google's latest activities. That is why InsideGoogle is more than a rehashing of Searchenginewatch news. InsideGoogle makes for worthwhile reading, but even more interesting is the extensive list of blogs Weinberg assembles concerning Microsoft, Google, Search Engines, Tech News, Non-English blogs, and blogs by Microsoft and Google employees. Check this list for additional blogs that can supplement what is covered in this article. We think this site can be effective for a keeping-up regimen that seeks an international perspective; others might find it marginal.

On Google Scholar
<http://schoogle.blogspot.com/>

T. J. Sonnderman, a research and instruction librarian in Newton, MA, maintains On Google Scholar. On Google Scholar is an expansive resource for keeping up with Google. Sonnderman writes "Wherein a librarian tracks a paradigm shift. Love it or hate it, the effect will be profound." Sondermann is right on target; Google is here to stay and librarians have a responsiblity to keep up with it. He pulls information from a variety of sources including library professional journals and newsletters, blogs, and Google itself. But Sonnderman can be less up-to-date than we like. A story about Peter Jacso's "Side-by-Side" search engine that compares Google Scholar to native publisher search engines was posted on April 19, 2005, but there were multiple stories about Jacso's engine months before that in a variety of sources. Sonndermann doesn't hesitate to add an opinion to Google developments. The commentary is almost exclusively about Google, but at times goes generic when blogging about non-Google library issues. The blog is updated regularly. While less up-to-date, comprehensive, and informative than our highly recommended sites, there may be some interest in On Google Scholar for its library perspective.

Sorta' Google

Search Engine Report
<http://searchenginewatch.com/sereport/>

Search Engine Report is an e-mail newsletter form Searchenginewatch. com. The newsletter is all encompassing, covering Yahoo, Google, Lycos, Ask Jeeves, and more. If something is new in the search engine world or causing news, then Search Engine Report has the story. The news items come primarily from two sources, Search Engine Watch (a blog) and SearchDay. While it would be interesting to have the news arranged by search engine or degree of importance, Search Engine Report uses just common chronological order to organize the news. Each posting provides a brief summary of why the news matters. Some of Search Engine Report's full content is available only to subscribers of Searchenginewatch.com. If you are serious about keeping up with Google, someone in your library should subscribe. If price is an issue, do not fret. The Search Engine Report tends to be the main source of Google information for some of the other blogs so some of the fee-based content may turn up elsewhere. While librarians are encouraged to use the free version of the Search Engine Report, we think the fee-based version of the service is highly worthwhile.

ResearchBuzz
<http://www.researchbuzz.com/>

ResearchBuzz, online since 1998, written and edited by Tara Calishain, is among the oldest sites on the Web dedicated to keeping up with search engines. Like Searchenginereport, it has free and fee versions. Since ResearchBuzz is all-encompassing, like Searchengineblog, the authors suggest use of the category "search engines" to limit searching and information to just about Google. The reader is taken to a page with Google entries back to 1999 in order by date. Clicking on any of the entries will take the reader to expanded entries. A Google entry is added almost every other day. There are some similarities in the types of Google news covered between Searchenginewatch and ResearchBuzz. While its news about Google is somewhat limited and may be slightly out of date, Calishain provides some useful tips that should benefit any librarian. It is not for serious Google Watching, but valuable for its tips about Google tools and search technique.

SearchengineBlog
<http://www.searchengineblog.com/>

Peter Da Vanzo, a search engine marketing strategist and industry commentator in Wellington, New Zealand, writes Searchengineblog, online since 2002. His blog is crisp and clutter-free. He pulls materials from a variety of American and European sources. He makes note of search engine events relevant to Australia and New Zealand. For example, he mentions an April 1, 2005 incident when Google dropped the google.com.au domain for several hours. This story was missed by many of the sites covered in this article. Recently, Peter Da Vanzo reported that he was going on vacation, and that Searchengine Blog would be left static for a while. Since the blog will not be updated for an undetermined period, we think it can be skipped.

Google Blogoscoped
<http://blog.outer-court.com>

Phillip Lennsen, a Web designer in Stuttgart, Germany, maintains Google Blogoscoped. Google Blogoscoped is the most unusual site explored for this article owing to its clever forum features and added value utilities. While the postings are mainly about Google, the blogger also provides interesting posts about aspects of Web design and important news about other search engines. One good example of the utilities Lennsen creates are his quick search tools that run Google in the background. For example, he developed a tool called "Actors." It quickly identifies the roles played by any actor. One of the authors queried Harrison Ford, and quickly obtained a comprehensive list of his acting roles. The tools may be perceived as more for amusement than research, but we think researchers will find them of value. The forum (discussion board) feature on Google Blogoscoped is highly active. Because the forum content comes from individual readers it can offer a valuable method to obtain news and updates about Google not found elsewhere. We don't recommend it for regular reading: however Google Blogoscoped is certainly worth a look from time to time.

Not-A-Lotta' Google

Phil Bradley's Blog
<http://www.philb.com/blog/blogger.html>

Phil Bradley's Blog has been online since 1998. His blog is designed to allow one to keep up on search engines, Internet searching, Web page design, and new Web features for librarians. He updates his page regularly, sometimes up to three times a day, and his posts are short and concise with a library focus. Phil Bradley takes from a variety of American and European sources including the professional literature. Google is reasonably covered. It's not highly recommended for developing or maintaining Google expertise, but librarians may want to consider Phil Bradley's Blog as a more generic way to keep up on topics of interest to information professionals.

CUSTOMIZING GOOGLE KEEP UP

Based on our experience, regularly reviewing a mix of these publications will effectively ensure that almost any article, newsletter, or blog post published about Google will become a part of one's personal Google universe. But we also know that even these hard working followers of Google are likely to occasionally miss an interesting story or two. There are times when a librarian or researcher wants to be alerted to stories about some specific aspect of Google. For example, a researcher may wish to learn how high school students are using Google for identifying prospective colleges. How about locating articles that focus on academic or public libraries using Google? These are good examples of when it is appropriate to customize a search for the Google keeping-up regimen.

We recommend two options for customizing Google watching. The first option is to take advantage of the alert services offered by search engines. Google and Yahoo both offer easy-to-use alerting systems. Setting up an alert varies only slightly in each. In Yahoo, performing any search results in an option to create an alert for that search statement. In Google, one needs to go into the alerts service to establish an alert based on a search statement. Alerts in either system require the establishment of an account, so this does call for the provision of some personal information. Once an alert is established, whenever either engine indexes a story containing the search terms, or it could be a Web site containing information related to the topic, the alert owner receives an e-mail message with a link to the article or Web site. One drawback of alerts is that they can easily, if not carefully prepared, result in the forwarding of too much information that is often irrelevant.

The other option is to make use of the RSS technology offered by a variety of search engines and news outlets. RSS technology makes virtually any news story a "feed" that can be automatically deliverable to a news aggregator such as Bloglines. A good example is provided by the news source called Findory.com that covers thousands of news sources and blogs. Any search results in the delivery of a unique RSS feed for that exact search. When one subscribes to the feed with his or her news aggregator, any time a new story related to that search query is published it is delivered to the aggregator. Both methods offer great convenience, but sometimes at the risk of being overwhelmed if the search statement is too broad. However, the RSS feed can be deleted and a new one constructed. Our personal preference is to use the RSS method because it is ultimately more convenient to capture the feeds in an aggregator for once-a-day review rather than having them come intermittently into an e-mail inbox. In addition, the RSS feed approach requires no registration with any engine or news source.

CONCLUSION

So, what do we recommend? What is the best strategy for keeping up with Google? The answer depends on each individual's needs and interests. It is likely that true Googleholics will want to take advantage of the full gamut of resources we identify. That will inevitably lead to receiving a fair amount of duplicate information but there are some slight variations, such as a particular blogger's perspective, that an enthusiast will find salient. For everyone else, we think a mix of selected resources will suffice for a robust regimen for keeping up with Google. Table 1 provides a chart that compares a variety of features for each resource. While any and all of these sources have some merit, only three received our "highly recommended" rating. We believe that librarians should

routinely follow all three of these resources to effectively keep up with
Google, both the engine and corporation. Beyond those three, each individual may choose to add one, two, or more resources as time and preferences allow. While a resource may be marginal in terms of the new or
additional news it can add to one's personal Google universe, the style
of a particular blogger, the frequency of the news, or the particular spin
put on the story can all add to the experience of keeping up. In addition,
we think it is a good idea to consider developing a customized search or
two that can be tracked as an alert or RSS feed.

Keeping up is all about time, or more often, our lack of it. The number one reason librarians fail to keep up effectively is insufficient time.
But time is our most precious resource, and it is incumbent upon us to
keep up as efficiently as possible so we maximize our available time.
Think of keeping up with Google as an investment of time. Like most
investments, there is risk. Keeping up will sometimes yield little news
or information of value, but without fail, those who keep up conscien-
tiously will be rewarded with a gem of information that is the return on
the investment. Granted, if something as significant as GooglePrint
happens we all hear about it in a short time. But the reality is that Google
is now a news machine, constantly generating stories both significant
and minor. Which are the ones we can afford to miss?

TABLE 1

Source	Google Gossip	Google Inc.	Google Research	RSS Feed	E-mail Alerts	Rank
Google Blog	Yes	Yes	Yes	No	No	Highly Recommended
Phil Bradley	Yes	No	Yes	Yes	No	Marginal
Topix	Yes	Yes	No	Yes	Yes	Highly Recommend
UBC Google Scholar	Yes	No	Yes	Yes	No	Marginal
Google Weblog	Yes	Yes	No	Yes	Yes	Marginal
Inside Google	Yes	No	No	Yes	No	Marginal
On Google Scholar	Yes	No	Yes	No	No	Marginal
Search Engine Report	Yes	Yes	Yes	Yes	Yes	Highly Recommended
ResearchBuzz	Yes	Yes	Yes	Yes	Yes	Marginal
Search Engine Blog	Yes	Yes	Yes	No	No	Marginal
Google Blogoscoped	Yes	Yes	Yes	Yes	No	Marginal

REFERENCES

Fallows, Deborah. (2005) Search engine users. Washington, D.C.: Pew Internet and American Life Project, 2005. Retrieved on April 27, 2005. <http://www.pewinternet. org/pdfs/PIP_Searchengine_users.pdf>.

Index

BOOK ORDER FORM!

Order a copy of this book with this form or online at:
http://www.HaworthPress.com/store/product.asp?sku= 5812

Libraries and Google®

____ in softbound at $24.95 ISBN-13: 978-0-7890-3125-9 / ISBN-10: 0-7890-3125-6.
____ in hardbound at $34.95 ISBN-13: 978-0-7890-3124-2 / ISBN-10: 0-7890-3124-8.

COST OF BOOKS _____

POSTAGE & HANDLING _____
US: $4.00 for first book & $1.50
for each additional book
Outside US: $5.00 for first book
& $2.00 for each additional book.

SUBTOTAL _____

In Canada: add 7% GST. _____

STATE TAX _____
CA, IL, IN, MN, NJ, NY, OH, PA & SD residents
please add appropriate local sales tax.

FINAL TOTAL _____
If paying in Canadian funds, convert
using the current exchange rate,
UNESCO coupons welcome.

❑ **BILL ME LATER:**
Bill-me option is good on US/Canada/
Mexico orders only; not good to jobbers,
wholesalers, or subscription agencies.

❑ **Signature** _____

❑ **Payment Enclosed: $**_____

❑ **PLEASE CHARGE TO MY CREDIT CARD:**
❑ Visa ❑ MasterCard ❑ AmEx ❑ Discover
❑ Diner's Club ❑ Eurocard ❑ JCB

Account #_____

Exp Date_____

Signature_____
(Prices in US dollars and subject to change without notice.)

PLEASE PRINT ALL INFORMATION OR ATTACH YOUR BUSINESS CARD

Name		
Address		
City	State/Province	Zip/Postal Code
Country	Tel	
Fax	E-Mail	

May we use your e-mail address for confirmations and other types of information? ❑Yes ❑No We appreciate receiving
your e-mail address. Haworth would like to e-mail special discount offers to you, as a preferred customer.
We will never share, rent, or exchange your e-mail address. We regard such actions as an invasion of your privacy.

Order from your **local bookstore** or directly from
The Haworth Press, Inc. 10 Alice Street, Binghamton, New York 13904-1580 • USA
Call our toll-free number (1-800-429-6784) / Outside US/Canada: (607) 722-5857
Fax: 1-800-895-0582 / Outside US/Canada: (607) 771-0012
E-mail your order to us: orders@HaworthPress.com

For orders outside US and Canada, you may wish to order through your local
sales representative, distributor, or bookseller.
For information, see http://HaworthPress.com/distributors

(Discounts are available for individual orders in US and Canada only, not booksellers/distributors.)

Please photocopy this form for your personal use.
www.HaworthPress.com

BOF06